WITHDRAWN

African Theatres and Performances

African Theatres and Performances looks at four specific performance forms in Africa and uses this to question the tendency to employ western frames of reference to analyse and appreciate theatrical performance. The book examines:

- masquerade theatre in Eastern Nigeria
- the trance and possession ritual theatre of the Hausa of Northern Nigeria
- the musical and oral tradition of the Mandinka of Senegal
- comedy and satire of the Bamana in Mali.

The book describes each performance in detail and discusses how each is made, who it is made by and for, and considers the relationship between maker and viewer and the social functions of performance and theatre in African societies. The discussions are based on first-hand observation and interviews with performers and spectators.

Osita Okagbue gives a fascinating account of these practices, carefully tracing the ways in which performances and theatres are unique and expressive of their cultural context.

Dr Osita Okagbue is Lecturer in the Drama department of Goldsmiths College, University of London.

Theatres of the World

Series editor
John Russell Brown

Series advisors
Alison Hodge, *Royal Holloway, University of London*
Osita Okagbue, *Goldsmiths College, University of London*

Theatres of the World is a series that will bring close and instructive contact with makers of performances from around the world. Each book looks at the performance traditions and current practices of a specific region, focusing on a small number of individual theatrical events. Mixing first-hand observation, interviews with performance makers and in-depth analyses, these books show how performance practices are expressive of their social, historical and cultural contexts. They consider the ways in which theatre artists worldwide can enjoy and understand one another's work.

Volumes currently available in the series are:

African Theatres and Performances
Osita Okagbue

Indian Folk Theatres
Julia Hollander

Performance in Bali
Leon Rubin and Nyoman Sedana

Future volumes will include:

Indian Popular Theatres

Indigenous Australian Theatre Practices

Polish Ensemble Theatre

Shamans in Contemporary Korean Theatre

African Theatres and Performances

Osita Okagbue

Routledge
Taylor & Francis Group

LONDON AND NEW YORK

First published 2007
by Routledge
2 Park Square, Milton Park, Abingdon, Oxon OX14 4RN

Simultaneously published in the USA and Canada
by Routledge
270 Madison Ave, New York, NY 10016

*Routledge is an imprint of the Taylor & Francis Group, an informa
business*

Reprinted 2008

Typeset in Galliard by
Integra Software Services Pvt. Ltd, Pondicherry, India
Printed and bound in Great Britain by
MPG Books Ltd, Bodmin

British Library Cataloguing in Publication Data
A catalogue record for this book is available from the British Library

Library of Congress Cataloging in Publication Data
Okagbue, Osita.
    African theatres and performances / Osita Okagbue.
        p.   cm. -- (Theatres of the world)
    Includes bibliographical references and index.
    1. Performing arts--Africa.   I. Title.
    PN2969.O33 2007
    791.096--dc22   2007005421

ISBN10: 0–415–30453–9 (hbk)
ISBN10: 0–203–94533–6 (ebk)

ISBN13: 978–0–415–30453–5 (hbk)
ISBN13: 978–0–203–94533–9 (ebk)

Contents

Figures

Acknowledgements

In the course of writing this book, I accumulated debts of gratitude to a number of people and organizations. I am especially indebted to the British Academy, the AHRC (AHRB) and Goldsmiths College for grants and a research leave that made field trips to Nigeria, Senegal and Mali possible.

I thank Professors Emmanuel Obiechina and Martin Banham, who have been my academic mentors. I am also grateful to Professor John Russell Brown for inviting me to write the book and for his patient editing and suggestions. During my field trips, so many people helped me: in Lagos my brother and sister-in-law, Ifeanyi and Oby Okagbue; at Nkpor members of my family; in Zaria Paul and Ngozi Obah; Faith Collingwood, who assisted me in London and Zaria; in Segou Ulla Santara, Mamadou Keita and Anadolo; and in Dakar Mike Idemili, Cheikh Seydi and Professor Mamadou Gaye. Thanks also to Zagba Oyortey for explaining the Krobo terms for 'play'.

But the greatest support came from my wife, Amaka, and my children, Solum, Chichi and Nedonna, who had to live with my absences from home and endured endless replays of 'boring' video tapes.

1 Introduction

Concepts of performance and theatre in Africa

What is theatre or performance in an African context? By what terms do African peoples designate their performances? Most African cultures and languages, in fact, seem not to have specific words for theatre or drama. But they, however, have terms that broadly encompass a host of performance activities, ranging from ritual to play, from sporting activities such as wrestling, boxing and hunting to masking, dancing, singing and acrobatic displays. It is also interesting that the descriptive verbs for these activities generally tend to be the same in a lot of African cultures. The Igbo of Nigeria, one of the cultures whose performance will be looked at in this study, is a good example. For them, the word *egwu* is used to refer to 'play', 'dance', 'song' and 'music'. The Hausa use the term *wasa* as both a noun meaning 'play' and a verb 'to play'. In Hausa the concept 'theatre' is expressed as *wasanin gargajiya*, which roughly translates as 'traditional performances', where *wasanin* means performance in general. The Hausa also have the expression *wasan kwaikwayo*, which is used to designate any kind of performance in which any form of mimesis or imitation play is involved. The Krobo of Ghana, according to Zagba Oyortey, use the term *fiem* to mean 'play' as in children's play and theatre; *fie do* means to drum and *do* also stands for song. The same can be said of other West African languages in which the various activities, which in English are generally classed as performance or theatre or drama, are very often designated by a single term. However, verbs are then used to specify which type of activity is being referred to. So for the Igbo, 'to play' is *igwu egwu*, 'to sing' is *igu egwu*, 'to dance' is *igba egwu*, 'to play music' is *iti egwu*, *iti igba* is 'to drum'. *Iti mmo* is 'to mask' or 'to play mask', *iti okpo* is 'to box' and *igba ngba* is 'to wrestle' while *igba oso* is 'to run'. The Igbo also have the expressions *ife emume* (literally meaning 'something that is done') to refer to any kind of public celebration and *ife nkili* ('something to look at') to mean any kind of public performance or spectacle. Thus, it is obvious that in African cultures, the concept of performance is rather a comprehensive one, and the fact that not very serious effort is made to put the various types of performances into compartments indicates an acute awareness that there are elements which these activities have in common. In this respect, they predate radical performance thinkers such as Richard Schechner, Eugenio Barba and Western European avant-garde theatre theory and practice, which moved theatre discourse into the domain of performance, away from the much narrower frame of dramatic theory and criticism.

In Africa, the idea of performance is very much about 'showing' and 'seeing'. It is about spectacle, a feast for the eyes. It can sometimes be an auditory feast for the ears, as Igbo *Ayaka* performances show. In such shows, people are already in bed or inside their homes while listening to the music, the songs, and the dialogue of the *Ayaka* performers as they walk through the town or village in the middle of the night. These night performers are not meant to be seen. For most African cultures, a measure of what is perceived as performance is whether or not the three elements of space, performer and spectator are present in the activity. The space can be anywhere, usually a village or town common, or any other open space, including public roads and family compounds. A performance happens wherever the spectator encounters and engages with the performer, and the two automatically define, and continuously redefine, the enveloping space of their meeting throughout the duration of the performance. Equally, their roles, as performer or spectator, go through a similar process of rene-gotiations and re-definitions as the performance progresses. The fluidity of the space is responsible for the constantly shifting positions of and altern-ating roles between spectator and performer in most African performance contexts.

However, although everyone is believed to be able to perform, it is also accepted that some people are much better at it than others, and that some derive more pleasure from doing it than others. This perhaps explains why in a lot of African performance traditions, no attempts have been made to formalize training processes since every individual, male or female, is expected at some point in their lives to take the stage. This could be in a performance *qua* performance, or it could be in some of the many volitional or mandatory rites of passage, such as weddings, initiations, naming ceremonies, and/or other status enhancement ritual performances that are part of most African communities' cultural life.

But how are these performance activities differentiated from other everyday activities? The first characteristic of performance events is that they take place in a time out of time. This means that performances are placed outside the usual work-a-day times; they are usually fitted in a time when the community is taking a time out, as it were, from the normal daily processes of life, of making or earning a living. Performances also take place in a time specially set aside and agreed by all parties involved. It means therefore that such events or activities also have an agreed temporal duration. Thus, there are formal openings and closings, and mechanisms in place which frame the spatial compass, as well as the temporal duration of these events. Secondly, such activities are used to mark special occasions or significant moments in individuals' lives or in the life of the community. The third quality of these events is that those engaged in them are very much aware of themselves as being on show, as being in the public gaze. Therefore, behaviours for the duration are designed and executed with this awareness in mind – the result being that such behaviours tend to be exaggerated, stylized, presentational or representational, and consciously done for the viewing other. The fourth is that performance activities in African cultures are not done ostensibly for any immediate material reward for the participants. They may however be done with a hope for possible future benefits for those involved in the doing or for those for whom they have been organized, and for the good of the community as a whole. And finally, these activities are marked out by the fact that they are sometimes done just for the joy and fun which they bring to all who take part.

Cultures and their performances

Cultures, according to Victor Turner, are most fully expressed and made conscious of themselves through their rituals and theatrical performances. Performances, he adds, declare our shared humanity, yet each suggests the uniqueness of the culture from which it originates. For Turner, we will understand one another better by 'entering one another's performances and learning their grammars and vocabularies' (in Schechner and Appel, 1990: 1). The ideas underpinning this vision of a world community based on mutual respect and appreciation of cultural differences seem not to have existed for scholars, such as Molly Mahood (1966), Ulli Beier (1967), and Ruth Finnegan (1970), in their assessments of African performance forms. Every culture has its own traditions of performance and theatre, its own forms and modes of artistic expression. Equally, each culture has its own framework and language for organizing, presenting, describing, and assessing its artistic impulses and manifestations, which include theatrical and performance processes. But the scholars mentioned above, instead of 'learning the grammars and vocabularies' of African performances, opted instead to read these performances using European critical terminology and vocabularies, subjecting African performances to Western analytic frames, with the result that there was a significant disjunction in their understanding and assessment, since these performances resisted, and sometimes totally refused Western categorizations. This resistance and refusal were ideational and structural since the impulses, processes and purposes of African theatres and performances were intrinsically different from those of Western Europe.

Only an ethnocentric tendency to approach the foreign through one's own can account for Finnegan's claim that:

> Though some writers have very positively affirmed the existence of native African drama, it would perhaps be truer to say that in Africa, in contrast to Western Europe and Asia, drama is not typically a widespread or a developed form... There are, however, certain dramatic and quasi-dramatic phenomena.... (1970: 500)

Not wising to waste time disputing Finnegan's critical framework and its implied embryonic primitivity of African theatre or performance forms, this book merely seeks to highlight the narrowness of such a critical framework, based as it was on the very limiting field of dramatic theory and criticism. Finnegan in her analysis listed what she considered to be the crucial elements of drama – these are, the idea of enactment, of representation through actors of persons and events, linguistic content, plot, represented interaction of several characters, specialized scenery, music, and dance. She found that it is very 'seldom in Africa that all these elements of drama come together in a single performance' (p. 501), and one wonders of course where these elements ever come together in a single performance. Yet, for her, drama in Africa is a minority and undeveloped form because all the elements hardly come together.

Although this claim has annoyed and engaged generations of scholars of African theatres and performances, a majority of these advocates of African 'dramatic' arts completely miss the point at issue. Finnegan may have been partially right in her assertion that drama, especially of the Aristotelian Western type, is not a very widespread form in Africa. But, she was wrong in the second assertion since where it exists, such as the *Kote-tlon* in Mali, the *Ekong* comic plays of the Ibibio of South-eastern Nigeria, and in some of the masquerade plays of West Africa, drama is well developed, and there is absolutely nothing 'quasi'or 'pre-drama' about them as our study of the *Koteba* in Chapter 5 will show. This study, however, is not concerned unduly with this kind of view, or with the now tired debate between the evolutionists and relativists about what is or is not drama or theatre in Africa. Scholars, such as Emmanuel Obiechina (1978), Oyin Ogunba and Abiola Irele (1978), Meki Nzewi (1979), Ossie Enekwe (1981), who represent the 'relativist school', have challenged Mahood,

Finnegan, Beier, and the African scholars who followed in their footsteps, such as Kalu Uka (1973), Joe de Graft (1976), Michael Echeruo (1981), James Amankulor (1981), and Nnabuenyi Ugonna (1984) – the last four belong to the 'evolutionist camp'. Unfortunately, the relativists fell into the trap of using the same narrow Western terms and classifications to challenge the Eurocentric viewpoints of the evolutionists, as well as explain African musical, ritual and theatrical performances. It seemed that in their determination to expose the inappropriateness of the essentially Western critical viewpoints, they go to extremes to try and prove that what Mahood had termed 'pre-drama' and Finnegan 'quasi-dramatic phenomena' are, in fact, full grown drama. Some of the performances studied here, such as *Bori* of the Hausa, *Jaliya* of the Mandinka, some Igbo masked perform-ances, are not and do not aspire to be drama, and they should never have been or be assessed now using purely dramatic frames of reference as was and sometimes still is the practice in Western theatre and performance scholarship.

Going through the arguments put forward by some African scholars, such as Amankulor, Enekwe and Ugonna on Igbo masking theatre, one is somewhat disappointed to find them defending Igbo theatre by trying to find similarities between it and Greek or Western models of drama – the very thing the evolutionists were doing. The only difference is that while the evolutionists, such as Echeruo and Uka, feel that Igbo masquerade performances are still some distance away from being drama, the relativists argue that for their respective African communities they are already drama in their own right. Ugonna, in particular, devotes so much time in his study trying to tease out an elaborate linguistic content and dramatic structure for Igbo masquerade performances that are absolutely alien to the form. Amankulor, in his own study, explores the similarities in aesthetic principles and performance processes and structuring between the *Ekpe* masquerade and Greek festival performances out of which Western classical tragedy evolved.

But all these efforts, in my view, were unnecessary. What the scholars failed to take note of and question is the issue of whether or not every performance, every theatre event, has to be drama. And second was their failure to make any distinctions between the terms 'drama', 'theatre' and 'performance'. Unfortunately, the imprecision in terminology still persists today in a lot of the critical writings about performance, not only in African performance and theatre scholarship, but also in performance and theatre discourses worldwide. All the critics involved in the relativists versus evol-utionists' debate on the nature and status of African drama, performance and theatre frequently used the three terms interchangeably in their essays and books.

However, Richard Schechner's *Performance Theory* (1977) helped to rescue discourses of drama, theatre and performance from the prolonged aesthetic and taxonomical hegemony of Aristotelian tragic drama, and the Western product-led fascination with the dramatic script as the be-all and end-all of the theatre process. Most writings about the theatre up to this point had concentrated on dramatic criticism, dramaturgy, dramatic structures and themes, and story and character; they were hardly about the process of making and receiving theatre, or the place and function of the spectator in this process. But, by moving discussion away from the restrictive frame of drama to that of performance, from the prototypical dramatic criticism of Aristotle's *The Poetics* and its numerous dramatic theory and critical off-shoots – these, by the way, usually exclude performers and spectators – to the more comprehensive analytical frame of performance theory, Schechner put forward a more inclusive framework for looking at the performance forms from across the world. His differentiation between the terms, 'drama', 'script', 'theatre' and 'performance' is very clear, and will be useful frames in a study of African performances and theatres.

Schechner suggests a 'model of concentric overlapping circles', with the outermost, largest and least strictly defined standing for performance, and drama, the smallest and innermost, being the most specifically defined (1977: 71). Theatre is the middle circle and shares in part the loose definition and inclusiveness of performance, and the strict definition and exclusiveness of drama. I will leave out Schechner's fourth category, script, because the performances studied are not script based. Looking more deeply into Schechner's model, three key facts become obvious. The first is that both drama and theatre are types of performance. Second is that drama is a kind of theatre. And the third, which is relevant in this context, is that not all theatres or performances are drama. Schechner also points out that while theatre and performance are about doing, drama and script refer to the idea or record of the doing or what is done, and as such are more concerned with the written. Schechner further differentiates between drama, theatre and performance by saying that:

> The drama is the domain of the author, the composer, scenarist, shaman . . . the theatre is the domain of the performers; the performance is the domain of the audience. (71)

And he concludes, using his oppositional dyad model of drama-script versus theatre-performance, that within cultures, to the extent that the drama-script dyad is emphasized, to that extent will the theatre-performance dyad be de-emphasized, and vice versa. However, a majority of cultures of the world, he argues, emphasize the theatre-performance dyad, while it is only modern drama, especially in the West, since the late nineteenth century 'which has so privileged the written text as to almost exclude theatre-performance altogether' (p. 73). Unfortunately, this privileging of the drama-script dyad still dominates Western performance practices and literature, in spite of the avant-garde non-western emphasis on theatre-performance. One can therefore begin to recognize the ethnocentric subjection of the mainly oral theatre and performance forms of African and other non-Western cultures to mainly literary derived analytical frames.

The polarization in thought in the seventies and early eighties about the existence or otherwise of native African drama, or how indigenous theatres and performances can 'develop' into drama mentioned earlier has remained. It is evident in the writings of newer scholars, such as Victor Ukaegbu (1996), who concludes his speculations on the future of Igbo masking theatre by suggesting that what should be done would be for the theatre to begin to identify more with individual struggles as 'a means of furthering its identification with contemporaneity and opening itself to a wider audience' (p. 267). Lurking here is a veiled evolutionist suggestion that indigenous African theatre should bow to the demands and pressures of modernity by ditching its traditional aesthetic principles and structures in favour of 'modern' Western European dramatic ones. That is to say, it should become more drama than performance or theatre.

The evolutionists–relativists debate, although framed in the context of Nigerian drama and theatre, could have been about drama, theatre and performance in any other place in Africa. Also, although it was wrongly framed as a discussion on whether an African indigenous performance form was drama or not, it was, because of similarities in performance practices between African cultures, in reality about notions and perceptions of drama, theatre and performance in Africa. The evolutionists, influenced by their exposure to Western theatre history and development, argued for African drama and theatre to evolve from African ritual and myth, in the same way that Greek classical drama evolved from Greek mythology and Dionysian rites. The relativists, however, counter by pointing out the cultural relativism and specificity of performance and theatre practices. For them, the Igbo have developed the kind of 'drama' which they needed based on the material available to them, and they perform it in a manner specific to them. It did not have to be like 'drama' or theatre or performance performed anywhere else. Thus, African drama or theatre does not have to be like European drama or theatre. The four performances studied in this book are all culturally specific, rooted in and formulated by their respective African contexts.

Both the evolutionists and Eurocentrics are right that drama as it exists in Europe is not a widespread form in Africa; and the Eurocentrics are also right that African theatre and performance forms are not drama. But the three European scholars were wrong to rely on only the drama criteria in their analysis. By using only 'drama' – a term which Schechner has shown designates a specific and circumscribed kind of performance – they excluded and on occasions completely dismissed a host of African theatre and performance forms, since most of them are not drama. By not recognizing their over-reliance on a narrow frame, and also by not differentiating between the dramatic frame and the relatively more inclusive theatre and performance frames, the evolutionists inadvertently perpetrated the mistakes of the Eurocentric scholars, by implying in their writings and utterances that drama is a higher and more developed form, which all 'rudimentary'or 'primitive' theatre and performance forms should aspire to develop into. And the relativists, while making the point that cultures have their performances, inexplicably were enslaved by the drama frame. They ended up trying to prove or convince their opponents that certain African performances, such as masquerades or ritual performances are drama when they clearly are not.

This study hopes to extend the ideas of scholars, such as David Kerr (1986 and 1995) and Andrew Horn (1981), by highlighting the imprecision in 'terminology and nomenclature' which has been present in discourses of African theatre and performance practices. A distinction needs to be made in the examination of African performances between 'drama' and 'theatre', and between the 'dramatic' and the 'theatrical' (see Horn: 181). The inability to recognize a 'generic distinction' is responsible for the tendency among African scholars of both camps to easily interchange the words 'drama' and 'theatre' as if they are one and the same thing. Granted that these differences are mostly subtle, but such non-differentiated usage ignores the 'fact that drama . . . is a sub-group of theatre with specific qualities, both formal and functional, which distinguish it from other sub-groups' (p. 193). A non-differentiated usage also ignores the fact that even within the broad family of performance, theatre represents a distinct sub-group, with unique characteristics which distinguish it from other sub-groups, such as sports, rituals, festivals and so on. Amankulor, de Graft, Enekwe, Echeruo, Ogunbiyi and Uka are consistently guilty of this imprecision and consistently interchange between the terms in their writings.

The performances in this study therefore are presented first and foremost as theatres and performances, and they are all discussed in performance and theatre terms, with the central focus being on the three key elements of performance – space, spectator and performer – their deployment, and the nature of the interaction between them within a performance process. Most of the discussion – even if it is the full-bodied dramatic sketches of the *Koteba* – will neither be about plot or linguistic content, nor about specialized scenery; rather, emphasis will be placed on what happens when the spectator encounters the performer in a designated space. It will also be about the processes of making and analysing the performances. How are the performers trained? How do they prepare for a performance? How do the spectators interact with the performance? What kinds of costumes are worn, and what kinds of props are used. Who makes these accessories of performance? What is the nature and use of space? How do the performers bring the diverse but interconnecting elements together? And crucially, how do the spectators assess this assemblage? Finally, it will be about what aesthetic or social benefits these performance forms bring to their respective communities.

Traditional and modern

This introduction intends to get rid of one other misconception about African performance and theatre. Quite often, discussions about African performances try to distinguish between the indigenous oral tradition and the literary tradition by using the terms 'traditional' and 'modern' respectively to designate them. However, as with the term 'drama', the terms traditional and modern are misleading, and grossly misrepresent the performance landscape in Africa. They also concomitantly misrepresent the relationship between indigenous oral theatres and performances and the literary drama and theatre. To begin with, the idea of traditional in relation to indigenous performances had come to imply something of the past, fossilized and no longer in use; whereas modern, on the other hand, is the current, the fashionable, the contemporary, and the actively in use. There is also a sense in which this usage suggests that the 'modernisation' brought about by colonization had completely eradicated these theatrical performance practices, and that where they are still to be found, they are more or less frozen museum pieces resurrected from time to time. This suggestion of stasis in the indigenous forms this book hopes to disprove.

The actual situation, however, is that the two traditions of performance in Africa are contemporaneous with each other, as the four performances chosen for study here show. The indigenous African performance and theatre forms survived historical processes and phenomena, including a culturally devastating colonial encounter. They have also managed to hold their own against the literary theatre and other syncretic popular perform-ance forms that emerged as a result of the colonial intrusion into African cultures and histories.

Using the term 'modern' to designate the literary drama and theatre implies that it is only this theatre which has a modernist vision or adopts a modernist perspective to themes, characters and processes. However, the resilience of the indigenous forms, such as the Igbo *Mmonwu* and the Bamana *Koteba*, lies in their ability to dialectically interact and nego-tiate with history. These negotiations, the study shows, are mainly them-atic, although sometimes they are structural. The indigenous forms are constantly reviewing and revising themselves in response to their ever-changing historical and cultural contexts. They withstood the concerted assaults of colonial politics and those of Christian and Islamic religions by engaging with, adapting and incorporating these intruding elements into their universe as a means of domesticating and coping with them. The Ijele masquerade of the Igbo, for example, exhibits an almost irreverent postmodernist appropriation of alien materials and threats in a process of discursive containment. Ijele successfully absorbed the colonial experience and presence of late nineteenth and mid-twentieth centuries, and of late has taken on board the jet bombers, fighters and military personalities of Nigeria's three-year civil war of 1967–1970. At the time I saw it again in 1997, it was already beginning to acknowledge and assimilate the presence of computers, satellite dishes and communication masts of the eighties and nineties era. In this way the Ijele is able to perform its primary role of representing the entirety of the Igbo universe. Its climactic dance at the end of each performance is usually a gigantic and graceful swirling move-ment of reflecting mirrors and images through which it is able to reveal to all the spectators a concatenation of key moments, objects and personal-ities of accumulated Igbo communal experience and history. Significantly however, it is also a history that is in constant motion, forever changing and adding unto itself, in the same way that the Ijele masquerade adds on to itself from year to year by adding newer images and objects to its ever growing frame. Thus, the Ijele, like the Igbo universe, which it represents, and like life itself, grows in size as it encounters and negotiates with history. The same can be said of the other performances being studied; the *Koteba*'s pool of characters constantly expands to keep pace with a constantly chan-ging and unfolding Bamana collective experience and history. The *Koteba*'s most recent character is the Been-to, usually an economic migrant like Wankyu, recently returned from China or Europe and out to impress everyone with his new knowledge and wealth. Mandinka *griots* are quint-essentially modernist in outlook as each *jali* (Mandinka for *griot*) forever lives and performs in the moment. A *jali* responds to the immediate and the remote past in his or her performance. While anchoring their narrative firmly in the past, he or she is still able to incorporate the here and now in the thematic landscape, thus enabling the past and the present to coexist in the same moment and mutually interrogate one another. Even *Bori* ritual performance, which, on the surface, may appear to be the most fixed and time-bound of the four chosen performance forms, yet its spirit characters are timeless entities, who are still as powerful and as influential as they have always been in the affairs of Hausa society. Besides, the *Bori* pantheon has been revised to now include Muslim and European spirits as a result of its continuing process of negotiations with and containment of alien threats.

Thus, to categorize these performances as being outside the 'modern' umbrella, as has been the case, shows how grossly inadequate and ultimately redundant such terms as 'traditional' and 'modern' are in dealing with such eclectic African indigenous forms. Besides, the expected evolutionary progression from the traditional to the modern suggested in the evolutionist viewpoint and those of Mahood and Finnegan has not happened and is not likely to happen in the context of African performance and theatre. The expectation was that a progression and transition needed to take place from the indigenous theatres and performances to literary drama and theatre. Looked at from one perspective, the two traditions are, in fact, tangential to one another, with each developing along its own lines. But, there is evidence in the literary theatre that after the initial phase of a slavish imitation of European models, more and more African dramatists are beginning to mine their respective indigenous performance traditions as sources and basis for their dramatic creations. The literary theatre is borrowing more and more from the oral tradition as is clear from many African plays.

Soyinka, for instance, is deeply influenced by his Yoruba cultural heritage, not only in his themes but also in the way his plays are sometimes structured. *A Dance of the Forests* bears imprints of Yoruba *Egungun* theatre in which ancestors and the dead are invited by the living during the latter's moments of need. Soyinka uses this idea, as well as indigenous storytelling techniques to weave a cautionary parable for Nigeria on the eve of her independence from colonial rule in 1960. Other playwrights influenced by African indigenous storytelling traditions are John Pepper Clark-Bekederemo in *Ozidi*, Efua Sutherland in *The Marriage of Anansewa*, Femi Osofisan in *The Chattering and the Song*. Werewere Liking has developed a theatre form based on *Ngue* – a healing and initiation ritual of her native Bassa in the Cameroon, and Zadi Zaourou's plays are based on the *Didiga*, a sacred hunter performance of the Bete people of the Ivory Coast. All these borrowings have one thing in common, they show the writers' acceptance of the indigenous African aesthetic and understanding of theatre and performance as a complex of multiple languages of dance, song, music, mime and, occasionally, dialogue. The borrowing, however, seems to be in one direction only. The indigenous theatres and performances – especially the ones being studied here – seem neither aware of nor in any way influenced by the literary, or any other theatre or performance forms.

Aesthetically, they have remained true to their original forms and processes, and where they have adapted new or foreign material, such as techno-logy (photography, film, video, and electric lighting), and to changing life patterns of their respective communities, these adaptive processes have not significantly affected, or interfered with, the essence of their performance practices and structures.

Performance, culture and society in Africa

There is a unique three-way relationship between performance, culture and society in all contexts of human existence. This relationship is a dialectical one in which the three mutually inform and affect each other in significant ways. Turner's statement that 'cultures are most fully expressed and made conscious of themselves in their rituals and theatrical performances' with which this chapter opened offers only a one dimensional view of this relationship, one in which the latter are just reflections of the former. However, Turner at the same time suggests the dialectical nature of this relationship. On the one hand, cultures provide the material subjects and objects out of which performances are made. On the other hand, in and through the process of performance cultures become self-aware and present themselves as cultures. This close relationship between performance, society and culture is reflected in the fact that every work of art belongs to its age, its nation and its geographical context.

The dialectic in this relationship between a work of art and its context occurs as a series of mediations and counter-mediations between art, culture and society. African performances constantly engage with, modify, and are, in turn, modified by their socio-cultural contexts. This dialectical view sees theatre and performance as constitutive social practices, which are part of the very complex social processes that make up African histories and contemporary realities. Thus, African cultures and societies inform and shape African theatres and performances, and the former are in turn revealed in and through the latter. It is a relationship of mutual affectivity.

Do the performances being studied here fit into this scheme of mutual affectivity between theatre, culture and society? First, the very existence and survival of these performances reflects the unending cultural politics engaged in over so many years between African societies and cultures and intruding or invading cultural forces. Second, their resistance to attempts to dismiss or marginalize them in the post-independence, postcolonial era says a lot about the enduring legacy of the colonial cultural devastation and hegemony which is expressed by the idea of 'colonial mentality'. Its continued existence in thinking and behaviour underpins the viewpoints expressed by the evolutionists; it is also present in the alternative viewpoint put forward by the relativists when they desperately try to prove that African indigenous performances are drama. They are unfortunately side-tracked into an unnecessary and meaningless defence of the existence of African indigenous performances and theatres, rather than examining their aesthetics and function as social art practices.

The four performances studied provide glimpses of this process of negotiation and mediation between the performances and their cultural contexts. *Bori*, for instance, is a ritual/religious performance, which by its very existence within contemporary Hausa society that is predominantly Muslim, reflects the battle between an invading colonial Islamic culture and an indigenous cultural practice; in the process *Bori* and its adherents/artists have become a marginalized minority culture and practice. The performances themselves reflect a continuing battle for the spiritual domination of minds within Hausa society. For while in theory a majority of the people has been converted to Islam, in reality however, these same converts watch and participate in the performances by supporting and soliciting the help of the *Bori* spirits during possession and trance events. The same religious pragmatism is reflected in the Igbo *Mmonwu* performances in which, although most Igbo people are now mainly Christians, the ambivalent relationship between the spectator and masked performer strongly reflects the conflicting pull that most Igbo people feel between their acquired Christian faith and doctrine and their indigenous religious belief in the existence of many spirits and the power of the ancestors and these spirits to influence human life and action. Thematically, these on-going contradictions are reflected in the performances as they take on board contemporary issues and realities. The theatres reflect the respective historical journey each society or context has made. They also reflect abiding and contemporary concerns. As old as the comic characters of the *Koteba* sketches are, they reflect Bamana society and culture today. But they are also about Bamana past and future.

What the theatres and performances do is to appropriate new experiences, re-present them, and thereby in the process acting simultaneously as social memories and refractive indexes of their respective communities. Each performance is in dialogue with history, affecting and changing history as much as it is affected and changed by history. They are also in dialogue with their respective cultures and societies, affecting and being affected by them. Performance, culture and society, therefore, can be said to exist in an intricate symbiotic relationship of mutually beneficial affect in which none of them acts, either merely as a reflective mirror or as a containing vehicle for the others. They are like the three legs of a cooking tripod, each needing the others for support and survival, and each enabling the others to perform the roles expected of them by their communities.

Choice of performance forms

The first consideration in the choice of performance forms for study was based on how widespread a form is across cultures, societies and regions and therefore fairly representative of the continent. The masquerade theatre is the form most likely to be found all over the African continent, and so it was the first to be chosen. The major extant masking traditions in Africa today are: in Nigeria, the *Mmonwu* of the Igbo; the *Egungun* and *Gelede* masquerades of the Yoruba; the *Ekine* of the Kalabari, the *Okumpka* of Afikpo, the *Okonko* and the *Ekpe* of Ngwa, Ohafia, Arochukwu and Arondizuogu, and the *Ekpo* of the Ibibio; in Sierra Leone, the *Ode-lay* and *Mammiwata* in Freetown; the *Dama* of the Dogon, the *Do* and *Koteba* of the Bamana and the Bozo, all to be found in Mali; further afield in Eastern and Southern Africa, the *Gule wa Mkulu* of the Chewa of Malawi and Zambia; the *Makisi* of Angola and Zimbabwe; the *Nkonde* of Mozambique and Tanzania. Most African cultures south of the Sahara have a masking theatre tradition of one kind or another. It became clear in the course of looking at African masking that across this vast geographical landscape and different contexts, the practices show very close similarities in terms of their stories of origin, organizational structure and support, actual performance processes, and social and aesthetic functions. The present researcher has chosen to focus on the *Mmonwu* tradition because my long participation in, and intimate knowledge of this theatre practice makes it the most suitable form for study.

The second type of performance chosen because of its wide distribution on the continent, is ritual theatre. The term needs explanation as it can be applied to a host of other indigenous performances in Africa, including the masquerade theatre and the *Koteba*. *Mmonwu*'s close association with ancestors and spirits gives it an aura of religion and ritual even when the context of a performance is clearly secular. The difference between them is that in *Bori* the ritual possession and trance is the performance, whereas in *Koteba* and *Mmonwu* the performances merely have ritual associations. The book will explore this religious dimension in detail in Chapters 2 and 3. Although not as widely distributed as the masquerade theatre, ritual performances are found in many African cultures. Of the various kinds in Africa, trance and possession rituals particularly fascinated me, and logically these became my second choice of form to study. But the choice was also because of their complexity, theatricality, and ability to transform performers into characters without the employment of any form of physical disguise, as in the *Mmonwu* and the *Koteba* theatre traditions.

The implications of this theatricality will be explored in Chapter 3 which will concentrate on *Bori*, a trance and possession ritual of the

Hausa, who live mainly in Northern Nigeria, but are also to be found across most northern parts of West Africa and southern parts of North Africa. I have specifically chosen *Bori* for three main reasons; first, because it is a tradition that I am very familiar with, and second, because of its long and established history and very developed state. And finally, *Bori* was chosen because the Hausa are a significantly large ethnic group who are dispersed across a large area of the region. Other major traditions of trance and possession performances in Africa are: in Nigeria, the *Orukororo* of the Ijaw of the Delta region and the Nago-Yoruba spirit mediums, found also in neighbouring Benin; in Eastern Africa, the spirit-medium performances of the Bunyoro and Alur of Uganda, and the Shetani cult possession performances of the Segeju of Tanzania; and in Southern Africa, the *Bira* of the Shona in Zimbabwe, the *Masabe* of the Tonga of Zambia and Zimbabwe, the *Ngoma* spirit-mediums, and the trance and possession performances of a host of Southern African Bantu groups in Mozambique, Angola, Malawi, Botswana and Swaziland. Spirit possession cults also exist in Ethiopia, Somalia, and in other parts of West Africa. In general, these trance and possession dances are mainly performed by women, but the possession cults also have other marginalized social groups as members.

One interesting fact to emerge from the exploration of these performance traditions is that of the widespread exclusion of women in a significant number of them. So far, no convincing explanation has been put forward for this exclusion. In Igbo masking theatre, for instance, women are never initiated and so can never participate as performers, since only through an initiation can an individual acquire the basics and the authority to perform. Women can only be spectators, and for them the mechanics of theatre-making and control is shrouded in mystery and secrecy. The irony however is that without the female spectators, Igbo masking theatre would lose a lot of its fun and impetus. It is surprising that women are also excluded from a secular performance, such as the *Kote-tlon* satiric sketches. *Jaliya* and *Bori*, of the four performances considered here, are the ones in which men and women participate in equal measure.

Koteba (*Kote-tlon*) was chosen because it is in many respects a totally different kind of performance. Unlike the others, it is not found across the continent, being unique to its Bamana culture, and it is more like a dramatic performance – having clear plots, stories, scene divisions, and relies mainly on dialogue. It is essentially a secular theatrical form, having apparently broken away from whatever religious connections it once had. The *Jaliya* of the Mandinka of Senegal and the Gambia was chosen because it also is quite different from the other three. While it shares the secularity of the *Koteba*, it is principally a musical performance which encompasses the very widespread art of the storyteller. But like all the others, it is also 'total theatre' in which song, music, dance, acrobatic displays, mime and sometimes dialogue are present in varying degrees and combinations. Of the four, it is the most individualistic, requiring formally and informally acquired performance skills and one of the most internationally visible African performance forms today. Although known by different names in different places, the art of the *griot* (*jaliya*) and *griots* (*jalolu*) can be found across the whole of West Africa – from the Cameroon in the east to Senegal in the west and Mauritania in the north-west of the region. Sharing a similar wide distribution as the masquerade, it can also be found in other parts of Africa, the closest example being the *Oriki* chants and praise-poetry performances of the Yoruba of Nigeria and Togo and the *Izibongo* of the Zulu of South Africa.

I have in my choices tried to reflect the unfortunate Anglophone, Franco-phone and Luso-phone divide, which is one enduring legacy of the continent's colonial history. For practical and logistic reasons, two perform-ances have been chosen from the two main zones of English and French, but because of the similarities in practices and processes of performance, a form from any one culture or society provides a good sample with which to analyse and understand other versions of that form. The practice of *Jaliya* in Senegal or the Gambia gives an insight into *griotism* in Guinea-Bissau or in Niger. Moreover, the Euro-zoning of West Africa as a result of colonization seems to have had no significant impact on indigenous performance practices and forms. The four chosen are in their respective native languages – *Mmonwu* is performed in Igbo, *Bori* in Hausa, *Koteba* in Bambara, and *Jaliya* in Mandinka. The first two come from Nigeria, while the other two are from Mali and Senegal respectively. The traditions and forms of theatre and performance studied in this book will give the reader a good insight into the dominant indigenous theatre and perform-ance forms of West Africa, and an introduction to those of the whole continent.

Each form will be explored in terms of contexts and occasions for performance, staging techniques, such as stage and use of space, props, costume and make-up, scenery; methods of training and rehearsal; systems and structures of management and organization of performances; methods and processes of creating and maintaining performances and reper-tory. Aesthetic principles underpinning performance are also considered, including the idea of 'total theatre' in which music, song, dance, mime, acrobatics, dialogue and story or *mythos* come together and are of equal value as languages and mediums of performance. Thematic concerns, social and aesthetic functions of theatre and performance in African cultures, the nature of the spectator–performer encounter and interaction, and means and languages of assessment of performances are also discussed in relation to these practices.

The book is divided into five chapters, each of which focuses on a specific performance event. Chapter 2 looks at *Mmonwu* of the Igbo of Eastern Nigeria for which the chosen location is Nkpor in Idemili Local Government Area of Anambra State. Chapter 3 is on *Bori* ritual of the Hausa of Northern Nigeria, for which field research was carried out in Zaria in Kaduna State. Chapter 4 is on *Jaliya* and is based on the *Mandinka Balundo* celebration held in Dakar, Senegal, while Chapter 5 on the *Koteba* is based on field observations in Markala and Segou, in Mali. The concluding chapter brings together the similarities and differences between the performances, and looks at the future of these indigenous oral forms in the light of urbanization and technological developments.

2 *Mmonwu*: Igbo masquerade theatre

Encounters with ancestors and spirits

Igbo masking is religious and theatrical, ritual and entertainment, and it is difficult, almost impossible, to separate the two. However, an understanding of the Igbo worldview is crucial to a study of the masquerade theatre. The Igbo universe is perceived as being made up of three planes of existence: the planes of the dead, the living, and the unborn. These planes correspond to the past, present and future. Crucially, Igbo religious thought espouses an essential dualism based on a notion of mutual dependence and affectivity between spirit and matter. Every object or phenomenon has both spiritual and material aspects that are mutually complementary and dependent. However, despite this, the Igbo accept and celebrate the primacy of the spiritual over the material. The world of the living (humans and animals) exists on the material plane, while the worlds of the gods, the dead or ancestors, and the unborn exist on the spiritual. For the Igbo, religion is a way of exploring, understanding and coming to terms with both the natural (material) and the supernatural (spiritual) aspects of their world. Through rituals they are able to establish an environment within which they can negotiate with the spirits believed to play major roles in their lives. Through rituals also, they are able to honour the gods, placate the spirits, and commune with their departed ancestors. Thus the Igbo universe, though it has the living at its centre, is spirit-centred. But while a clear distinction is made between spirit and matter, there is an acceptance of the interconnectedness and movement between them. Transference from one plane to another can easily be achieved through specific rites of transition. Igbo masking is one such socio-religious rite of transference, and the mask is the 'most tangible manifestation of the link between the living and the dead' (Awoonor, 1975: 70). Two other such rites are birth rites (to enable movements between the world of the un-born and that of the living), and funerary rites (to facilitate transition from the human world to that of the ancestors).

Conceptually, Igbo masquerade characters are ancestors or spirit forces that have taken on material form and returned to the human plane at the invitation of the living. Masking is thus a highly developed socio-religious activity whose sustaining ethos is that it enables the Igbo to establish a physical relationship and communion with the spirit world of their ancestors and deities. The ancestors and spirits constitute a community of souls and entities whose beneficial contact is constantly needed and sought by the living. The ancestors, spirits and gods are ideas born of the Igbo collective imagination but which need to be made flesh periodically in order for immediate physical contact and interaction to be effected. This physical manifestation of the spiritual on the material plane ensures that the continuities between the different worlds of the Igbo universe are kept alive through the masking theatre, with its explicit symbolism and performative dynamism. Igbo ancestors and spirits are able to participate physically in human affairs as masquerades.

Although the masked characters are, in general, regarded as dead ancestors or spirits who have returned for a communion with the human community, they are also recognized as human actors playing roles before a critically appreciative audience. The sense of playing with ancestors and nature spirits is never far away in any encounter between an Igbo spectator and a masquerade character. And this is in spite of the overwhelming religious significance and the ritual envelope within which this encounter usually takes place. Igbo masking, therefore, like all theatres around the world, involves the performance paradox of 'invisible presence and present absence': in a masking encounter, there is the visible character (an ancestor, a spirit, an animal, etc.) and the invisible performer (the masker). The simultaneous co-existence makes Igbo masking a theatrical encounter as well as a ritual since the spectator is capable of perceiving and accepting the paradoxical presence and absence of both. The masked performer constantly challenges the spectators with his absence but at the same time he confronts them with the 'obvious' presence of the character. At a religious level, the masked figures are ancestors or supernatural beings, but also at a purely theatrical level, the spectator sees these figures as characters in fictional situations. It is this playful challenge, and the willingness of the audience to accommodate this paradox that brings about the magic of theatrical performance. This is made possible by the mask, which is the soul of Igbo indigenous theatre, because it provides the basic and enabling metaphor for dramatic characters and situations. The mask is a coded plane of signification for the characters and the fictional or real situations that develop in their semiotic encounter with the spectators.

Although masking is widespread in Igboland, this study will concentrate on one tradition, as the best way of defining and maintaining focus.

However, one sub-tradition's practice cannot be a basis on which to construct a homogenizing aesthetic theory: so the *Mmonwu* (*Mmo* or *Mmanwu*) tradition studied here is merely one among many, unique in itself, although sharing many common features with a host of other sub-traditions. The focus here will be on masking in Nkpor, a town in Anambra State of Nigeria. I will be using this masking practice because it is one that I know very well, having actively participated in it for a considerable length of time.

Occasions for performance

A broad range of occasions lend themselves to the appearance and perform-ance of masquerades in Igboland. These include festivals, sacred and secular ceremonies, funerals, and sometimes periods of crisis or major breaches and threats to social cohesion and stability. A group may decide at any time to present its masked performance, but most try to do so around certain festival and seldom during the rainy or farming season. The dry season guarantees a rain-free performance, as well as maximum attendance by spectators who are then free of any work pressures.

The main occasions in Nkpor are initiations or *ima mmo*, which literally means 'knowing the masquerade' and is the formal introduction of young boys into the secret art of masking. The second is *ime ntu* – a boys' masking event that provides the first opportunity for initiated boys to make their own masks and perform with them. Third are festivals such as *Enemma* ('beholding beauty or spectacle'), *Ifejioku* (yam harvest festival). Other occasions are Christmas, Easter and New Year celebrations, *uno onwu* (funerals), *ibuputa mmonwu* ('bringing out a masquerade' or private outings) and judicial performances. These occasions exist throughout the Idemmili masking area, and specifically for this study I will be looking at an *Enemma* performance, which I watched in March 1993.

An *Enemma* festival performance

Festivals are an integral part of Igbo social, political and agricultural calendar, and every Igbo community has a series of them. They are public celebrations of events, which are considered to be of significant value by a community. In Nkpor, events that invite such public celebrations are those that involve the worship of local deities, mark the agricultural cycle, or those that celebrate life crises of individuals or the community. *Enemma* is the biggest festival in Nkpor, and it exhibits the major characteristic of fest-ivals, which is inclusiveness. Every masquerade type or group in the town is free to participate. Both performers and spectators need no invitation to take part. *Enemma* belongs to the whole community, as a celebration of the collective spirit of the town and a moment of transition between two seasons. Unlike the funeral, initiation and judicial performances in Nkpor, *Enemma*'s celebratory nature provides the theme and flavour for all participating masquerades and groups, irrespective of the underlying ethos or idea behind individual performances, set of skits, or sketches. The festival usually takes place in late February or early March. It is timed to precede or coincide with the first rain of each year. I watched and recorded the festival in 1993 and 1994.

Enemma has a set structure made up of three phases: a ritual veneration or worship in the morning; a family feast in the afternoon; and a general communal open-air entertainment in the evening. We will be concerned with the third phase during which the masquerades feature. The appearance of the masquerades marks the highpoint of the festivities. I chose *Enemma* as the event to analyse for two reasons. The first is that as a festival, the theatre offered is far richer and more representative of the community's theatre tradition and style than the single mask display of the other contexts. The second reason was because Igbo masquerade theatre is not, strictly speaking, a story- or character-led theatre, but more of a symbolic spectacle, which makes analyzing it using dramatic frames as both the evolutionist and relativist scholars mentioned in the previous chapter (pp. 4–12) inappropriate since it is not drama. The festival was an event in which the rich symbolism, the collage of moving images and colours, and the spatial fluidity of this theatre could be fully realized and appreciated.

In scale, *Enemma* is quite grand and lasts an entire day. A full *Enemma* would expect to present close to three hundred different masquerades for an intense four hours in which the central performing venue would be teeming with performers and spectators, both colourfully clothed and fluidly interpenetrating each other's space. But for the 1993 performance, only about seventy masquerades took part, and a majority of these belonged to the three groups that I will be discussing later. The spectacular thing about *Enemma* was that as many masked characters as could be accommodated in the space performed simultaneously for different sections of the audience. This mode of staging can best be described as composite since various scenes and pockets of action were happening at the same time (Okagbue, 1987: 159). The result was that both spectators and performers were constantly on the move, as each masquerade wanted to be seen or to interact with as many spectators and in as many locations as he/she possibly could. The spectators for their part engaged with as many performances and masquerades as they could. The festival is ideal for the masquerade theatre, by providing a spatial envelope in which independent and unrelated masquerades or other performance activities can take place simultaneously or separately.

For this *Enemma*, I was a special guest of the Ochammili Cultural Group, a mixed age masking group from Ububa Village, who were presenting their Ochammili masquerade for the first time in the festival. This meant that I had the opportunity to observe the group's preparation from their rehearsal venue – some two miles away from Ilo Obofia, the venue for that year's festival – through the journey to the performance and back in the evening for the cooling down phase. So, for the team and ourselves the performance began quite early. Even though the festival performance was scheduled to begin at around 2.30 p.m. and go on until around 6.30 p.m., people began gathering at the Ochammili rehearsal compound from about midday. My team and I arrived at approximately 12.30 p.m. and, by the time we got there, most group members were already assembled and putting finishing touches to their costumes, the musicians were tuning their instruments, while others generally chatted to one another or helped out in other ways. At about 1.30 p.m. the musicians began playing a slow rhythm, intended as a warm up for actors and spectators alike. It was also a signal that everything was in place for the emergence of the masquerade characters.

But first, the group had to search for the masquerades – this phase is known as *icho mmonwu*. The musicians continued with the slow rhythm for a while before they rose and began circling the compound – there were five dancers in front, followed by five instrumentalists and one singer. All of them wore yellow T-shirts and short brown skirts underneath which they wore khaki shorts. On the front of each T-shirt was painted a bold image of a giraffe (ochammili) on top of the group's name.

The rhythm suddenly changed to a faster beat and the dancers in response changed to energetic and rhythmic stamping, running and dancing, as they frantically looked everywhere and called out loudly to the masquerades to appear. The flutist's distinctive sound could be heard as he plaintively called upon the masquerades to inform them that all was set for the procession to the festival arena. There were acrobatic displays by the dancers – including double and triple somersaults, and highly energetic dances and movements. There was no specific pattern to the dance, and neither did the movements at this stage appear to have been choreographed. This went on for about ten minutes, until the music changed yet again, this time to a slightly slower processional beat, with a melodious lyrical accompaniment:

> *Obodo Nkpor, unu anugo na Ububa tili*
> *Mmonwu ana kpo Ochammili*
> *Obodo Nkpor, unu anugo na Ububa tili*
> *Mmonwu ana kpo Ochammili*

Mmonwu ana kpo Ochammili
Na odi ebube
Mmonwu ana kpo Ochammili
Amaka
Nkpor, mmonwu aputa ilo
Obodo Nkpor, mmonwu aputa ilo

(Nkpor town, have you heard that Ububa has produced
A masquerade called Ochammili
Nkpor town, have you heard that Ububa has produced
A masquerade called Ochammili

The masquerade called Ochammili
Is dignified
The masquerade called Ochammili
Is beautiful

Nkpor, a masquerade has come out to the square
Nkpor town, a masquerade has come out to the square)

As the song came to an end, the music changed to another quick beat
and a new dance routine with complex patterns of leg and body movements began. The dancers squatted really very low, legs apart, upper body
and head held straight, and holding this stance they made short rhythmical forward jumps with their hands parallel to the ground, the left fully
extended in front and the right, hooked at the elbow, making small slicing
movements while the left was held steady. In this posture – lead dancer in
front and the others forming two lines on either side – they rhythmically
moved forward. On getting to the end of the compound the lead dancer
turned right and the two lines behind turned, one to the right, the other to
the left and danced back towards the musicians; then in again to repeat the
sequence. This highly energetic dance was designed to achieve two things.
The first was to keep the waiting spectators entertained, and second, as a
cue for the first masquerade to emerge from the dressing room – a little
brick house to the right of where we sat. The first to come out was Onuku
(Fool). Onuku was dressed in a dark bluish loose-fitting costume. His face
was quite striking because of its prominent features – bald head made more
obvious by a wide and protruding forehead, sagging eyelids, a wide mouth
with a bit of his tongue showing in the corner, ears that were almost flat
on the sides of his face, and very bushy eyebrows. He had large and sad
eyes. A combination of all of these features gave him a vacant, sad and silly
countenance (**Fig. 2.1**). Onuku's other striking feature was his enormous
genitals – a very large scrotum represented by a big white pouch which
hung prominently between his legs. He constantly cupped it while running

Figure 2.1 Onuku (Fool).

or dancing or thrust it lewdly at people. His entrance was greeted with much joy, especially by children and younger members of the audience whom he proceeded to gleefully chase around the compound in his characteristic loping and ungainly manner of walking, running or dancing – arms and legs flailing and flapping about, and his outsized genitals bobbing from side to side. Everybody seemed to like Onuku, he embraced anyone within reach, occasionally making sexually suggestive hip movements or humping at anything or anyone within grabbing distance. Having made a frenetic run around the arena, chased and copulated with as many objects or people as possible, he dashed back to the dressing room, an exasperated restrainer following in his wake.

While we waited for the other masked characters to get ready and come out, we decided to make a quick dash in a car to the festival venue. Spectators were already gathering and taking their places – some sat on chairs, some climbed the trees that ringed the arena, while some stood right around. Collectively, they framed a fairly big performance space in the middle (**Fig. 2.2**). About nine colourful canopies were placed at regular distances round the arena, with chairs placed in rows inside and between

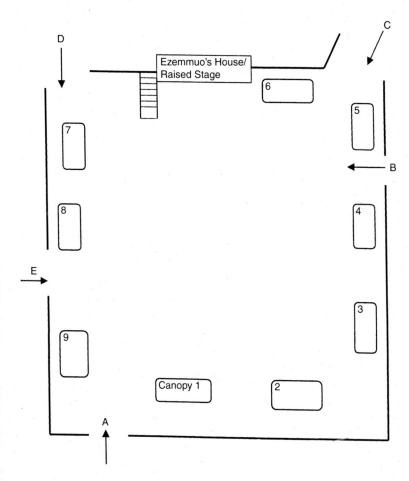

Figure 2.2 Diagram of Ilo Obofia/Enemma arena and stage.

them. Three big gaps A, C and D and two small ones, B and E were left for entrances and exits. Some masked performers were already in the square entertaining the assembled spectators. These included Mmonwu Akolo – the satiric night masquerade who delights in exposing moral and social misdemeanours. He was busy regaling the spectators with satiric songs about recent events, and he spiced this with some comic banter. He picked on anyone who passed by who had not acknowledged him. Another character, dressed in a white caftan and white helmet to match and holding a small staff in his left hand and a leather fan on the right, was clumsily weaving in and out and falling over the rows of chairs between B and C, and then turning round to blame the bewildered spectators for tripping him. He pretended to be creating order among the seated members of the audience, while in reality he was causing much chaos, especially among the female members and children who ran away each time he approached where they sat. A third character dressed as a young woman delighted in sneaking up behind, or in between, female spectators, and in a female voice would begin a conversation with them until the unsuspecting spectator(s) realized they had been talking to or been standing very close to a masquerade. Of course, this often led to mini stampedes as the women rushed to get away from 'her' – it is the tradition that women and the uninitiated always run away from masked figures.

While all this was going on, Akuezuozo (also known as Ezemmo or king of the masquerades) arrived with his retinue of about six – made up of his flutist, and personal assistants. Akuezuozo is also regarded as the archetypal ancestor and hence the respect he enjoys and his role as the custodian of the community's cultural heritage and patron of the festival. He came through Entrance A, and slowly made his way across the arena to its right end where a raised house or stage had been erected for him. From this vantage position he surveyed and oversaw the entire evening's performance (**see Fig. 2.2**). Part of Akuezuozo's duties and performance was to declare the evening open, welcome each group and give them permission to take the arena, and he also brings the event to a close. Gingerly climbing the steps of his house and taking his place, Akuezuozo stood up and blew a few toots on his elephant tusk to all corners of the arena to formally signal his arrival. He then handed the tusk over to one of his assistants, and sat down. Another assistant handed him a whole kola nut and he proceeded to perform the ritual oblation, which always precedes the breaking of kola nut in Igboland. Finished, he gave a piece each to his assistants. A cup of palm wine was handed over to him and he poured a libation, with each drop of palm wine on the ground he called on the gods and ancestors to come and partake of the celebration and to bless the performances about to follow. He then sat down to await the arrival of the first performers.

While those in the arena waited, we rushed back to the Ochammili compound to join up with the group. Mmonwu Awusa (Hausa Masquerade) was just emerging from the dressing room as we entered. He was a foreigner from the North and this was suggested by his *baba riga* – a traditional two-piece Hausa attire-ethnic facial marks, and his ability to 'speak' Hausa. Around his neck hung a green silk scarf and his two hands were covered in white gloves. Because he was a petty trader, he carried a small tray expertly balanced in his left hand. His performance was mainly trying to sell items from his tray to spectators. He came straight to offer us his wares to buy – kola nuts, biscuits, sweets, cigarettes and matches. Like Onuku, he too was a favourite of the audience and he engaged in a lot of trade banter with them. As soon as he emerged, he was greeted with shouts of:

Spectator 1:	Aboki, zo!
Spectator 2:	Aboki, weta oji
Spectator 3:	Aboki, ina kwa na?
Mmonwu Awusa:	Ina ga jiya
Spectator 2:	Ya ya dei?
Mmonwu Awusa:	Lafiya lau
Spectator 1:	Aboki, weta oji
Mmonwu Awusa:	Ka wo kwudi
Spectator 1:	Akwoi kwudi mana!
Mmonwu Awusa:	Tau, kawo kwudi
Spectator 1:	Ga kwudi
Mmonwu Awusa:	Tau, na gode. Na gode Allah!
(*Spectator 1*:	Mister, come!
Spectator 2:	Mister, bring kola nut
Spectator 3:	Mister, how are you?
Mmonwu Awusa:	I am well
Spectator 2:	How goes it?
Mmonwu Awusa:	No problem
Spectator 1:	Mister, bring kola nut here
Mmonwu Awusa:	Bring your money
Spectator 1:	There is money (indicating his pocket)
Mmonwu Awusa:	Ok, bring it (extending his right hand)
Spectator 1:	Take the money
Mmonwu Awusa:	(taking the money) Thank you. Thank you, God!)

At last, he succeeded in selling some items – one person bought a piece of kola nut, and another paid for a stick of cigarette. The happy trader collected his money, turned and did a brief dance to celebrate his success,

Figure 2.3 Mmonwu Awusa waves to 'Customers'/Spectators.

and soon was off to another side of the compound where more willing customers were beckoning for him to come over (**Fig. 2.3**).

As Mmonwu Awusa sashayed across advertising his wares, Adamma, the daughter of the household, appeared. She was dressed in shiny golden yellow long blouse and trousers to match, the blouse had a multi-coloured anchor embroidered on it, the point of the anchor stopping just above her breasts. Her features were sharp and finely presented, and she wore a wig of full and well combed black hair and large golden coloured earrings. On her left shoulder hung a small red leather handbag, and on her right hand a small fan with which she fanned herself. At first she stood shyly by the doorway until persuaded by her guide to come out and introduce herself. She came across to where we stood and executed some dainty ladylike dance steps – and forever shy, she never looked at us throughout her introductory dance but kept her head turned away or fixed to the ground. However, there was nothing shy about her dancing as, through hand gestures, body movement, and the soft and gentle manner in which her feet touched the ground when she danced or walked, she tried to convey the seductive grace and suppleness of a young maiden. This was made all the more noticeable and appreciated by the common knowledge that the actor performing the role was a man.

She was soon joined by the Police Sergeant, who, as soon as he got to the centre, did his own little introductory dance in which he demonstrated his role of guard, enforcer and one who had to create space for other characters to perform by keeping the spectators in check. To reinforce this, his main props were a baton in one hand and a long cane in the other. Sometimes, he got so carried away in his dance that he had to be reminded by either the spectators or other group members to do his job of protecting Adamma and clearing the space. At which he promptly terminated his dance and with the cane swishing in the air set off to chase the encroaching spectators away from where Adamma was dancing. Her introduction over, Adamma was led back to the dressing room by her guide, while the sergeant remained in the arena, swishing and dancing as he waited for the remaining characters to appear.

A few minutes passed by, before Adamma's parents, Nna Mmo (Father masquerade) and Nne Mmo (Mother masquerade) emerged. Nna Mmo wore a green tunic with golden yellow stripes and hem on top of a long skirt of the same material and design. His face was painted a bright pink, and on his head he wore a red crown. He wore gold beads around his neck, and on his right hand was a leather fan and across his left shoulder, an elephant tusk which he supported with his left hand. Both parents wore white hand gloves, black shoes and white socks. Nne Mmo wore a rich blue blouse on white intricately decorated *kente* wrapper, and a second neatly folded *kente* wrapper was placed on her left shoulder. In her right-gloved hand she held a white horsetail whisk. On both wrists she wore huge bangles made from elephant tusk. An elaborate head-tie made from brown chiffon completed her attire. The couple were accompanied by Ezeikolobia (a hunter), and Police Inspector. Both wore military-style uniforms – Ezeikolobia's was dark blue, while the inspector's was dark grey with a small green-white-green Nigerian flag on the left breast and a row of medals on the right. Ezeikolobia carried a single-barrelled gun and on his helmeted head a hunter's glow lamp (**Figs 2.4 and 2.5**). The inspector immediately went to the front to protect the wealthy head of the household and his wife by clearing the road of traffic. Onuku and Adamma followed some distance behind the others.

Apart from Ezeikolobia who straightaway was crouching and intently scouring the ground in search of animal footprints, the others came straight to where we were. The couple did a slow dignified aristocratic dance to introduce themselves. The dance was characterized by its seeming effort-lessness and a tendency to hold the body stiffly upright, with minimal head and leg movements. Nne Mmo occasionally got down quite low in her dance, as both a mark of respect for her husband and a demonstration of her feminine suppleness – and as with Adamma, the fact that she was

Figure 2.4 Nna Mmo, Nne Mmo and Ezeikolobia emerge
from the dressing-room.

played by a man added to the excitement with which this was received.
Nna Mmo proudly acknowledged this homage by fanning and embracing
her as she got up. The entrance of the couple and their dance marked the
end of this phase.

With all members of the family ready, a procession of performers and
spectators began to make its way from the rehearsal compound to a second
compound about three hundred metres away. The musicians led the way,

Figure 2.5 Police Inspector directs traffic.

followed by the dancers, and then Mmonwu Awusa, Police Sergeant, Ezeikolobia, Onuku; some distance behind came Police Inspector followed closely by Adamma; Nna Mmo and Nne Mmo were last. On both sides of the road, walked the spectators. The second compound was where the Ochammili (Giraffe), Anukaibie (Zebra), and Akum (Hippopotamus) masquerades were being readied for the day's performance. Akum belonged to another theatre group. When the procession had arrived at the second compound, the music changed to the quicker *icho mmonwu* beat again, to which dancers, masquerades and a few spectators heartily joined in and kept dancing until the first animal character emerged from its enclosure. Anukaibie, the zebra, was performed by two actors – one person was the fore legs and front, the other the hind legs and rear – thus movement and dance had to be carefully coordinated between the two. Once out of the enclosure, Anukaibie's every movement was done to the beat of the music, and to the persistent entreaties and praises of the flutist. The sight of this huge animal threw Ezeikolobia into a frenzy of excited attempts to shoot at it. Unfortunately for him, but to the delight of the audience, he kept missing the target because of being pushed and shoved about by the crowd. Even when he thought he had had an accurate shot, the animal nonchalantly flapped its ears, flipped its tail from side to side and galloped down the road towards the festival venue. Exasperated, Ezeikolobia threw his hands and gun up in the air, and shook his head in disbelief. Occasionally, he went up to the spectators to complain about his misfortune, expecting sympathy from them. But often he got none, which spurred him on to scamper after the departing animal.

After Ezeikolobia came Inspector leading Nna Mmo and Nne Mmo, proud owners of the exotic animals which they were going to show off at the festival. Behind them came Mmonwu Awusa, and meanwhile Sergeant was busy trying to clear the road for the appearance of Ochammili, the giraffe, who apparently was the pride of the family. When some semblance of order was created, this big and majestic animal emerged from its hiding place at the farthest end of the compound. Loud cheers from the waiting spectators and group members greeted his entrance. Ochammili was approximately ten feet in height, and six feet between fore and hind legs. Its body looked very much like a real giraffe – an earthy brown patchwork of skin, a very long neck and tall front legs that enabled it to reach up to the trees without difficulty. The head and long ears could be manipulated to swivel and flap. Like Anukaibie, the role of Ochammili was performed by two actors, and its shape and size made greater coordination demands on the performers. Once it was out of its enclosure, the procession began its journey towards Ilo Obofia, but only after Ezeikolobia had made another futile attempt to gun the gigantic animal down. Meanwhile, Anukaibie had stopped a few hundred metres down the road to wait for the others, so that they would all arrive at the performance venue together. The sight of these two animals galloping or striding majestically down the road, accompanied by the human characters, musicians and dancers and spectators, was a spectacle to behold. The two animals stopped from time to time to rest, and this enabled the musicians and dancers to get to the performance venue to warn of their impending arrival.

At this point we left the procession to make our way to the venue so as to be there when the group arrived. The arena was now full, with little pockets of activities happening here and there while the audience waited for the big masquerades. As soon as the festival announcer heard the music and saw the dancers rushing into the arena, he announced that Ochammili was on its way. There was a buzz of excitement and anticipation among the spectators, and a few jostled for better viewing positions. The dancers and musicians made their way round the arena once, before Police Sergeant came in swishing left and right with his cane as he cleared the way, closely followed by Onuku, who ran excitedly from one end of the arena to the other. Police Inspector was the next to enter the arena, acting as bodyguard to the rest of the family, Adamma in front, and her parents closely behind. Meanwhile, Ezeikolobia was lurking behind a clump of bushes by the right side of Entrance A, gun primed as he waited for the approach of the two animals. Some distance behind the family was Anukaibie, and bringing up the rear, Ochammili. The group made their way across the arena to the foot of Ezemmo's raised stage to pay their respects – this was done by the group's staff bearer striking the *oji* (a rattling staff) into the ground three or four times and leaving it there on the last strike. Akuezuozo acknowledged them by blowing a few times on his tusk and motioning the group to centre stage. The announcer called on all other groups or individual performers to clear the stage to allow the Ochammili group to perform – each group was allowed approximately twenty minutes performance time. The staff bearer then retrieved the staff and led the group to the middle of the arena.

The performance consisted of each masquerade doing precisely what they are known for and had been doing at the rehearsal ground and all the way to the venue. Onuku chased and ran around, trying to engage in sexual acts with anyone near enough to be grabbed or occasionally scampering away in fear whenever either Anukaibie or Ochammili turned in his direction. Mmonwu Awusa traded with spectators or exchanged words in Hausa with them, but all the time keeping out of the way of the big animals or protecting his goods from spectators trying to steal them. Sergeant threatened members of the audience who encroached into the performance space, and occasionally getting challenged by them. Ezeikolobia kept skipping around as he searched for the best position from which to have a good shot at the two animals, while spectators pleaded with or bribed him to let Ochammili and Anukaibie alone to perform. Adamma from time to time identified members or sections of the audience and went to dance for them and receive gifts of money and praise from them in return. Some male spectators flirted with her, but she shyly avoided being touched by them nimbly dancing away from their groping hands or covering her genitals with her hands and fan. However, she gladly allowed close contact with female spectators. Her parents proudly displayed their family and immense wealth, symbolized by the two exotic animals, which they kept as pets, while Inspector hovered protectively in front of or around the couple. Anukaibie and Ochammili, the main attractions, dashed and galloped around the arena, occasionally threatening to go into the audience only to be stopped at the last minute by their restrainers from crashing into the canopies in which sat some members of the audience. The climax of this collage of moving images and bodies was the energetic dance of the two animals in which they swirled, jumped, galloped and danced while the actors inside still managed to keep to the rhythm together and suggest the movements of the respective animals. This brought loud claps and applause from the audience, who were well aware of how difficult it was to achieve such teamwork. The cheers and music built to a crescendo before crashing to bring the performance to an end. In the background, other individual masquerades were also keeping the audience occupied on their own – dancing, singing satiric songs, engaging in comic banter, or trying to intimidate the spectators into giving them money. The Ochammili group exited to great applause, the attendants and guides leading the two animals straight back while the rest of the family carried on performing on their way home.

As the group left the arena, Mmonwu Akolo began his performance which took him from one end of the arena to the other. This character was just a big rotund mound of grass, about six to seven feet tall and four feet in circumference. He hobbled along as he walked or ran. Mmonwu Akolo is renowned for his satirical songs about events in the town. When we arrived, he was comfortably positioned by Entrance A, which led into the arena and generally had a go at passers-by. As he came by where we stood, he stopped to give me a severe reprimand because I was not at home when he stopped in front of our house to greet me on his way to the square. I placated him by offering some money, which was grudgingly accepted by one of his attendants before he moved on to another target. Completing a turn of the arena, which included stopping at the foot of the raised stage to pay homage to Akuezuozo, he returned to his previous position (**Fig. 2.6**). When the *ogbo* had quietened a bit, Akuezuozo stood and tooted a few times to attract the attention of the spectators. When he felt that he had their attention, he handed the tusk back to one of his assistants, and received his fan from another and fanned himself a few times. At last he spoke, although inaudible his gestures made clear his displeasure that sections of the audience were being unruly and encroaching into the performance space.

The stage was cleared for the Akum Group, and as had happened with the Ochammili group before them, the staff bearer went to the foot of Akuezuozo's house and stuck the *oji* into the ground to signal their arrival. Akuezuozo repeated the same ritual of blowing on his tusk and asking the group to take the stage. The musicians were the first to enter, accompanied by Police Corporal, a couple, their daughter, and Di Nta (a hunter). Apart from the difference in colour, their costumes were similar in design and signification to those worn by their Ochammili counterparts. As the previous group had done, each character performed their well-known routines round the arena, such as Di Nta trying to shoot Akum, Corporal keeping order and protecting his employer's family and property, and the wealthy couple proudly strutting about. The daughter, however, was bold and flirtatious and had to be kept in check by her guide, unlike Adamma before her. The group did not have a character similar to Mmonwu Awusa. As before, the spectators showered them with money for their performance. Attendants busily collected the money, which would go into the group takings to be shared out at the end.

Figure 2.6 Mmonwu Akolo and spectators.

While Akum was performing at one end of the arena, a malevolent looking Dibia (native doctor) masquerade appeared very close to where I stood. He was so ugly that it was very difficult to look at him without a feeling of terror; his charred teeth and large eyes glaring back at me through the camera screen was disconcerting. He threatened harm and mayhem if he was not appeased before I or anyone dared to take his photograph or capture him on video without his permission. The mask face, with bold scarifications and exaggerated features, was meant to suggest power, terror and danger. He carried his own *oji* in his right hand, in his left was a little pot of medicine and on his back hung a live lizard and a live cockerel, and all kinds of amulets. One member of my team went over and offered him some money, and this made him come over to where I stood. I asked if I could record and photograph him, and he indicated through his assistant that I could. He directed a barrage of words at us, most of which I could not decipher but which were translated as boasts about his exploits, his immense power and his unique ability to strike fear into his enemies and friends alike. I offered him more money, which was received on his behalf by his assistant who also played a wooden gong for him. Deciding that he had given enough of his attention to us, Dibia darted across to the opposite side of the arena, having apparently spotted another patron. Meanwhile, all the women and children on that side took to their heels, or looked away when

they were courageous enough to stand their ground. Dibia made a few
more of these darting runs before concluding his performance at the foot
of the raised stage, where he paid homage to Akuezuozo. Acknowledged
by the latter, he turned and left the arena to make his way home.

Close on his heels from the opposite entrance came the Enemma
Group. The dancers were the first to enter the arena through Entrance
D, followed by Police Constable, a Sergeant, a hunter, daughter, father
and mother. Finally, Enemma (Beautiful Antelope) followed and, unlike
Ochammili, Anukaibie and Akum, went straight to pay homage at the foot
of Akuezuozo's stage. Enemma was a striking animal to behold, its body
was yellow-orange with tinges of chocolate brown. It had a beautifully
carved head with two large eyes that looked very much alive, and ears that
flapped from time to time. It had two antlers and a mane of brown hair,
which covered the whole of its neck and all the way down to its chest. Its
dance consisted of rocking and rolling movements designed to show off
the beauty and size of this animal. After dancing for a while, it knelt down,
shaking its head from side to side and flapping its ears (**Fig. 2.7**).

Akuezuozo acknowledged the group and they moved into the centre
of the arena to perform for the audience. The climax of Enemma's
performance was a quick loping forward and backward movement, ending
yet again with the animal kneeling down in the centre of the arena. As it
knelt, Akum re-entered from Entrance B to do its final dance – a circular
movement, followed by bobbing, lolling and swaying to represent moving

Figure 2.7 Enemma (Beautiful Antelope) enters the arena.

in water. All the while, his Di Nta who had been stalking him tried desperately through the moving bodies to get a shot at him. A spectator however intervened by offering him some money to spare the animal's life, a bribe that he gladly accepted and moved on. But by this time it was getting dark and the group guided Akum out of the arena through Entrance A to begin its journey home. Enemma got up as well and exited with her group through Entrance D. Akuezuozo allowed a few minutes to pass before he too got up, and tooted on his tusk to get the attention of everybody; he expressed his hope that they'll meet again the following year, then he blessed the crowd and wished everybody a safe journey back to their homes before he slowly climbed down from the stage. His flutist followed him closely, heaping praises on him as he made his way through the throng of spectators. His progress was very slow since he stopped every so often to exchange pleasantries and banter with spectators. This was the signal that *Enemma* was over for another year. He did stop to pose for the camera, and in response to taunts from some spectators who said that he was rather too old and could no longer dance properly, he did some 'laboured' dance routines, and holding his waist he ran around a bit to demonstrate his undiminished agility. I later learnt that the actor who played this character was in fact twenty-four years old. And in return for his 'geriatric' exertions he received more money and a chorus of applause from the spectators (**Fig. 2.8**).

Figure 2.8 Akuezuozo (Ezemmo) poses for the camera.

We then made our way back to the Ochammili group's rehearsal compound where the members were already assembled and enjoying light refreshments. All masked performers were by then divested of their costumes and masks, except for the four actors who played Ochammili and Anukaibie. They still had their trousers on and were engaged in the customary final acknowledgement dance round the compound, with the flutist behind them. The flutist called each animal's tune to which the two who played it demonstrated that animal's movements before taking their seats to join in the merriment. Members discussed and assessed how the day's performance had gone – about what had gone well and what had not. This postperformance analysis continued until well into the night, but we left them at about eight o'clock, at the point when they began discussing how much money they had received and what they were going to use it for.

Management and organization in Igbo theatre

There is a perception, especially among outsiders, that African traditional performances erupt anywhere, anyhow and at any time, almost as if they happen without any pre-planning. Part of this perception, I believe, is given credence by the belief of most African peoples that everyone can perform and thus no form of training is required. Coupled to this is the fact that there has never been any pressure for people to specialize as actors, dancers, musicians, directors or designers. Certainly in Igboland, an excessive interest and involvement in performing is frowned upon because no one is expected to make a living out of it, no matter how talented or good they are. Igbo masking theatre, like all theatre, is a composite art form, which brings together a multitude of artists working in different mediums, and thus it essentially requires skills in extensive organization and management. The study will concentrate on the various kinds of training, which would have been undergone by members of the Ochammili Cultural Group, prior to and in the making of their performance. I use this group because they and their process are typical of masquerade groups and the process of organizing a performance in Mmonwu theatre.

The group, I understand, came together in 1991 and decided to organize a performance with Anukaibie as the main animal character, but the carver had made a botched job of the mask head and shape. The group decided to go for Ochammili instead. The carver made a better job of this. They, however, decided to keep both, but the group's name changed to Ochammili Cultural Group. Members came from a broad range of interested men in Ububa Village – between the ages of twenty to forty-five years. Criteria for membership included having been initiated, an ability to perform (either as dancer, actor, musician, organizer), interest in the theatre, and financial ability. Financial ability was important because of the huge cost envisaged in organizing such a large-scale performance. The performance was expensive because of the number of masquerade characters that had to be designed and costumed, the costumes for the dancers and musicians, as well as the musical instruments to be bought.

Training

While it is non-formal, training is not absent in the masking theatre. Rather, the method used for training of actors, dancers, singers, musicians, designers and so on is unique and in keeping with the non-formal method of socializing the young into new roles and responsibilities in Igbo society. The first stage in the process of becoming a performer in the Igbo masking theatre begins with a formal initiation into the masquerade cult. As masking is exclusively a male-only activity, initiation is open only to young boys of between nine years to thirteen. According to Nnabuenyi Ugonna,

> *mmonwu* initiation known in Igbo as *ima mmonwu*, which literally means 'knowing the spirit', is actually a kind of process of education into the complicated stagecraft of mmonwu drama and the systematic unraveling of the seemingly mysterious representation of the mask as a 'visible spirit'. (1984: 50)

Another scholar, Odita (1970) sees initiation as both a prerequisite and an auditioning process for individuals to become either performers (mask wearers, dancers, singers, instrumentalists) or just members of the masking fraternity who perform other supporting roles within the town's masking theatre tradition. However, like the masquerade practice itself, initiation procedures vary across Igboland – from the highly extended period of initiation that sees members graduate through a series of stages and grades of seniority (twelve in all in Ebem-Ohafia) in the *Ekpe*, to the one night intensive affair which is the practice in most of Central Igboland. In between, there are the Afikpo *Okumkpo and* the Nsukka *Omabe* and *Odo* traditions where formal initiation takes up to three months, during which the initiates are given 'exclusive lessons in the village adult life and crafts in areas including the traditional village customs, the art of hunting and material survival, in family crafts along with the playing of their appropriate grade of masquerade' (Onyeneke, 1987: 85).

In Nkpor, initiation takes place in one night when the initiates are given their first chance to participate actively in a masquerade show. But the initiate is merely introduced to the art and practice of masking, as well as given the go-ahead to fully take part. The actual learning process continues all through life, and through participation in subsequent performance events. Thus, every member of the Ochammili group would have undergone an initiation at different times in the past before being allowed to join. Being a member of the group then allowed them to acquire newer skills as well as learning a specific masquerade performance.

Training is, on the whole, non-formalized, and non-professionalism in art practices in Igbo society has meant that specialization in specific aspects of the theatre has not happened. This means that performers and participants are never differentiated in terms of experts and non-experts. But it would be erroneous and misleading to suggest from this that Igbo theatre artists do not train to become accomplished performers and theatre makers. Experienced performers, in fact, refresh their techniques or learn new skills to help them remain at the top of their craft. There are no schools or training institutions for traditional theatre and performance. Neither is there an apprenticeship system as exists in some other cultures for the formation of artists, such as there is in *Jaliya* in Senegal or *Bori* musicians in Hausa culture – these two traditions will be looked at in Chapters 3 and 4 respectively. In Igboland, rehearsals for specific performances or masquerade shows provide contexts for new artists to acquire their initial training, and for experienced ones to learn new skills and techniques while refreshing and re-polishing existing ones. Each new performance is thus a challenge for experienced performers, and an entry point for the newly initiated.

One of the main qualities of Igbo masking theatre is the desire for and encouragement of versatility in all participants. Every member of a performing group has the chance to contribute in different capacities, including the major task of performing one of the masking roles (in a multi-mask play) such as Ochammili. They can also perform the main masked character in a performance such as the *Ijele*. Individuals thus train to dance, choreograph, make and play various instruments, participate in the chorus as singers, as acrobats, prop makers and carriers, or as assistants and guides to specific masquerades. They can be called upon to perform any of these roles at any time during a performance or in a different performance. However, over time some performers come to be recognized for their skills in performing certain roles so that they end up making these roles their own. Generally speaking, depending on the size of a group, up to three individuals understudy for one role, but usually a strict order of 'seniority' or preferred performer exists, based on skill and experience. Competition however is very often more for the acting roles than for the others, since the masquerades are the central attraction in this theatre.

Rehearsals

Rehearsals are much more than just getting ready for a performance, memorizing parts, learning specific music cues, dance steps, and other stage business. They are also contexts for training. This may explain why they are usually very long – a process that can take from between six months to, sometimes, more than a year to learn a new performance. Curiously enough, the informality, which characterizes many other aspects of Igbo masking, is often discarded for more formally structured stages of a rehearsal process. Every group goes through these stages, beginning with the first decision of which masked play/performance a group wishes to learn. The next stage is preliminary exchange of visits between the teaching group and the learning group. Between the two groups a time frame is agreed for the process to commence and conclude, with the first outing of the new play in its new home. After this is agreed, the first rehearsal begins, in which the teaching group arrives and takes up residence in the trainee group's village or neighbourhood. Members of both groups are paired, usually according to roles. Training consists of the teaching group performing, watched by the hosts who then copy what they have seen, and so on until both groups are satisfied that the rudiments of the performance has been acquired. These include the basic dance steps, character mannerisms and movement, character sketches and scenarios, and the musical accompaniment. It is necessary to point out here that the learning group do no just copy and reproduce what the teaching group has taught them; each performer is expected to grasp the basics of their role and then proceed to creatively make it their own. This phase can take from between four to eight weeks. After the guests have left, the hosts will then carry on rehearsing on their own, sometimes bringing in local experts to oversee or comment on their progress. Sometimes, leaders or specific members of the departed group are asked back to clarify or help out with difficulties that the host group are unable to sort out on their own. Towards the end of the rehearsal, the visitors return for another week of final rehearsal and polishing of the performance, and they usually stay for the first outing to provide support mainly, but also to help out if the need arose during the first performance.

Rehearsals are usually held in the evenings because performers have to go to their day jobs. The Ochammili group rehearsed for approximately six months to get their performance ready. Members of the group included, a primary school teacher, two coach drivers, one taxi driver, three motor mechanics, an electrician, a bus conductor, a vulcanizer, three shopkeepers, traders, a bricklayer and a few unemployed and apprentice youngsters. Rehearsals lasted well into the night, and typical sessions lasted from between four to six hours. Another reason why rehearsals take place at night and often in a secluded venue away from prying eyes is because night time helps maintain and reaffirm the mystery and secrecy which surrounds masking activities in Igboland. Night also gives the performer a safe cloak of darkness in which to practice and learn new steps and roles, make mistakes and be criticized and corrected by teachers and experts. Although most performers carry in their bodies and minds, memories and techniques gained from previous performances and roles, every new performance or role is unique and thus will demand new interpretations, styles and applications of previous knowledge and techniques.

For many members of the group Ochammili was not their first *mmonwu* performance – a few of the older members had been involved in up to seven or eight major performances in the past, but for some of the younger members, it was the first. For all group members, the initial stages of getting the performance ready were tentative, unsure and error-strewn. Also, the improvisatory nature of the masquerade theatre meant that even after months of rehearsals, nothing was really fixed or codified with the result that the performers would always be called upon to recreate their roles anew each time they stepped out to perform. To be able to do this, performers were taught, first, to master the basic elements of a role, and second to learn how to be comfortable in themselves as performers who had to perform to a very vocal audience who would comment directly on their performances. Learning to cope with this unpredictability of what the audience might say or do was concentrated upon during rehearsals by members and selected onlookers interrupting or shouting out as they learned their parts. It was the same for the musicians who while retaining the central beats had to improvise all the time, both in rehearsal and in performance.

Rehearsals usually take place in the compound of one of the members, sometimes in that of the group leader, if there is one. Sometimes it takes place in the home of the group's patron. However, some groups choose public venues such as a village square or a clearing in a nearby bush. The Ochammili group held their rehearsals in the compound of their patron. They chose this rehearsal space because of its size, location, as well as the security and secrecy which it offered. The patron's role is that of adviser and supervisor during the rehearsal process, but continues throughout the life span of the performance and group.

Although non-professional, the Ocahmmili group took rehearsals very seriously, and non-attendance and disruptive or unproductive behaviour were not tolerated. Strict rules and guidelines on how members conducted themselves were drawn up and agreed, and fines were usually imposed and collected for unexplained or unapproved absences or for minor disruptive acts. The Igbo principle of democratic cooperation of equals governed the group's organization of its activities. Each person brought into the production process whatever talent he possessed. Although the group started without chosen leaders, leadership did eventually emerge, and some members began to take leading roles in artistic and organizational matters. It is important however to point out that these leaders never functioned or were designated as directors, producers, stage managers or choreographers in the Western theatre sense. Again this illustrates the difficulties of comparing, on a like for like basis, performances and other social practices from different cultural contexts. Each culture, as pointed out earlier (see p. 4), is unique and designs practices that may sometimes be unique to it, and so, casting decisions and task distribution in the Mmonwu theatre are different from those in other theatres. The criteria for assigning tasks to members was on the basis of individuals taking on roles or showing a flair, or having done similar teaks before. Unlike in Western theatre, these individuals did not expect to be and were not paid for these roles and services, just as other participants and contributors received no payment.

Staging Techniques

The most common setting for traditional African theatre performances is the open-air space, with an arena staging style. Very often this is a multi-purpose communal space in which other communal events, besides theatrical performances, are held. The idea of a building or a fixed structure to house performances is unknown. Most African performances reveal the African idea of and desire for non-permanence and a non-product conception of art – art as disposable, ephemeral, existing on, for, and in the moment of its production, use, and appreciation. In the case of theatre, it only exists at the moment of encounter between the spectators and the performers in the designated or found space. Everything within the performance space is fluid, shifting, and there are no boundaries between spectator and performer, who constantly shift and sometimes interchange roles. In keeping with and as a result of this fluidity, there is reluctance in Igbo theatre to designate a permanent space or erect a fixed structure for performances. Arising from this also is the need to have police characters or marshals whose performance/responsibility is to ensure that, despite this shifting spatial relations, spectators leave enough room for the actors to perform. Igbo masking theatre exhibits all these qualities of non-permanence in many ways and ultimately, the performances leave behind traces of themselves only in the memories of the spectators, unlike in Western theatre where there are scripts and scores which predate and outlive a performance.

All it takes for a performance to take place is the presence of the performer and spectators to transform an ordinary space into a symbolically charged performance space. This in a way predates Peter Brook's (1969) idea of the 'empty space'. Igbo masquerade theatre, like most African theatres, seems to suggest that a performance will always find and define its space, once the other two elements are present and willing to engage with each other. The masking theatre does not depend on scenery or a previously defined stage. At the *Enemma* festival, it was the actual encounter between the performers and spectators, which defined the arena stage, while both performers and spectators contributed towards creating the visual spectacle. The only position seemingly fixed was the makeshift raised stage/house for Akuezuozo.

The flexibility of Igbo masquerade space makes the theatre easily accessible. Little wonder that the idea of spectators paying to watch a performance is never considered, and in some instances where it has been tried, as in *Uzoiyi* Festival in neighbouring Umuoji, it was found to be impracticable, extremely unpopular and against the spirit of theatre in Igbo culture. Performers, first and foremost, want to be watched – they, in fact, are prepared to contribute to put their shows together, and all they ask for is the appreciation of the audience. Members of the Ochammili Cultural Group contributed large sums of money to put together their performance, and the last thing on their minds was recouping the sums they had contributed. As far as I know in Nkpor, no attempt has ever been made to introduce gate fees, as this would be completely contrary to the communal spirit in which the performances are conceived, offered and received. But overall, this has a lot to do with the space as well, because since there are no securely enclosed spaces for performance, it is practically impossible to collect any money or keep people out. The spectators will always be able to see the shows, from the top of trees or windows of high buildings around the arena, should organizers introduce gate fees. I do not foresee the masquerade theatre ever going indoors: performances in secure spaces exclude, whereas Igbo theatre, and *Enemma* in particular, includes.

So, despite efforts by some scholars (see Amankulor, Enekwe and Ugonna in Chapter 1) to give Igbo masquerade theatre a formalized staging structure, this theatre, in my view, resists such formalizations. It prides itself on, as well as benefits from, its flexible staging style because it ensures that its inclusive and participatory ethos is maintained at all times. It is a theatre whose staging space is primarily a fluid, constantly expanding and contracting arena stage in which gods, spirits and humans meet, coexist and intermingle freely as they create the spectacle. In analyzing the proxemic principles underlying Igbo traditional theatre, Ugonna is correct that:

The indigenous African theatre is abstract in the sense that the theatricality is realized more by symbolism and the mental disposition of
both the actors and the spectators than by the effect of actual staging
or environment. In other words, in mmonwu . . . illusion of reality is
achieved more by the use of abstract symbols than by the recreation
of physical environment . . . and . . . through a prior knowledge of the
mythic content of the drama and not necessarily as a result of a realistic
representation on the stage. (48)

Describing the staging of *Enemma* performance can hardly be straightfor-
ward because of its multi-spatial and multi-local nature, and the impact
of this on my viewing perspectives. My being attached to the Ochammili
Cultural Group meant that my viewing location kept changing all through
the day. I had to cover the entirety of their preparation, but I also had
to cover the festival as a whole. The locus of performance shifted between
three widely dispersed spaces, depending on what was happening at any
particular time of that day. The first location was the rehearsal compound
where the actors playing the human characters put their costumes and
masks on and introduced themselves to the initial audience. By the time
my team arrived, the spatial arrangement was already set. The musicians
sat under the shade provided by a tree located towards the left wall of the
compound as one walked in. Directly in front of the gate and slightly to
the right, a row of chairs were placed on a pavement which ran the length
of the main house – that was where we sat. Further down and built into
the left wall was a small out-building – just one room. Ordinarily, this
serves as a store room for the owners of the compound, but during the
performance it became a changing room for the performers. The area in
between the three positions was the performance space for each masked
character to perform their introductory routine before returning to the
dressing room. Spectators formed little pockets all over the compound and
around the performance space. The second location was where Anukaibie,
Ochammili and Akum masquerades were readied. It was just an open space
in front of a house inside another walled compound. There were three
separate enclosures made from palm fronds, approximately twenty feet
apart, which were used to hide the animals from view while they were being
costumed – each enclosure was later pulled apart to reveal the character
when the two actors were in their positions inside the animal structure.
The enclosures were placed in such a way that the three formed a triangle.
Anukaibie was in front while Ochammili and Akum formed the base of
the triangle. Hippopotamus, although belonging to another theatre group,
shared the space with the other two because it was very convenient and
not too far away from the festival venue for the animals to get to. When

the Ochammili group arrived in their *mmonwu* search, they stopped some distance from the enclosures so as to give the animals some space to prance about and the actors to get used to the weight they had to carry and to each other before setting out on the bumpy road to the village square. Once the animals were in tow, the entire road to the square became active performance spaces since the performers remained in character and the spaces and the characters transformed ordinary people into momentary spectators.

The festival venue itself was an oblong shaped open-air space, approximately half the size of a standard football pitch. It was ringed with big trees, the branches of which provided additional viewing positions for young and more adventurous spectators. There were five entrances and exits (**see Fig. 2.2**) and as much as possible, the festival organizers kept these open to let groups in and out of the arena. From where I stood, Ezemmo's raised stage was on the right, in between entrances C and D. The brightly coloured canopies provided some sun-shaded sitting and standing places. About twenty male marshals dressed in bright yellow T-shirts also stood at intervals. They kept order among the spectators, as well as ensured that enough space was always left for the performers. On the whole, the atmosphere was one of relaxed jollity – people chatted to those close to them or called/waved across to acquaintances on opposite sides. The *ogbo* (central performance space) itself was completely empty, there were no stage props or decor, since the masking theatre does not rely on these for its visual impact or for communicating with the audience, and so Finnegan's idea of 'specialised scenery' is redundant in the Mmonwu context (see p. 6). Whatever props needed were brought on, either by the actors themselves or by assistants. These were promptly removed once the characters left the *ogbo*. Since communication and the spectacle of this theatre depends a great deal on the masquerades themselves, on their dances and movements, much effort is concentrated on designing the masks, the costumes, and the choreography, all of which help to bring the masks alive during performance.

Design

Design in Igbo masking theatre can be examined on three levels: mask design and construction, costume design, and stage design. But of the three design components, only the mask carver and the tailor are specialists of a kind. The carver's job results from his innate talent but, like other artists in Igbo society, he does not make a living solely through carving. The designs for the setting, costume and props are the responsibilities of the group members or individual owners of a mask. For their costume, a group may just hire the services of a tailor to do the sewing, while the overall design concept would come from the group, in which case the tailor makes no original contribution to the performance. The carver in much the same way is not responsible for the mask idea or concept; he merely helps an individual or a group to realize their ideas in plastic form, usually for a small fee. The Ochammili group came up with the idea of the number of animal and human characters for their performance, before they commissioned the carver and the tailor to help them translate this into masks and costumes. The design for the set very much depends on the space available. For *Enemma*, the setting was designed by the festival committee, with some advice from some of the town elders. They decided where to locate Akuezuozo's raised stage, and it was obvious that they had taken into account the uneven ground surface of the square by choosing the end where the land was least undulating. The committee was also responsible for the seating arrangement and where to place the canopies, as well as choosing the running order for the performers and groups – the latter was, however, also dependent on which group or individual masquerade got to the performance venue first. The main aim of the committee in designing the *ogbo* was to leave the space open and flexible, thereby making it easy for groups and individual masquerades to adapt their performances to the festival space. All performances are usually blocked or choreographed with this in mind. The main thing that groups aim for is to make their performance flexible and easily adaptable to any setting or location. Most performances aim for longevity and so expect to be performed at different venues, at different times and by different actors. At the festival, only Akuezuozo's stage was fixed because it was needed to provide orientation for other performers. However, another year, this position could be shifted to another part of the arena.

Mask design

A major feature of Igbo masking theatre is the high degree of abstraction in the conception and design of masks, irrespective of whether they are masks just for the face or the overall envelope in which a character appears, such as the faceless Mmonwu Akolo. Igbo mask theatre is a symbolic art form, and thus hardly any attempt is made to create realistic portrayals of characters, even in the more recent facial masks, such as the human characters in the *Ochammili* performance. The carver often does not aim to capture a realistic human face as such. However, through lines, strokes and general placement of features he tries to suggest essences or ideas or motifs of the character. For instance, Adamma was meant to represent the Igbo idea of virginal beauty – smooth and radiant skin, high cheek bones, clear and innocent eyes, fully formed mouth, slightly pointed nose, rich and shiny black hair. Onuku's mask, on the other hand, was blank, had vacant eyes, pallid skin, wide and protruding forehead, a leering tongue to suggest both his stupidity and rampant sexuality. Akuezuozo's face, while slightly resembling a human face, was, through a series of distortions and exaggerations, suggestive of inscrutable power and knowledge – the ethnic scarifications indicated that he belonged to a bygone era when facial marks were used to signify age and levels of social achievement. The audience was presumed to have the semiotic competence to decipher these abstracted essences, helped of course by the *mythoi* which accompany and inform the characters or the contexts in which they appeared. Thus, watching and appreciating a masquerade performance is an exercise in reading and judging characteristics and behaviour in relation to what the designs, the music and the dance are saying or suggesting together. It is a multi-language experience, which demands different levels of semiotic engagement and competence from the spectators.

There are as many mask types as there are Igbo ideas and experiences. The masking theatre is not just about faces carved in wood or other materials. The masks can be anthropomorphous, theriomorphic, or therianthropic. They can be distortions and/or abstractions of a face or quality such as Akuezuozo, or amorphous bundles of raffia or grass such as Mmonwu Akolo, or innocuous heaps of cloth that rise and shrink during performance such as Orimmili Obue Ota (Ocean that Swells and Shrinks) or Wonder Masquerade. But, in general, ideas, concepts and notions, such as beauty, ugliness, power, force, strength, terror, wonder, elegance, chastity, strangeness, inscrutability, wisdom, nobility, agility, mystery, and wealth are predominant design motifs in Igbo masks. Sometimes, one finds a combination of more than one of these motifs in a single mask. Akuezuozo is a good example – his face, while being extremely distorted and ugly, was still suggestive of power, wisdom, inscrutability, nobility, wealth which are symbolized by the red cap and feathers on his head (see Fig. 2.8). In Nkpor, only men of status are allowed to put on red caps, and the number of eagle feathers on a cap indicates the wearer's level of achievement in both politics and wealth. Akuezuozo's physique – enormous chest and potbelly – helped to reinforce these qualities. Others were Ochammili and Enemma, very big, strong and elegant animals who surprised and thrilled the audience with their spectacular agility and grace in movement and dance.

In general, masks signify their identity through symbolism. However, newer masks, such as the human characters at *Enemma* were quite close to realistic human faces. But carvers still managed to keep the faces general, generic and distant – thus, while they were made to look human, their colour or facial scarification made them foreign, remote and other. They

Figure 2.9 Police Sergeant (bluish face) and Mmonwu Awusa (facial marks).

were types and not specific individuals (**Fig. 2.9**). Akuezuozo, for instance, was just a symbolic ancestor, while Adamma was just a beautiful young woman and her name simply means 'beautiful daughter'. The other characters – Mmonwu Awusa, the police officers, the fathers, mothers and daughters, and hunter masks – all had generalized human faces with realistic costumes and props to match, but no person-specific traits or names. Through design and colour codes, Igbo ideas of mystery, beauty, elegance, wealth, authority, power, wisdom, foolishness, strangeness and otherness are represented by and through the groups of masquerade characters.

Costume design

Costuming in Igbo masquerade theatre is primarily used to help conceal the body and thus the identity of the performer. It therefore contributes significantly in maintaining the mystery and mythology that spirits are present whenever a masquerade appears. It may seem that the artistry and beauty of the costume are secondary to the need to accentuate and maintain the mystique surrounding masking. This is more so in individually made and owned masquerade characters, where concealment is the primary goal and the desire to suggest a specific character is secondary. However, as one moves to group masquerades, artistic considerations in costume become important, and they sometimes supersede the need to conceal. This, I suppose, is because group masking is more about spectacle, and not much effort is really made to hide the identity or identities of the major masked performers. The classic example is the Ijele in which at the end of each performance, the actor emerges from the enclosure as himself, but still wearing the vest and trousers made of the same material and design as the Ijele itself. He dances to the adulation of the waiting audience, and in doing so announces to all that he had been the Ijele masquerade for the day. The same thing happened when we got back to the rehearsal compound at the end of *Enemma*. The four actors who had performed Ochammili and Anukaibie came out still wearing the forelegs and hind legs costumes of the two animals to dance round the compound as part of the cooling down process.

Most groups go to great lengths and effort to make their masks colourful and beautiful so that their performance will be long remembered for its artistic flamboyance and impact. This is where costuming can become very significant in what it can contribute to the overall visual affect of a performance. And the bigger the mask, the more the care that goes into the choice of costume and colours, not only in terms of the masks, but also in terms of the often large number of performers involved, from musicians, singers, attendants to the supporting dancers. The costume design for such an array of performers has to take into account colour and material coordination needed to achieve harmony, or contrast, and sometimes to establish levels of thematic significance and importance of roles. Thus, the more central a character is to the performance, the closer to the key colour(s) that character's costume is likely to be.

An awareness of these principles of design was amply demonstrated by the Ochammili performance. There was a predominant use of brown, green and yellow to costume the major characters, and the supporting performers. Ochammili was costumed in rich earth brown, the colour scheme then radiated from this inner ochre outwards until the bright yellow of the dancers and attendants. Adamma wore a gold-yellow attire with dark brown trimmings because, like Ochammili, she was the pride of her parents. Both Nna Mmo and Nne Mmo had variations of yellow, green and brown in their costumes, which aligned them closely to Adamma and Ochammili. However, more individuation was achieved by allowing other characters to have their own colours and unique costumes. Mmonwu Awusa wore white with a green scarf and trimmings. Police Inspector, Sergeant and Ezeikolobia wore shades of khaki cotton uniforms. Onuku's costume belonged to him alone and had nothing in common with other characters, both in colour and style. Only he, of all the human characters, was not costumed in a clearly identifiable human style of dress – in fact, his ill-fitting jumpsuit costume identified him as neither-nor, a marginal figure who existed outside the norm or codes of behaviour. The Fool is a special character in Igbo masking theatre, with each fool being unique in themselves, and not like any other, both in dress, behaviour and mannerisms. The prominent element in Onuku's costume was the white pouch in between his legs, which contrasted quite sharply with the dark blue of his jump suit. The effect of this was to highlight his scrotum, a significant feature of what he stood for – licentiousness.

What united all the costumes in the *Ochammili* performance was that individually and collectively, and in conjunction with the masks, they helped to establish the presence of the other worldly or fictional world in the human world. And as with the set design, what underpinned costume ideas – design and choice of material and so on – was a desire to marry the costumes to the appropriate movements and dances which the performers had to execute. The mask ultimately becomes itself only when it is moving or dancing and the beauty of the costumes became manifest when they were in use.

The emerging trend in masking costume in Nkpor is a move towards realistic costumes to match the increasingly realistic mask faces, especially for the human characters whose clothes are based on current fashions. This is rather surprising since in the past, all masked characters were made to look as far removed from and unlike humans as possible – such as the facial distortions, abstractions and bodily disfigurements of Akuezuozo, Dibia and Mmonwu Akolo. Further distancing is achieved by the very non-human costume of raffia gowns, the intricately patterned and coloured applique cloth of Agbogho Mmo, and the metallic bodice of Ebiogwu, Ozokwamkpo and Odogwu. These costumes were clearly meant to be theatrical, to signify the non-humanness of the masked characters, and the extra-daily nature of the activity for which they were intended. But Akuezuozo, Nna Mmo, Nne Mmo, Adamma, and Mmonwu Awusa wore realistic human clothes, and so did the two police officers, whose uniforms, badges and insignias of rank were as close as possible to real ones. In the past these would have been merely suggested or hinted at. Akum, Enemma, Ochammili and Anukaibie were costumed to make them look as close as possible to the real life animals they were representing, and from a distance one could easily mistake Ochammili for a real giraffe.

Performer-spectator encounter and interaction

Whatever the context, Igbo masking theatre cannot exist without its audience. This is because, to a large extent, every masked performer depends on the participatory responses from the spectators. Igbo masking, not being based on story, dialogue or fixed plot, relies on the *mythoi* of the characters or sketchy symbolization, which require the encounter between masked performers and spectators for performance and meaning to be activated. The spectators are therefore very much part of the theatre making process.

Spectators are of course aware of this responsibility, thereby making them a very demanding audience. They vocally praise a performer when he has performed well and show their disapproval if they felt the performance was not good. Unlike audiences in Western European theatre and other cultures, Igbo audiences do not keep quiet or wait until the end of a performance to register their feelings or render judgement. Instant critical comments are part of Igbo performance, and the performers also reserve the right to register their own disapproval of a very unhelpful or uncooperative audience. In fact, Igbo masking clearly demonstrates the idea, now central to performance theory, that a performance is a collaborative venture and interaction between space, performer and spectator, and that a performance could hardly exist in the absence of any of these elements. Thus, a mask has no life or meaning until it encounters and interacts with an audience. It does not have a pre-worked out performance, skits or scenarios or a fixed plot until the audience helps it to develop one. Mmonwu Awusa was a good example of this mutually dependent collaboration between a masked character and spectators in the generation of a performance text. As I was busy recording the performance, he kept coming to me to offer me items from his tray to purchase. I could not do this because I was concentrating so much on the video, and feeling ignored he became rather angry and stopped his performance entirely. When some spectators teased him about his sulk, he let loose a flurry of Hausa, which his assistant translated as: 'When the right hand washes the left hand, the left hand washes the right, and both will become clean', a popular proverb about mutual dependence and cooperation between people. He felt he had done a turn for me by posing for the camera, and so expected me to buy something from him in return. Taking his point, I stopped filming for a while to buy some kola nuts and sweets off him, after which he thanked me – in Hausa – before sashaying off to ensnare other potential customers on the other side of the arena.

The five contexts identified earlier support different kinds of performer–spectator relationships, with each kind allowing a different level of participation. The governing principle, just as in its proxemics, is the desire to constantly move the audience, from passive to active spectatorship. One moment, they are on the sideline watching the masquerades display their skills, and the next they are in the thick of the performance, dancing, singing and assisting the masked performer(s) in the making of the performance. However, among the audience members, the levels of participation required or allowed are often determined by gender, age, and whether or not the person is an initiate or an *ogbodu*. This is because these criteria affect where individuals are positioned during a performance. The male elders and other adult initiates are often positioned in front, while the women and young girls are at the back. Some new initiates who are lucky find places crouching in front of the elders and are thus guaranteed a good view and maximum participation. Thus, in some performances, such as the initiations or judicial contexts, there are no female or uninitiated members of the audience. Overall therefore, context and space significantly affect or determine spectator involvement. The highest level of participation is often achieved in the spacious arena setting of *Enemma*, with its composite staging. Here, multiple pockets of dramatic activity happen simultaneously, and respective sections of the audience are dragged into becoming spectacular performing bodies for other sections to watch.

The masquerade theatre operates an encounter-participatory structure because the masked figure is a being from another realm that enters the human realm, a fictional character that enters into the real world to engage with its inhabitants. The nature of this engagement is participatory for both masquerade and spectator who need each other for a performance to happen. And wherever they meet becomes the stage – it defines their engagement but they also define the space by their meeting. In this theatre we find the perfect example of the idea that a performance only exists in the moment of encounter and engagement between performer and spectator within either a pre-agreed or an accidentally found space.

Function and social relevance

Art has always been perceived as being functional within most African societies, and this sense of function is embedded in the aesthetics. Igbo mask theatre shares this functional notion of art. It, in fact, is more implicated in this than most other art forms because, by its very nature and contexts, it is very much part of the socio-religious fabric of Igbo life and society. This theatre exists to perform three key but closely related functions: ritual, socio-political and aesthetic. Every occasion when masking theatre takes place manifests these functions, but none more so than *Enemma* which performs all three.

Through the mask, continuity between the human and spiritual worlds is made possible. The dead ancestors and forces of nature, such as Akuezuozo, Dibia, and Orimmili assume material form as masquerades to return and commune with the living, provide them with information and knowledge to enable them cope with the uncertainties of life. In a sense therefore, the theatre enables the Igbo to practically perform or live their religious beliefs and faith. But also at the psychological and psychic levels, through giving form to the formless or making the invisible visible, Igbo masking enables them to understand and control their universe through performing as it were their anxieties and fears, their joys and sorrows, their successes and failures. Masking provides a context and mechanism for communal soul searching and therapy. The principle that the devil you know or can see is better than the angel you only hear about underpins Igbo religious thought and the masking theatre which has grown out it. By giving material form to these supernatural forces of their universe, the Igbo are able to interact, play, question and make demands of the spiritual world.

Ijele masquerade is the best example of Igbo masking theatre providing the Igbo with a mechanism and context for dealing with or fixing experiences within the Igbo collective memory. Ijele grows in size and complexity with age as images and objects representing new experiences are added onto the mask frame – from the khaki-clad and helmeted colonial district officer of the late nineteenth and early to mid-twentieth centuries, the colonial police and court messengers of the same period, flashy cars, bicycles and motor-bicycles of the thirties and forties, to the gun totting soldiers, jet fighters and bombers of the civil war in the sixties and seventies, and now there are television sets, computers and all the latest fashion accessories such as satellite dishes, masts and mobile telephones. By adding on these new experiences and developments in technology, Ijele becomes a dancing and moving chronicle of Igbo experiential realities, as well as a semiotic indicator that these experiences have become part of Igbo collective consciousness. Ijele is often described as the Igbo world in motion. Presenting this visual and mobile tapestry of Igbo experience periodically acts as a reminder to the spectators of what territories and moments Igbo history has traversed.

Individual mask characters and sketches are also added to the communal repertoire to reflect individual as well as communal encounters and experiences of the outside or the other. A new development at *Enemma* was the inclusion of characters that were more of European than of African origins. The fathers, mothers and daughters in the Ochammili, Akum and Enemma performances all had bright pink faces and pointed noses, while the officers, hunters, Onuku, Mmonwu Awusa had different shades of dark skins – chocolate brown, darkish blue and Grey. For the Ochammili group, however, these characters were not Europeans, just distant others and giving them a pink complexion seemed the best way to signify their strangeness and otherness. In the past they would have been differentiated from the Igbo by giving them different ethnic facial marks, strange looking costumes or props. But a Europe that is far away and yet accessible is very much a fact of Igbo life today, and what better way to represent the other than by making her/him come from a far away place.

The mask's greatest function for Igbo society, however, is its capacity to provide a reflective mirror with which the Igbo examine and make commentary on themselves and their neighbours – their belief system, social organization and institutions, polity, moral codes and guides for individual and collective conduct are held up for scrutiny and revision if necessary. This is usually the responsibility of satirical masks such as Ayaka, Onyekulufa, Osonigwe and Ogbazuluobodo – all these perform mainly at night and the actors are usually not masked. But when they appear during the day as Osonigwe did at *Enemma*, the identities of the performers have to be hidden somehow. Osonigwe appears in daylight as Mmonwu Akolo – the clump of grass that secretly collects information about people. At the festival, this character picked on people and satirized them through songs in the hope that such people would be forced into changing their unacceptable behaviours. Other satirical masks include the Ulaga (a sharp-tongued bird character), the ugly Awuka and the pot-bellied Ntolumafo, whose features and distended physiognomies are meant to warn people about the dangers of social and biological excesses.

Although the last three characters did not perform at the *Enemma* event, together with Akuezuozo, Dibia and Onuku, they embody the Igbo principle of moderation and balance, force married to wisdom. Many of the group performances at the festival explored this as a theme. Onuku, in particular, illustrated an absence of balance and moderation, psychologically in his insatiable desire to copulate with anyone or anything, and physically in his movement which is totally lacking in coordination and dignity. Ochammili and Enemma, on the other hand, reflected the opposite – they were huge and yet graceful, powerful and yet tender in the way they moved and danced.

Masquerade performances such as *Akum*, *Enemma*, *Ijele* and *Ochammili*, with their large entourage of characters, displayed and reflected Igbo social life, especially the notion of the ideal family – a rich titled man and caring father and husband, a dutiful and supportive wife and mother, a happy and obedient daughter, Onuku (who sometimes is the rascally no-do-good son, loved and tolerated in spite of his failings, exotic family pets (like Akum, Enemma, Ochammili and Anukaibie) whose size and rarity made them symbols of immense wealth and prestige, police bodyguards, and the family hunter. There was also a place in such an affluent household for the odd stray or foreigner, such as the kola-nut and cigarette selling Mmonwu Awusa – also tolerated in spite of his occasional lapses in local cultural etiquette and inability to speak the local language. In celebrating this ideal of family life, the performances were asking the spectators to identify with and aspire to such an ideal in their own lives. In the same way, social deviance, amoral or unsuccessful characters were lampooned or severely criticized to make such behaviour or characters abhorrent and unacceptable to the audience.

Initiations function as contexts for teaching male children the codes of conduct and roles required of them in the society. It is symbolically a place and a means of transforming boys into men. The structure of the initiation as a series of trials or contests is designed to celebrate and encourage manly courage, endurance, initiative, leadership, honesty, comradeship, and trust-worthiness in the young boys, which should become their attributes and mode of behaviour in future life. An initiation, by transforming boys into men, places a degree of responsibility on them to behave in accepted ways expected of men in Igbo society. Initiation also reveals to young Igbo boys the highest secrets of the land, thereby placing them in a privileged position as repositories of communal history, knowledge and wisdom. It prepares and authorizes them to use this theatre to achieve its other functions, through their participation in and maintenance of the masking tradition.

The greatest function of the masquerade theatre, however, is still its aesthetic contribution to the well being of the community. Ultimately, the masking theatre provides great pleasurable spectacle to its audiences. Masking, as a composite art form, is a site for the coming together of a variety of Igbo arts. Every masking event is both a celebration and a reaffirmation of the Igbo collective spirit and its cultural heritage. This is because in it the performer and the spectator, despite the assumed spiritual and physical opposition and distance between them, are able to meet and interact in a play of mutual deference and need. The atmosphere at *Enemma* was a joyful and celebratory one, in which there was evidence of an overflow of goodness and well being by all participants. People seemed happy to be alive and sharing in the moment with other happy human beings.

Enemma had brought together different organizational and artistic expertise – performers, carvers, tailors, organizers and community leaders. Months of preparation were spent putting the festival together. And all these skills were put on display for the appreciation and assessment of the audience – performers were assessed on their performances, carvers, tailors and prop makers on the masks they had carved, costumes they had made or props they had provided; while festival organizers were assessed on how well they had organized the venue, how well publicized the event was, and on how smoothly the festival programme had gone. Every element contributed to make the festival successful. It was a theatre in which the various art forms met as equals without the privileging of any form over the others – they all became veritable languages of communication for dealing with and articulating the community's collective experience and history, in the same way that *Bori* in the next chapter is a celebration and affirmation of autochthonous Hausa cultural history and experience.

3 *Bori*: A Hausa ritual theatre

Bori cult and its social background

To understand the uniqueness of Hausa *Bori* performances, one needs to look at both the Pre-Islamic and contemporary Hausa society. The Fulani conquest of Hausaland, through the *jihad* of Othman Dan Fodio, was completed by 1804, and formally established Islam as the dominant religion of the entire Hausa territory. In the process, and as a necessity for achieving such dominance, pre-Islamic cultural practices were either annihilated or extremely marginalized. But, although Islam finally took root, it did so upon a deeply entrenched pagan foundation, which still exerts considerable influence on much of rural Hausa thought and life. Wall's study of 'illness and well-being' in Hausa culture suggests that,

> The coming of Islam posed a potential threat to . . . traditional beliefs, but as in the case of other states of the central and western Sudan, the Hausa kingdoms adopted Islam only as an adjunct to general court procedures and rituals. Rarely did Islamic practices extend to the mass of the population and in times of crisis traditional beliefs often reasserted themselves, pushing Islam aside. (1988: 118)

One of these was *bori*, a religious practice based on belief in the existence of spirits who were seen as active participants in and influence on human affairs. *Bori* – a cult of spirit possession and trance – has remained one of the most resilient of the pre-jihad Hausa ritual practices. It is hardly surprising that such a practice – predicated on the belief that most human problems, especially diseases and misfortunes, are the handiwork of spirits whose wrath or displeasure the afflicted humans may have incurred – is still strong today among a majority of Hausa people. They see no contradiction in being Muslims and yet consulting *Bori* experts to appease the spirits through ritual offerings and possession performances. The performances

I watched in Zaria, Kaduna State, were part of on-going programmes of therapy for patients by 'Dr' Saadatu, the *Magajiya* or mother of a *Bori* compound at Ungwan Rimi, and Alhaji Wakili, the *Sarkin Bori* (Leader of the *Bori*) of another group based in Ungwan Fulani. At both events I was shown the patients for whom the performances were being organized, before and after the performances, to demonstrate the efficacy of the ritual.

The establishment of a Muslim socio-political ethos in Hausaland had brought about a significant shift in gender roles and relationships. Whereas in pre-Islamic society, women traditionally held titles and participated actively in public affairs, they are now placed in extremely sub-ordinate positions in areas which became completely Islamized – in Islamic law women are regarded as minors. In most aspects of public life they are completely marginalized, the ultimate exclusion being the practice of wife seclusion (*purdah*), referred to locally as *auren kulle*. In *purdah*, these women are not allowed to be seen in public and their circles of social intercourse are severely restricted to close relatives, or persons approved by their husbands. The prevalence of women as *bori* devotees may well be the attempt by a marginalized group to make use of an equally marginalized religious practice as a form of redress or a context for developing and main-taining solidarity and individual or group expression. With this instrument they try to subvert the authority and dominance of the men folk and the Islamic laws which keep them down. *Bori* also provides a therapeutic and playful outlet for the emotional and mental stress brought about by their social marginality.

Bori involves spirit possession of cult members, collectively known as *yan bori* (children of *bori*) or *masu bori* (owners of *bori*). All manner of diseases, ranging from simple muscle twitches to extreme forms of paralysis, and from minor headaches to raving insanity, are believed to be manifestations of the anger or displeasure and visitation from the spirits. The only way to make peace with the angry spirits and secure a cure is to 'dance *bori*', that is, become possessed or cause someone to become possessed by the afflicting spirits. *Bori*, therefore, falls under the category of Turner's (1968) 'cult of affliction'; its practice being primarily related to healing and medicine. To perform *Bori* is an act of faith in the existence and power of the spirits to relieve the human community of its ailments. In this respect, it is essen-tially a religious performance and, like the Igbo *Mmonwu* performance, a mechanism through which the non-Muslim Hausa are able to actualize their interdependent relationship with spirits and deities.

Bori is based on an elaborate pantheon of spirits which the Hausa have created in their own human image and to whom they have ascribed human characteristics, social gradations, patterns of behaviour and relationships closely similar to those which exist in Hausa society. Jangare, the mythical city where the spirits live, is a world filled with numerous spirits and deities. It has a divine hierarchy and a network of kinship relationships. However, the relationships between the spirits are only vaguely defined and change according to which part of Hausaland one is studying. This vague definition of relationship patterns is obvious in the performances themselves, which are often without elaborate story lines or plots. One is reminded here of the relativist argument in the introductory chapter that cultures devise performances based on their world and its needs, and that such a performance needs to be judged based on this understanding (see p. 13). The performers rely mainly on characteristics ascribed to the spirits by the human community in their interaction with the spectators. The structural relationships of husband, wife, daughter, son, brother, sister, master, slave and so on come to prominence when the spirits interact with each other, as illustrated by the husband and wife pairs of Gwagwari Dan Mama and Halima Madam, and Mai Gizo and Siriddo in the Gidan Wakili performance. Dan Mama and Halima Madam arrived together and were close to and aware of each other throughout: their dance was well choreographed and flirtatious, the husband protectively holding the wife when they entered and departed.

Gidan wakili performance

Of the two performances that I watched, I will use the Gidan Wakili performance, which took place over two days in early August 2004, and was more elaborate and altogether seemed better organized. It was also structurally more amenable to study. Usually, a *Bori* performance has a fairly fixed programme, especially the order in which the songs are played or the spirits called. The performance began with the preparation of the space – a small mat was placed in its centre, followed by a ritual purification of the space and an invocation of the spirits to ensure a good performance. Chairs were set out for the musicians, and about three chairs for my team; another mat was set down stage left of the musicians for the Sarkin Bori and his entourage. Others who wanted to sit brought their own chairs, while the majority stood in a horseshoe formation, with the musicians forming the base (**Fig. 3.1**).

Day One began with an evenly paced programme of music, singing and dancing. The opening songs and dances were an invocation of the patron or favourite spirits of the group, beginning with a song to Sarkin Makada, the patron spirit of drummers and musicians. Then it proceeded to an invitation to the spirits expected to feature in the two days performance event. Everybody was free to join in these dances, and many, including members of the audience, went into the arena and began to dance. It was

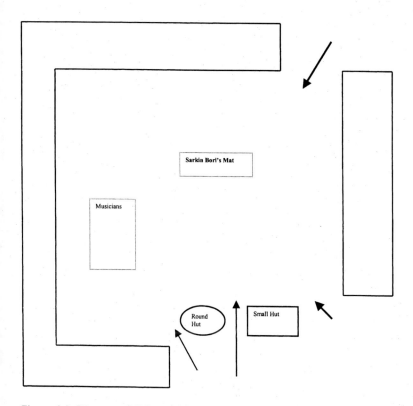

Figure 3.1 Diagram of Gidan Wakili compound/*Bori* stage.

a free dance intended as a warm-up for the performers and the space. As is the custom, the songs of the most senior or older spirits were played first, then those of junior or younger ones. Makada's *kirari* was followed by Baka Doguwa's (she is also known as Inna, The Tall One, Matron of Jangare, wife of Sarkin Arjannu, head of the spirits, and Supreme Mother):

>The Black Tall One
>The mother of Mai Gizzo
>The mother of Siriddo
>The mother of Auta
>The mother of all the spirits

As soon as the musicians began the song, some cult members gradually took up a position at the opposite end of the stage directly facing the musicians. While they were getting into position, people were still trooping in and finding places to sit or stand. Outside of the line now formed by the spectators, some of the performers were still busy applying their make-up or getting into their costumes. After a few minutes, the music changed to Kuturu's music and then to Sarkin Rafi's. As soon as Rafi's music was played, a cult member emerged from one of the side rooms fully dressed in the basic *Bori* costume of *gwado* (a thick hand-woven brownish-white wrapper tied tightly round the waist and reaching slightly below the knee). He had just this on, with a loose-fitting white shirt on top, and his entrance was the signal for members of the audience to withdraw from the arena and for those coming in to settle down. He made straight for the musicians and began dancing very closely to where they sat. For the first part of this dance, he stood on one spot and alternately lifting both feet and slowly bringing each down, as if caressing the ground with the landing, while his hands swung leisurely outward with the lifting of each foot and then came together in front as the foot touched the ground. Two other cult members, now fully dressed in Buzzu farmer costumes – darkish-brown leather shirts, belts and straps, on which hung an assortment of mirrors and metal objects, and odd looking black wigs made from horse hair – were busy blackening their faces with charcoal and ash from a fire-place nearby.

After the stationary dance, the dancer turned and moved away from the musicians to the centre of the arena where he turned again and, still maintaining the same feet movements but changing the arm to an up and down forward swing, danced back to his initial position in front of the musicians, and then he switched back to the previous on-the-spot movements. He was soon joined by a second dancer, another male, also dressed in a *gwado*, a black T-shirt, and black trousers. Unlike the first dancer, his *gwado* was way down his legs, just a few centimetres above his ankles. He wore a white Hausa cap, but soon took this off and handed it to another non-costumed member. With three dancers, the music noticeably changed in tempo to a faster and more urgent beat from both *garaya* [fiddles] and the five *buta* [shakers]. The singing also quickened in pace and the dancers responded to this change with more spatial and gestural movements – one dancer would move up to the musicians to dance briskly before them, while the other two moved to the opposite end, dancing on one spot while waiting for the first to finish and turn round. A second would start out and the two would meet in the centre as they changed places in front of the musicians.

This went on for a while, but stopped with the entrance of Wakili (the group's leader and most senior performer) in his *sarkin bori* regalia accompanied by his entourage of about seven people. He was dressed in a rich damask three-piece *baba riga*, an elaborate white turban and an iron staff (the last two are symbols of his office as *sarkin*). A male

Figure 3.2 Sarkin Bori and entourage.

assistant carried a bright multi-coloured umbrella of green, blue, yellow and orange, to protect the *sarkin*'s person from the scorching July sunshine (**Fig. 3.2**). The music changed again to acknowledge his entrance, with the lead musician calling out the *sarkin*'s praises which the latter acknowledged with a wave of his right hand. He then moved slowly to his reserved space where a seat was brought for him. His entrance marked the commencement proper of the day's performance. As if to welcome the *sarkin*, one of the performers, dressed all in white (trouser, caftan and *gwado* tied to reach just below his knee), did a few quick steps which took him to kneel down before the *sarkin*, the latter reached forward and touched him slightly on the back (a routine which all subsequent dancers would follow). Once touched, the dancer took off at high speed in a combination of skips, jumps and brisk dance steps which took him round the arena, and then into the centre from where he effortlessly leapt into the air to fall on his buttocks, arms and legs stretched out in front – this is called a *jifa*, and it is one of the central elements of a *Bori* performance. He did this a number of times, each time as high as he was physically able, and gradually the leaps were now in the direction of the *sarkin*. For the last three leaps, he turned so that he landed facing away from the *sarkin* and near the latter's feet with the last fall. On landing, he crossed his two hands above his head while leaning away from the *sarkin*. The latter acknowledged his display and show of respect by touching the bent back with his right hand. The *sarkin* then took his seat, with his retinue arranging themselves on either side.

The first dancer approached, knelt and touched the ground close to the *sarkin*'s feet and immediately spun round with a huge leap into the centre of the arena, and from there he strode back to the *sarkin* and then leapt into the air to perform his first *jifa* and landed facing the *sarkin*. He was up in a flash, and two huge strides took him back into the centre and once again he took off into the air and spun in mid leap to land facing in the direction of the *sarkin*; a few more leaps took him towards the mat and, manoeuvring himself with his final leap, he landed as the first dancer had done with his back to the *sarkin* and two hands crossed in front. Again the *sarkin* touched him to acknowledge his display. The second dancer took his turn and was similarly acknowledged. By this time three more male dancers had joined them, and the six moved quickly round and round the arena to a changed beat and song from the musicians. As they performed this circular dance, a group of eight cult members dressed as Fulani women took up a position left of *sarkin*'s group. They were all dressed in white hand-woven wrapper and short blouses of the same material. On their heads they carried large hemispherical calabashes which the Fulani use for carrying or storing dairy products, and loads of beads and cowries shells adorned their hair and blouses. The soles of their feet were painted with camwood. They were Barhaza and her group of Fulani maidens. They soon took the stage, accompanied by two male dancers dressed as the Buzzu brothers, Mai Gizzo and Dan Auta, for Barhaza's dance. The designs of Mai Gizzo and Auta's costumes were similar, except that Mai Gizzo's was dark brown, Auta's white, like the women's. Both had cowherd's sticks, which they carried on their shoulders as they danced. This dance, which was the climax of the performance on Day Two, is a courtship dance. It also encapsulates much of Fulani culture, as well as illustrating Barhaza's personality – coy, pretending to be shy and reserved while in fact she is reputed to be a wayward woman.

The point of this dance is for the women to be able to dance, weave intricate patterns with their hands and feet, and swirl round in both directions, while balancing the calabashes on their heads without the support of their hands. To begin their dance, the women moved into the arena in a single file, with Auta and Mai Gizzo at the rear. The first formation was a single line formation in which the leading woman turned inward so as to be following Auta, with a little space between them. The dance itself consisted of the left leg leading with a two step V movement and the right following in a straight line, with both hands slightly forward, hooked at the elbow, and palms facing upward. The men repeated the same feet movement, but

their elbows rested on both ends of the sticks, arms pointing inward. Each
dancer took a certain number of steps and then twirled round on the spot,
first to the right a full turn and then to the left another full turn, before
resuming the forward circular movement. Because they all started out at
the different times, there were always one or two twirling while the others
were moving forward. This gave the line of dancers a shimmering and
unrolling appearance. Their inward and outward twirling movement also
suggested a spiralling column of a tornado, another indication of Barhaza's
emotional disposition. They executed this movement formation three times
round the arena before changing, this time four of the women and one
of the men went to take up positions at opposite ends of the arena, one
group stood backing the musicians. They repeated the same movements –
little shuffles and twirls – but this time the two lines of dancers moved
towards each other to meet in the centre. Then each twirled round both
ways before returning to their starting positions. This pattern was repeated
five times, and each time the twirl and turn became more energetic, and
still the women never touched the calabashes.

The music changed and the group of dancers returned to the circular
formation, but this time the dance involved each person taking two steps
with the left leg outwards and then one step inwards with the right. This
dance brought a lot more of the dancers' bodies into use, further challenging their attempts to balance the calabashes on their heads without the
support of their hands. This was done while they made three turns round
the arena. It was then dissolved and another formation began in which,
first, three of the women danced forward from the lower end towards the
musicians who sang some praise lines to Barhaza. The three stood and
danced in front of the musicians before doing a half-twirl to start their
journey back to the starting line. As they twirled and turned another two
female dancers started out and they crossed each other in the centre. This
pattern was repeated until it was Mai Gizzo and Dan Auta's turn, at which
point the music changed to the manic breathtaking rhythm of the *buta*
and the insistent wailing and strumming of the *garaya* to denote the two
characters' pagan and wild personalities. The two dancers responded appropriately with furious stamping, spinning and twirling dance movements, all
beautifully done in time with the music. Both they and the music stopped,
to be replaced by a new slightly slower rhythm and two performers wearing
white military uniforms with epaulets and so on.

This was Kafaran's music. Kafaran is a foreign spirit from North Africa or
Europe, and he is leader of the soldiers – these came with him. Their dance
had precise leg movements with arms stiff by their sides, as if they were in
a military parade. Again the music changed to the equally fast and raging
tempo of Babule's praise chants – Babule is the spirit of fire. Soon, the two

dancers were joined by a group of five dancers, four females dressed in very bright red, and one male in green holding two bundles of twigs which were later used as flame throwers. A very tall figure in body-length black attire, with a bright red trimmed short skirt, who apparently was Babule himself, completed this group. Their dance was mainly a frenetic circular quick stepping/stamping movement which, when punctuated by the fast music and singing, visually resembled a fire raging through very dry grassland. This dance then transformed into a slower in and out foot-movement, with light stamping, to signal the arrival of a group of foreign pagan spirits. And to reflect their famed military prowess and organization, their dance (again performed in a circular formation in the centre of the arena) was characterized by precise hands and feet movements, accompanied by the clicking of their heels and military salutes. They dissolved this circle for solo dance routines which each performed in front of the musicians. The solos retained the same feet-movements of the group dances, the only difference being that this time the dancer stayed in one spot with the left arm holding the waist while the right was held straight out holding a red scarf or short staff. Each dancer ended by spinning round on the spot while still maintaining the same extended hand position.

This dance was followed by another group of seven male dancers, which included the three that opened the performance, performing a series of *jifa* falls each. However, there was a slight variation this time as the first dancer instead of just kneeling to be acknowledged by the *sarkin*, rather sat at his feet while a second dancer came, knelt before the first who touched him on the back, before the latter took off to perform their own leaps and falls, to end up in between the outstretched legs of the first. The same routine was repeated by the others until all seven were seated stretched out in front of the *sarkin*. They then quickly got up and did one quick run round the arena in a free kind of dance, before they were replaced by the two Buzzu farmers, each with a hoe and a leather bag on the left shoulder. In their dance which followed, they mimed digging or cultivating the land with hoes or occasionally switching to cutting down bushes with their machetes. To show their skill with the hoe, they threw them high up in the air and caught them as part of the dance.

A subtle change in the music announced the entrance of Sarkin Yaki or Chief of War, also known as Barade. He was dressed in a white shirt and baggy trousers, a white turban covered his head completely, probably to indicate his Arabic origin. He carried a long sword in his right hand, its sheath hanging loosely by his left shoulder. His dance was mainly of body swerves and feints, as if he was evading or striking imaginary foes. He then went into amazing magical displays in which he kept cutting himself furiously with the sword – he cut his tongue, his stomach, legs, arms, neck, and he tried to gouge his eyes out. But being the powerful spirit and warrior that he is, his body seemed immune to the sharp blade of the sword, as he carried on dancing. At one point another cult member offered their back which was cut and struck quite hard a few times, but still nothing happened. To bring his routine to an end, he was joined by the brothers, Dan Auta and Mai Gizzo, but he broke off again for one more demonstration for the *sarkin*, the musicians and then the audience. The latter applauded him.

At this point, there was a brief interlude in the music and dancing during which the *sarkin* and his retinue rose and went round the arena, first to thank the musicians, and then the audience for coming to be part of the performance. He addressed the audience through the *maroka* or praise-shouter and then went into one of the side rooms for a change of costume. While he was gone, people milled around, and the performers took a short break – some to smoke and some to have something to drink. When the music began again it was to call Halima Madam, and she entered accompanied by two of the red clad dancers who had been part of Babule's group. She was nicely and richly dressed, her whole body covered by a beautiful dress which reached right down to her bare feet. Her head was totally wrapped in a scarf made of the same material as her dress. She was shy because she concentrated very intently on her feet while she danced: she would not look up or at anybody but had a little smile on her face as she danced. Soon, the *sarkin* returned and took his place again. The dancers then began the routine of going to him and kneeling or bending to be touched by him before they proceeded to take centre stage. In the meantime, the Fulani maidens went back to stage left to place their calabashes. The *maroka* freely announced or amplified whoever spoke and had paid him to do so. And for the rest of the evening, the performance returned to the free dance in which anyone who wanted could join. For the whole of Day One and for about two hours of Day Two, we were treated to a rich menu of vocal and instrumental music, spectacular displays of intricately choreographed dance sequences and formations, as well as unbelievable *jifa* leaps and falls. All the performers wore very colourful and distinctly individual costumes, but there was no attempt to induce possession on the first day.

The second day started pretty much as the previous day. There was general music to which the members again danced, and then there were some more displays of *jifa* falls. However, the fact that in the centre of the performance space a bigger mat had been laid out was an indication that there was going to be induction later on. The preparations and dancing had been going on before we arrived at 12 noon. By 1 p.m. the stage was set and the mediums entered, one at a time, and sat on the mat, facing the musicians, who by this time had changed the music from the slower chanting and dancing beat of the introductory section to a much faster tempo. Wakili, now divested of his *sarkin bori* regalia of the previous day, was busy circling the mat, dancing, intoning and occasionally talking to or instructing the waiting mediums. All the while the tempo of the music kept building up and the rhythms were becoming more complicated and persistent, as the beats per second increased. The audience waited, excitement and anticipation mounting as they sensed the sudden stillness of the mediums who, it seemed, had withdrawn into themselves, almost unaware of their surroundings. This seemed to be the cue for three of the *buta* players to get up and move forward to the mat. The intense music, Wakili's exhortation and the deafening shakers (the *buta* or gourd rattles, usually played very close to mediums as they sit on the mat prior to possession) began to have the desired effect (**Fig. 3.3**).

Figure 3.3 Mediums being induced.

Suddenly, one of the mediums, the one sitting right in the centre of the mat, stiffened and his face became immobile. This extreme stillness slowly transferred to a few other mediums, while the audience's excitement went up a notch in response. Soon, the initial stillness was replaced by slight tremors at first, then gentle trembling which soon turned into involuntary spasms and shaking that gradually became so intense that the mediums' bodies were wracked and contorted in every possible way. This was accompanied by the customary glazed eyes and copious frothing and foaming at the mouth that indicate that a medium is about to become fully possessed. The eyes signal that they are no longer themselves, but merely vehicles for the spirit. The medium at the centre was the first to become fully possessed, and it was not long before it became evident that he had become possessed by Sarkin Rafi, Chief of the Rivers and the Water Wells. The first sign that it was Rafi was his outstretched left leg and folded right leg on which he sat (**Fig. 3.4**). Recognizing who he was, the lead musician quickly changed to Rafi's *kirari*, heaping praises on him as the medium proudly beat his chest with both hands, and uttered words and sounds which we could not pick up because of the loud music. The three gourd players moved closer to the medium, shaking the rattles loudly and intensely round his head, the purpose being to hasten possession, while the lead musician sang and played the praise chants on his *garaya*:

> Sarkin Rafi, the king of the river
> The one who possesses all the senses at the hem of his clothes!
> The one who plants in the farm of his in-law!
> The one who when the guinea-corn grows well will consume it!
>
> Sarkin Rafi
> The one who goes shopping on the day when there is no market
> The mad one with a quiver of arrows and a bow
> The one who shoots his arrow not caring where it comes down
>
> Sarkin Rafi
> The one who settles quarrels with a large pestle
> The one who harvests guinea corn from his in-law's farm before it has
>   ripened
> The mad one who when he goes right his senses go left.

This seemed to please him immensely and he responded with three *jifa* falls, before being stopped by Wakili and an assistant. Rafi was now fully in possession of the medium, and the gourd players moved onto two other mediums, who by now were shaking and twitching uncontrollably. They alternated between the two, and while these two were being induced,

Figure 3.4 Wakili welcomes Sarkin Rafi.

a fourth medium started her preliminary twitching and foaming at the mouth. Soon the identity of the second spirit became clear. He was Kuturu, the leper, also known as *Madaki* (or Chief Counselor) of Jangare. The medium was crawling on his hands and knees, and his legs and hands were curled inwards. He hooked his eight fingers and only his thumbs stuck out to give the impression that he had no fingers at all and so was unable to pick or hold on to any thing, and nor could he keep at bay the imaginary flies that were following him around. His music was instantly played to welcome him. Because of his senior position among the spirits, Kuturu is highly respected and as soon as cult members and spectators recognized who he was, many went up to him to be touched by him. Rafi had by this time left the mat and stood directly facing the musicians, who promptly returned to his praise chant. In response, Rafi did some more *jifa* falls and landing spectacularly on his buttocks to the applause from the audience. As his music continued, he hit his chest quite hard, three times with his left hand and three with his right, and he then collected a handful of sand, and poured this over himself believing it to be water. This was a cue for his assistant to go off to get a bowl of water, which he gently sprinkled over Rafi. This calmed him just momentarily but soon he was up and off in search of more water to pour over himself to cool himself, with the assistant in tow. Kuturu also left the mat and crawled around on the hard ground with much difficulty, while his assistant and some audience members fussed over him.

The third medium was now becoming fully possessed with foam copiously coming out of her mouth and her eyes glazed. The index finger of her raised right hand was pointing repeatedly to the sky as she held an inaudible conversation with beings who the audience could not see. Gradually, she stood up and instantly adopted a stiff, aloof and haughty aristocratic pose, and the musicians recognizing the presence of Dan Galadima, the Prince, quickly switched to his *kirari*. She walked straight out of the mat, without even acknowledging the musicians or taking any notice of what was happening around *him*, began to pace about the arena and throwing imaginary objects at the spectators. The latter scrambled to catch some of whatever it was Dan Galadima was throwing at them. The prince is known to be wasteful and also prone to bouts of wanderlust. The fourth medium, now fully possessed, stood up and cupped her two hands by her side and immediately an assistant came forward with two short carved wooden sticks which he placed in the medium's hands. He also brought her a red rimmed pair of sunglasses and a red sash to complement her red costume. Finally, an unlit cigarette was put in her mouth. This spirit was a sort of military person as 'he' mostly marched around the arena, or stood at attention by clicking his feet together, or saluted other spirits and the musicians or spectators who came to offer him money. Once fully costumed, the medium went and stood in front of the musicians to acknowledge the praise chants used to welcome him. After him came Babule, the Chief of the Fire Spirits. His features were contorted as if a fire was raging in his belly when he was becoming possessed, and once it became clear who he was, an assistant offered him a piece of red cloth which he proceeded to wave about as he stomped around the arena.

Some of the mediums were not possessed on the day, and they either quietly left the mat or occupied themselves as assistants to their possessed colleagues. But one female medium remained on the mat, she was quite still and her eyes were closed. The *buta* players converged on her as the lead musician changed the beat to a slightly slower tempo from the fast beat of the other inductions. The medium was humming under the barrage of sounds from the *buta* and the two *garaya* (fiddles). Gradually, she began to twitch as the shakers intensified their playing and the overall tempo of the music quickened again. The twitching increased, and her body seemed to acquire a life of its own. Her eyes opened and there was a hint of a smile on her lips, but it was a smile beyond her control. All the while her body shook involuntarily, and with one jerky movement she got into a squat. In this position, she was still wracked by spasms and occasionally shook her head and pounded the earth with her two hands as if the whole experience was extremely unbearable. The shaking gradually became rhythmical and soon in time with the music; it soon developed into a mini dance, in which she kept pointing her index finger in different directions of the arena. As is customary for junior spirits, she sang her own *kirari* to announce who she was:

> Siriddo is for Palaka
> Siriddo is for Mai Gizzo
> Siriddo is for Auta
> Siriddo is for Barhaza

Once she began her song, an assistant hurriedly brought her a long cattle herd's stick. She then stood up, and putting the stick across her shoulders, she did a few steps of the *Barhaza* dance before proceeding to stand in front of the musicians to be formally acknowledged by them.

A host of other spirits came in between Rafi and Siriddo. These included Sarkin Dangwoda (the thief, who mischievously hovered on the periphery of what was going on in the centre while trying to steal things from the unwary spectators), Sarkin Arna (the Pagan Spirit, who stumbled along in a drunken haze and occasionally fell flat on his back and went to sleep), his son, Sarkin Piti, Kafaran (the bespectacled European Spirit who carried a note pad and pen with which he furiously made note of events), the brothers, Dan Auta (Last Born), Mai Gizzo (the Wild One with the Matted Hair) and Palata, Gwangwari Dan Mama and Balkissu.

The finale was the possession of Wakili, the *sarkin bori* and most senior medium of the group. When all the mediums to perform had become possessed and were interacting with spectators or each other, Wakili came to centre stage. He began by walking round the arena in very quick steps, and occasionally skipping, but from time to time he stopped to listen to/direct the music. Suddenly, with one quick movement he swished the metal rod which he had been using as a walking stick across his waist, and for a man approaching seventy-five, these feats of agility were amazing. The rod wrapped itself completely round his body and had to be uncurled by an assistant. His hands free, he began the free dance, which the other mediums had been performing the day before. It was a simple dance in which his hands were stretched out in front and raised slightly above shoulder height, head held still, eyes fixed intently on the musicians. The left leg first traced a zigzag pattern on the ground, and the right leg followed in short forward steps. On getting to the musicians, he completed this phase by bringing his hands down and then turning round to return to the position from which he started, and the sequence was repeated. For Wakili's preparatory sequences, the music went through varying tempos – from the slow and monotonous twang of the *garaya*, to a quick urgent challenge/plea to the lurking spirit to reveal itself. Occasionally, the *buta* players moved in and out to punctuate the sound of the *garaya* with their complex and equally compelling rhythm. Wakili slowly went down on one knee, eyes still fixed on the musicians and soon, his whole body went into spasms, and at last he was sitting with his two legs folded underneath him. His palms were on the ground facing down, and he began slowly to roll his head from side to side. This was the cue for three of the *buta* players to move in to draw the spirit out. They played very close to the head and ears of the now foaming and shivering Wakili (**Fig. 3.5**). Everything seemed to stop, including the other spirits who appeared to subdue their own activities for the arrival of this spirit. The body wrenching and frothing at the

Figure 3.5 Wakili becoming possessed.

mouth continued for approximately ten minutes and then the spirit spoke
to announce his identity. As soon as he began to speak, the music stopped
and the *maroka* took the microphone and repeated whatever the spirit said,
and inserting welcoming exclamations in between. There was great excitement among the spectators, especially the female members. The newly
arrived spirit dashed off into the welcoming arms of women seating behind
the musicians. They cuddled him and some stroked his hair, something he
seemed to enjoy immensely. After a while, he emerged from the women's
area and made his way to a small room by the left entrance, accompanied
by the female medium who had just played Siriddo and a male assistant.
A few minutes passed before both emerged, he as a Gwagwari Dan Mama
and she as Halima Mata Madam, the wife of all the Fire and Foreign
Spirits. To thunderous claps from the spectators, they advanced towards
the centre of the arena, he very boldly strutting and displaying his costume
and assortment of body props, and she rather timidly hiding her face and
only nudged forward by her husband. The music joined in praising her:

> Halima Mata, the mother that stops children from crying
> Halima Mata, the mother that stops women from crying
> She dresses like an Arab woman
> Halima, the one from the Buzu Tribe.
> Halima, daughter of Tuareg serfs
> Wife of non-believer Dan Mama
> Greetings Madam

This did the trick and Halima's eyes beamed and she took some tentative
dance steps forward. Together, the couple did a fuller but flirtatious version
of the *Barhaza* dance. It was a beautifully choreographed cow herd's
dance – their long sticks across their shoulders, the left feet leading by
stepping in and out while the right feet more or less spun on one spot. This
dance differed from Wakili's dance earlier because, instead of the right feet
following, it actually traced a circle which meant the dancers more or less
spun around as if caught in the swirling vortex of a tornado. The dancers
twirled a full circle and then changed direction, and it was the dancers doing
this – one person going one way, and the other another or moving towards
each other and then backing away again in such a synchronized way – that
was the beauty of the dance. It seemed to be the central dance, which
underpinned the two days performance. As they danced, they were joined
by a now very filthy looking Sarkin Rafi, and by other mediums who were
no longer in character. Some spectators joined too. This went on until Rafi,
Dan Mama and Halima got in a line, the music changed and they returned
to the zigzag dance which took the three towards the musicians to bring
the possession section to an end. While the three left the arena to cool down

and change out of their costumes, the dancing continued. The performance concluded with the sharing of the takings from the two days; this was done by the leader of the musicians. The money shared out included the sponsorship fee, which I had paid, and donations from the spectators. Gifts included trinkets, cloths of various kinds, perfume bottles, packets of cigarettes, and soft drinks. The money and gifts were shared out according to position and the instrument the musicians played, with the most senior members or instrument players receiving a larger proportion of the takings. The same went for the mediums and other members of the group.

Organization of *Bori*

As a cult of affliction, one principal route of entry into the *Bori* cult is through a curative rite, known as *girka* (which means 'boiling'). *Girka* usually takes place over a period of days, up to one week in some instances. The members or *yan* or *masu bori* belong to a society of the 'formerly afflicted...whose obligation is expressed by the acceptance of the role of spirit medium ever after' (Besmer, 1983: 22). While one can speak of *Bori* as a single cultural practice in Hausaland, the organization and running of compounds or groups is often local and individual. And also, while there may be uniformity in the basic hierarchy of the spirits and the structuring of performances, the actual number and types of spirits that appear and the duration of their stay depend on the decision of each compound and its head.

My initial impression was that *Bori* was a women-only cult. There was also a suggestion that these female *Bori* members were prostitutes – the term 'prostitute' in Hausa loosely refers to any unmarried person, whether female or male. However, membership includes homosexuals, transvestites or other 'deviant' or marginal individuals, such as the sick and the mentally ill. The only 'really' male participants, I had thought, were the hired professional musicians and the *maroka*. Occasionally, some groups have a *sarkin bori*, who was a nominal head and performed a mainly administrative role. Some all-female groups have a *sarkin bori* to serve as the legitimate face of the group. The *sarkin* is often installed by the local *emir*, to whom he pays tribute like any *sarkin* in the town or district is expected to. The Gidan Wakili group completely changed this perception, led as it is by Wakili, as *sarkin bori*. He was not just an administrative head, as was demonstrated during the performance described above. He, in fact, was the *Yar Maguru* (the Chief Guardian of the Initiate) at the *girka* ceremonies of all the members of his compound, and a few other neighbouring compounds as well. At nearly seventy-seven years of age, he still actively performs. He alone supervised the induction sequences on Day Two, and his own possession performance was the climax of the two-day event.

The Gidan Wakili performance took place on the outskirts of Zaria on a Saturday and Sunday. This group was large and their compound was much bigger than that of any of the other groups I watched in the area. Their performance was very elaborate, colourful, and well organized. The group's management structure was quite effective. A few office holders took part in the negotiation and execution processes of the performance over the two days but Wakili, as *sarkin bori*, was the sole leader of the group. There were three sub-groups, one was led by a *magajiya* and each of the other two by a *shugaba* (leader). There was a single secretary (*Akawo* or *Sarkin Takada*, Chief of the Book) who was responsible for administrative co-ordination, including group bookkeeping and contract notes and receipts for clients. For the performance proper, there was a *maroka* (master of ceremonies/praise shouter or announcer), *masu kiro* (grooms who assisted possessed mediums and who sometimes interacted with and interpreted between the spirits and the audience). Other officials whose specific roles I could not figure out were *Sarkin Fili, Mata Markin, and Sarkin Filini*. A striking thing about the group was the professionalism in the way they organized their activities – the staging arrangements were detailed and strictly followed, there was a resident orchestra of about ten musicians (two *garaya* players, five *buta* players, and some hand-clappers); they also had their own standby generators and loudspeakers, as well as technologically enhanced native instruments, such as electronically amplified fiddles; a diverse and apparently well maintained wardrobe; and an efficient secretarial personnel which promptly wrote a contract for the show and subsequently a receipt for the fee which I paid. In all, there were about fifty members in this group. Most members earn their living mainly from *Bori* activities, especially performances and medicinal services. The group's lead musician was also a fully initiated *Bori* member, contrary to the widely held belief that the musicians are outside the cult.

Training

There are two methods of performer training in *Bori* – one for actors and one for musicians. These two methods reveal a lot about *Bori* practice, especially the relationship between cult adepts and the musicians who support their performances. While an actor's training takes a more or less informal route, the *Bori* musician has to go through a formal period of training. Hausa music is a professional activity and *Bori* cults depend on these highly trained and skilled artists. Training is by apprenticeship to masters over an extended period of time, and formal instruction during training takes the form of regular demonstrations by the teacher, observation and copying by the learner, and finally correction of the learner by the master. The duration of training varies depending on individual talent and application to mastering the technique and conventions. There are principally two kinds of musicians – vocalists and instrumentalists. The vocalist also plays an instrument (usually the *goge* or *garaya*), while the instrumentalists in a group sometimes chip in as chorus or respond to the vocalist's calls or questions. The *Bori* musicians first learn to be professional musicians under a master, and then they become specialists by learning and mastering the very complex musical scores (*kirari* and *waka*) of the individual spirits and the order in which they are played during performances. Fidelity to accepted patterns and lyrical accuracy in the songs are expected and are the bases on which a musician's performance is judged. As there are up to a thousand spirits or deities, learning the entire corpus of *Bori* songs is a huge task and responsibility for the musicians. This is because the music usually controls the performance since only through it is possession achieved. It is also the music that often explains the actions of the spirits when they are in the arena.

Two types of musical training can be identified in Hausa society, and the choice of which type individuals or sponsors opt for is often dependent on the kind of kinship relationship between teacher and pupil. One type is where the two are related as kinsmen, either as maternal or paternal; in which case training becomes a simple case of inheriting the craft from an older relative. The second type is through a formal apprenticeship in which master and apprentice may not be related in any way. But, in general, for *Bori* musicians, kinsmen by far outnumber non-kinsmen as teachers or masters and this reflects the hereditary nature of *Bori* cult practice and membership as a whole. The lead musician of the Wakili group, for instance, had been taught by a close relative, and so was the second *garaya* player who had been taught by his maternal uncle. However, indirect kinsmen are more common than direct kinsmen are as teachers. On the rare occasion when a trainee musician seeks a non-kinsman as a teacher, it is often the result of factors such as a prestigious teacher being available and whose association with the pupil would help ensure the successful start of a career, or when no suitable relative is available to act as teacher. But whichever type of training opted for, the basic principles and method of learning are always the same. There usually are no written contracts or agreements between the pupil, his sponsors or parents and the teacher. However, it is generally understood and accepted by all parties that the teacher will assume both professional and social responsibility for the pupil for the duration of training and even beyond, unless, of course, the pupil after the training period decides to move to another town far away from his teacher's area of coverage. During training the teacher becomes a 'father' to the pupil, and he is treated and addressed as such by the latter. The teacher reciprocates by treating the pupil as his own son or son-in-law, and for the latter, irrespective of his age in relation to the teacher's biological sons, he is assigned the status of the youngest son of the house.

Training involves a slow graduated process in which the pupil must first learn to play the simplest instruments, oftentimes starting with make-shift or improvised models of these instruments, before he is allowed to practice on those which require greater skill. If a pupil is studying under a *garaya* teacher, they will spend the early part of their training – that is, until they are about eight or nine – experimenting with various kinds of 'improvised noise-makers' before progressing to small *buta* (gourd-rattles). These makeshift instruments are usually made by the pupil themselves from all kinds of materials – imitation shakers are made with empty cans filled with pebbles or tiny stones, and *garaya* from a flat piece of wood with two nails at both ends and a piece of nylon thread or wire as a string. What he learns at this stage is mainly how to keep a basic beat with the gourd rattle – the teacher demonstrates with a real *buta* and then invites the pupil to accompany him. When this simple stage is mastered, the teacher then introduces the *garaya* – that is, he plays his *garaya* and the student joins in with his makeshift *buta*. From this period onwards, training becomes a series of mini performances in private between teacher and pupil. The main learning outcome of this method and stage is for the student to understand how his *buta* rhythm fits with his teacher's *garaya*'s melody – this knowledge is essential if one wanted to play as part of an ensemble. In Hausa culture, as in other African cultures, musical performance is understood as a dialogue – either of harmony or confrontation – between the various instruments of an ensemble, the vocalist and the chorus on the one hand, and on the other, between the ensemble and the dancers, and through them, the spirits.

Part of training involves the pupil, even from an early age, attending as many of the teacher's or group's performances as he is able to keep awake in. And even though the pupil may fall asleep in some of the perform-ances their interest in and membership and participation are encouraged through small payments from the proceeds from the shows. From these simple beginnings, the pupil gradually moves up the instrument ladder, and by age thirteen they can actually buy their first real instrument with their savings from the payments, with the approval of the teacher of course. The pupil, from this point on, is allowed to practice on his own within the privacy of the compound, and then from time to time he performs for the teacher, who assesses his performance. If thought good, the teacher can invite the pupil for some relief work during long nights of performance. Once this stage is reached, it is accepted that the teacher's responsibilities are practically over, and if the pupil so desires – and most do, since staying around might set them in competition with their teacher – he can move out to seek work elsewhere on his own, or to put together a music group of his own in which he will become leader.

There is a gender preference in instruments played by *Bori* musicians – instruments played by one sex are usually never played by the other sex. Female ensembles, mostly non-professionals, tend to play *kwarya kidan ruwa* (hemispherical calabashes placed face down in water and played with two sticks), whereas male musicians, mainly professional, either play the *garaya* (two-stringed plucked fiddle), *goge* (single-stringed, bowed fiddle), *buta* (gourd-rattle), or *kwarya*. These four are the main instruments for *Bori* music, although there are a few others used infrequently by groups. Female ensembles tend to play a single family of instruments, the *kwarya*, within which there is a gradation from junior to senior. But male ensembles tend to make use of instruments of contrasting types or families, and there are two principal kinds of ensembles based on which instrument the leader plays. A *garaya* ensemble is made up of a main *garaya* player accompanied by perhaps a second *garaya* and a host of *buta* players, while a *goge* ensemble has a main *goge* player, and another *goge* with *kwarya* accompaniment. This combination of instrument families or types is never mixed or interchanged – such as *goge* with *buta* or *garaya* with *kwarya*. The Wakili group was a *garaya* ensemble and consisted of two *garaya* players and five *buta* players (**Fig. 3.6**).

Figure 3.6 Bori musicians and their instruments.

Actor training

Training to become a medium is different. In the past, cult members were not seen, nor did they see themselves, as purely professional performers. Increasingly however, many groups and members are beginning to see themselves as professional *Bori* troupes or practitioners. In fact, a significant number, such as members of the Wakili group, now earn a living from their cult activities. As a cult, membership of *Bori* is through *girka*, an elaborate initiation process in which initiates are 'made' into vehicles for the spirits and are said to have become the horses or mares of the gods – *doki* if they are male and *godiya* if they female; when possessed a medium is seen as being 'ridden' by the spirit. *Girka* is a preparation for a life-long practice of performing the spirits by the new member. Initiation establishes a permanent bond between the initiate and the spirits invoked by the *Yar Maguru* during the ceremony. There are two kinds of members. The first are those who underwent *girka* as a curative rite, and the second are those who choose to become members out of interest. The latter formally approach a cult, are interviewed, and sometimes character references are sought before the individual is finally accepted. But they have to undergo a *girka* initiation ceremony like the afflicted members.

As in the *Mmonwu* theatre, at no specific time during initiation is the *Bori* initiate formally taught how to perform any of the spirits. Actual learning comes from a widely available cultural knowledge of the characters, and by watching other mediums perform. So, acting a role is done within a set of conventions and expectations but these also allow individual creativity, interpretation and embellishment of the role. Flexibility and a physical ability to move from role to role is also encouraged since it is possible in the course of one performance event for a medium to become possessed by as many spirits as time allows. In effect therefore, unlike in some Asian performances, such as *No, Kabuki, Kathakali,* and so on, in which actors are trained to play specific roles or characters, the *Bori* performer can move through a whole range of characters in a short period of time, sometimes as many as five or six in one performance. Some of the mediums at the Wakili performance were possessed by more than one spirit. Wakili himself moved from his role as *sarkin bori* and facilitator of the induction process, to becoming a Buzzu spirit, and then Gwagwari Dan Mama for the finale. Learning to perform in such a context entails mastering the mannerisms, movements and the basic improvised sketches of each spirit for whom she or he can become a medium. The performer also has to learn to master and be able to respond to the musical cues that indicate the arrival of each spirit.

In general, cult members do not have a sustained or extended formal system through or within which they learn how to perform or master their roles. Instead, like other performance genres in Africa, acquiring the techniques of acting or performing a specific role takes place in the process of actually doing it. Members of *Bori*, like the young initiated boys in Igbo masquerade theatre, get the license as it were to perform through the *girka* ceremony in which they for the first time make formal acquaintance with spirits. How they then embody these spirits when possessed, it was claimed by the mediums I spoke to after the performance, is outside their control since it is believed that each spirit takes control and the medium is merely a 'horse' or 'mare' under the power and direction of the riding spirit. The performer who was possessed by Rafi insisted he could not remember any of the things he did, such as pouring sand and dirty water over himself, hitting his chest so hard that he had to be restrained from time to time, or blessing a young child and her mother. In theatre terms, the performer learns from having watched experienced mediums, and is able to create whichever character is required by using this knowledge and information about the traits, behaviour, mannerisms and so on of the spirits.

Occasions for performances

Generally speaking, *Bori* performances can be classed under two headings – private *bori* (*borin gida* or *house bori*) and public *bori* (*wasan bori*, *bori* play or social *bori*). The two types demonstrate the idea of mutual transformability between ritual and theatre based on function and or context. While *girka* is ritual and private, social or *wasan bori* is play, secular, public and solely for entertainment. The Gidan Wakili performance fell in between the two, having been organized for me and was open to the public. But it was also done as a curative rite for one of Wakili's patients. *Girka* can either be performed as a curative ritual for a patient afflicted by the spirits or just as an initiation rite for a new member. In both instances, it is a special occasion and usually involves spirit possession and is open only to cult members and close relatives of the afflicted or intending new member. The spirits have to be invoked during *girka* because it is the mechanism or context for the afflicted and their supporters to come into direct contact with the causative spirits in order to appease them and become cured of their affliction. In the initiation of a new member, *girka* enables the afflicted or initiate to imbibe the essences of particular spirits whose *doki* or *godiya* (horse or mare) they'll become for life. Theatrically though, through *girka* mediums acquire the rudiments of their roles. They are then expected to develop and perfect these as they perform subsequently after initiation.

Occasions for the performance of *wasan bori* range from weddings, through political rallies, to festivals involving a whole community, and up to national festivals of the arts in recent years. Affluent individuals can also commission performances – each performance that I watched was organized specifically for me, although they were tied to on-going programmes of therapy. The difference between them and other private shows was mainly that even though they took place in secluded *Bori* compounds, audiences of non-members were allowed to watch.

Themes

In many ways, *Bori* does not differ from Igbo masquerade performances or *Jaliya* of the Mandinka. For instance, in *Mmonwu* the same masquerades or spirits will appear, but the context in which they appear will give meaning to their performance; a funeral performance, for instance, will differ from a festival or a judicatory performance. In *Jaliya*, the same praise lines and the same musical patterns are repeated, but occasionally modified slightly to take into account the client and the context. But the nature of *Bori* as a cult of the afflicted means that performances are celebrations of the unique relationship between the cult adepts and their spirits. This implies that most performances are religious in both theme and tone, even when the contexts are ostensibly secular and playful, such as the Gidan Wakili performance. Their ritual-religious functions are inextricably woven into their entertainment or theatrical functions. Because no individual stories or narratives are involved, secular themes are not usually explored directly or in any detail, as in *Kote-tlon* or African literary dramas and other syncretic African theatre forms, or as Echeruo (p. 12) and Ukaegbu (p. 11) advocate for Igbo *Mmonwu* theatre to go beyond its ritual and communal base in order to become secular dramatic performance. But *Bori* and *Mmonwu* explore secular themes; what they not do is explore individuated themes as Greek and Western dramas do. What is presented in *Bori*, as a reminder to the human spectators, is the ultimate power and omniscience of the spirits, and the need for the human community always to show respect and to be willing to defer to the authority of these repositories of power and influence. But, in the construction and demonstrations of some of the characteristics of the spirits, and often manifest in the praise chants, the human community is able to use these as commentary and censure of individual behaviour. Spectators recognize the spirit behaviours and are able to relate them to those within their human community. The theme of harmony and peace with the spirits being central to both individual and communal well being seems to underlie every *Bori* performance.

Bori characters

Characters in *Bori* are as numerous as the Hausa imagination can encompass. Its pantheon is a complex hierarchical structure that, like the human culture that created it, replicates the whole range and patterns of human relationships and individual traits found in Hausa society. What is expected of mediums whenever they become possessed by any of the spirits is clear and provides both the drama and the framework for evaluating performance abilities. The pantheon is divided into houses, and each house is made up of a male head, his wife, sons, daughters, adopted sons and daughters, grandsons and granddaughters, and other members who may not necessarily be cognate relatives of the household. Knowledge of this is helpful in understanding the hierarchy, as well as the relationships between the spirits. However, there is not total agreement among cult members about which spirit belongs to which house, and this is further compounded by the occasional haziness about relationships between the spirits. The view presented here is based on the relationships as described by the Wakili group and so reflects the Zaria version of the social structure of Jangare.

The major spirits are Sarkin Aljan Sulemanu (Chief of the Spirits) and head of the first house in Jangare. A medium possessed by him is expected to be bossy, commanding and getting those around him (including the spectators and the assistants) to do things for him, rather than do them himself. He acts like a chief and maintains an air of aloof superiority and indifference to what happens around him. Inna, his wife, is also known as Fulani Woman, Matron of Jangare, Bafilatana, Baka Doguwa, or the Tall One. She has a very complex personality and, because she is believed to be responsible for paralysis of the limbs, those possessed by her move about holding a curled up arm, and sometimes the mediums lie sideways and rock backwards and forwards. Dan Galadima (the Prince or Noble Youth) is the gambler who often throws cowry shells at the spectators. He dresses very fancifully and is a typical aristocrat who doesn't care much for who or what are around him but is single-minded in pursuit of his own pleasures and interests. He is also a spendthrift, who throws all his money away without the slightest worry. Dan Galadima is believed to cause wanderlust and so his medium just walks around the arena or paces like a nobleman. Occasionally, he condescends and sits and holds court as members of the audience come to bring their problems or cases for him to look into. Dan Galadima (he was performed by a female medium) at the Wakili performance just wandered around the arena showering the spectators with imaginary gifts with the latter 'catching' and 'putting' them away. Occasionally, he just stood still, head straight and hands held stiff and slightly apart, in a dignified pose while junior spirits came and knelt at 'his' feet to be blessed.

Mallam Alhaji is the king of the Muslim spirits, who unfortunately did not appear at the Zaria performances. He is described as a devout Muslim who has performed the pilgrimage to Mecca, and walks about bent over with a shuffling gait, mutters and coughs a lot as he reads his holy book and counts his prayer beads. He is very popular with the spectators, who consult him for his immense knowledge, wisdom and medicinal skills. He was not a favourite of the Wakili group, as all the spirits at this performance were pagan/bush spirits or foreign and non-Muslim. Mallam Alkali, the learned judge is another prominent Muslim spirit and was also not present at the performance. He just sits on a mat and counts his beads while hearing, adjudicating or dispensing justice in cases which the spectators bring to him. Another popular character is Sarkin Rafi; he is the Chief of the Rivers and Streams. He is Sulemanu and Baka Doguwa's son but adopted by his uncle, Biddarene and his wife, Magajiya Jangare. One of the prominent spirits at the Gidan Wakili performance, he was the first to appear and the last to depart. He is known for his wild striding steps which are regularly interrupted by his spectacular *jifa* falls. He constantly searches for water to pour over himself. He is very strong and wild and his mediums have to be constantly restrained by assistants to prevent them from physically injuring themselves. Rafi repeatedly beat his chest, occasionally stiffened his hands and legs and yet, when he calmed down, he engaged in verbal and gestural exchanges with his restrainers, other members and a few spectators. When a young child was brought to him, he took her in his arms and began to wipe her face and entire body gently with the hem of his now very wet and dirty *gwado*. As he did this he was intoning inaudibly over the child. When he had finished, he handed the young girl back to her grateful mother who offered some money to him. He did not touch the money, which was accepted on his behalf by one of his assistants. Rafi's a wife is Nanaaishe, who unfortunately did not appear at this performance.

Barade, also known as Sarkin Yaki or Chief of War, is Sarkin Rafi's brother and regularly travels with him. He appeared at the performance, a ferocious character who scared the spectators. His magical sword display had the audience in awe and wonder but nobody came forward when he asked for volunteers to demonstrate on. Another regular spirit absent at the performance was Makako, the Blind One. This spirit wanders about like a blind person, and is usually led by a boy with a long stick; spectators are expected to give alms to him. Kuturu, the Leper, another prominent spirits was present at Gidan Wakili. He is Jangare's senior counselor, and his other titles include *Urban Dawaki* (Father of the Horses), and Leader of the Horsemen. His medium crawled on hands and knees, with a pained expression on his face. As part of his performance, Kuturu pretended to brush away invisible flies from imaginary sores. In his *kirari*, two key facets of his personality, his fearsomeness and his amusing antics, are celebrated. Kuturu is a complex and well-respected character in Hausa society because his power is very visible in the large number of people afflicted by him. Performing him seemed quite demanding and very painful because of the contorted posture that the actor had to assume and maintain. Plus, his opposing comic and serious traits also challenge the acting abilities of the medium. The latter had his fingers curled and spread apart, and he crawled all over the uneven ground, while trying to cope with the 'flies'. Occasionally, he tried to stand up or pick an object from the ground, but each time failed miserably and his frustration was evident in the scowl on his face. Kuturu is an important character in Jangare, being a senior member of Sarkin Sulemanu's court. Only the most senior and proficient members of a cult become possessed by him. As such, his appearance during a performance – which is not very frequent – always creates a lot of excitement and awe among the spectators. The moment he appeared, a loud cheer went up from the spectators.

Sarkin Arnaa is the Chief of the Pagans and appeared at the Wakili performance. Given the predominance of Islam in Hausaland, this major representative of the infidel is not usually presented flatteringly. His main problem is drunkenness, which is all he lives for and this is made worse by his deep-rooted hatred of Islam. His medium danced and walked in a very disjointed manner: legs wobbly and arms flailing; his general movement was jerky and he often bumped into things, people and other possessed mediums. He finally ended up falling on the ground in a drunken stupor and lay there for a long time. He had to be carried to the side by his grooms. Mai Dawa or Owner of the Bush, sometimes also called Mai Baka or Owner of the Bow, the Bowman, Adamu or Gajere (Short Man). This is another multidimensional character, reflected in his many names. He is an expert hunter, who fears neither man nor beast and is called the short man because he constantly adopts a crouching posture. His medium carried a bow and a quiver of arrows which from time to time he aimed at imaginary animals and sometimes at the spectators. He also carried an axe which he used to chop down imaginary undergrowth or slay wild animals to the beat of his *kirari*. His performance had stylizations of the basic movements of hunting or slashing with an axe, all done in a crouching position. Barhaza, Inna's younger sister, is Mai Dawa's wife. She was presented as a shy Fulani woman who kept hiding from the crowd – this of course is a Hausa stereotype of a pastoral Fulani woman. In fact, her assistants had to restrain her as she kept wanting to run away to hide when approached or startled by noise. She spoke only when spoken to and in a very low voice; her Hausa had a very strong Fulani accent. Other characteristics were evident in the performance when the medium went about imitating milking and churning gestures to her music. Finally, there was Umaru Sanda ba Buga or Umaru, Stick for Beating, sometimes seen as the European spirit. He carried a pen and pad and pretended to be writing with them. At the Wakili performance (he was performed by a female medium) he wore dark sunglasses, behind which he peered contemptuously and suspiciously at everything around him. A modern spirit, he smoked cigarettes and at one point had two comically sticking out of the corners of his mouth and alternated between them. His dance resembled a military march and his assistant brought a special chair on which he sat very close to the musicians. He wore western European style clothes – a red baseball-cap, shirt and trousers, and white shoes. The audience found him comical and endearing.

Other characters whose chants were played on Day One or appeared on Day Two were Mai Gizo, Dan Auta, Siriddo (Auta's wife), Palaka (Mai Gizzo's wife), Jadu Mai Dan Hanu, Duna, Kafaran, Sarkin Piti, Gwagwari Dan Mama and his wife, Halima Mata Madam, Babule, Buzu and Balkissu (Buzu's wife). A host of other spirits not featured at the performance can broadly be classed as belonging to: Muslim spirits, Pagan spirits, Warriors, Youthful spirits, Children of Small-Pox, and Bush spirits.

This gives some idea of the variety of characters which mediums can be expected to perform. Their characteristics are distinct and fairly well known – especially the bush spirits who are mainly animal characters and whose behaviours mediums reproduce. The mannerisms and characteristics by which spirits are identified are also the main basis on which mediums' representations of them are assessed. They are expected to reproduce the demeanour of the occupying spirit with the appropriate voice, movement and actions. Thus, if Mallam Alhaji (the Moslem scholar) possesses an adept, the medium is expected to walk with a learned stoop and constantly count his prayer beads while reading from an imaginary Koran. The medium playing the spirit of Sleeping Sickness will automatically doze off, even in the middle of a conversation or a lively dance. There is no confusing the characters and it is their distinct way of interacting with the audience and sometimes with one another that constitutes the drama of *Bori*.

What this diversity indicates is that *Bori* performers are very versatile actors whose bodies are required to go through a broad range of muscular deployments in any one performance. And if, as was claimed by group members, mediums did not have a choice over which spirit possessed them and at what time and for how long, once within the performance space their bodies had to be willing and ready vessels for the arrival and passage of the spirits. This tuning process happened during the pre-possession free dance which preceded the performances. This phase lasted almost six hours – the whole of the Saturday's performance and for almost two hours on Sunday. The spirits came only half way through the performance on Sunday.

Staging techniques and design

Like other traditional performances in Africa, *Bori* performances are often in the round (arena) and in the open. However, with different *Bori* contexts, the structure, character, and size of the space often determine the staging arrangements. Thus, whereas an open, village square *Bori* performance can have a complete arena staging, an initiation or a special performance, such as the one I watched, can take place in private compounds or a *gidan bori* (*bori* house) – the shape and size of the compound gave shape and scope to the staging arrangement and spatial configuration.

However, whatever the shape of the space, and spatial configuration a group opts for, the internal staging, particularly the placement of musicians and mediums for the preliminary dance sequences, is fairly standard – they are usually positioned at opposite ends of the arena, facing each other and the mediums dance towards the musicians. These positions ultimately determine how the spectators are placed. This fixed position, however, does not apply to possessed mediums who, wander everywhere because the spirits are in control and have the freedom of the space: every other person has to readjust to them, move and shift position as they do and so on.

A *Bori* stage is divided into two main interactive spaces. The first is the actual stage space which is occupied by mediums, musicians and assistants, and in ritual performances such as *girka*, by the guide or *magajiya*. The second outer space accommodates the audience, who can either completely envelop the performance space (stage) as they did in the Gidan Wakili performance, or leave some gaps through which the performers pass. Complete envelopment was possible in Gidan Wakili because the compound was a big rectangular space measuring approximately forty-eight feet by sixty-four feet (48ft x 64ft). On one side was a long building with two ends jutting out, and opposite that was a second long straight-line building which formed an entrance with one end of the main building. On the right were two small round huts and one granary – one side of the granary created another entrance with the other end of the second building. Spectators came in mainly through this entrance. The positions of these structures, especially the smaller buildings, and the location of the *sarkin bori*'s mat created a square space used for the preliminary dances on both days. An extra enclosure at the end of the main building, directly behind but forming part of the jutting end acted as a costume/dressing room. The opening formed by the two main buildings provided exits and entrances for the performers coming from the dressing room. The main building had an awning which provided a shade for the mainly female spectators who sat behind the musicians, among whom Wakili had gone to be mobbed and caressed. The two main gaps, down stage left and right, served as exits and entrances for the spectators. Within the space enclosed by the spectators, three areas were marked out – backing on to the awning were the musicians, to their left and centre sat Sarkin Bori and his retinue on Day One, and at the other end, facing the musicians, were the cult members in a single line formation. The space at the centre of the arena – between the three positions identified – became the induction space on the second day. When the time came for this part of the performance, a large mat was spread for all intending mediums to sit on to await the arrival of the spirits (see **Fig. 3.1**).

There were no fixed elements or structures on the stage – everything was mobile and most of the props and stage objects, such as chairs, mats, umbrella, swords, machetes, bicycle and so on, were brought on stage either by the performers or stage assistants, as needed, just as they were in the *Mmonwu* and *Koteba* performances. These items were removed immediately after use to make way for new ones needed by other spirits. Most of the props used were specific to the characters. Special props referred to as *tsere*, act as aids to possession – such props are believed to attract the spirits who they belong to. The main props included a machete, dagger, sword, bowls, a metal rod, walking sticks, a bow and arrows, a bicycle, pestle and mortar, two fire blowing bundles of twigs, the decorated calabashes of the Fulani maidens, note pad and pen, a fly whisk, sunglasses, hoes, cigarettes.

Costume

The stunning and flamboyant colours of the costumes were the most striking element in this performance – from the flaming red, white and black outfit of Dan Galadima, Babule, and Sarkin Yaki, to the dark smoky brown and ochre of the Buzu farmers, and from the black and brown glittering mirror-covered tunics of the huntsmen and the bush spirits to the white embroidered hand-woven blouses and wrappers of Barhaza and the Fulani women. These were complemented by the everyday, but equally beautiful colours of the musicians' caftans, *baba riga* and Wakili's *sarkin bori* regalia – both equally stunning in their elegance and elaborateness. Mediums constantly changed costumes to signal which character was present at any specific point or period in the performance. Wakili, the group leader, changed his costume twice as *sarkin* on Day One, and twice again on Day Two when he performed a Buzu spirit and when he became Dan Mama (**Fig. 3.7**, also see **Figs 3.2** and **3.5**).

Figure 3.7 Gwagwari Dan Mama and Halima Madam.

Costume plays a significant role in *Bori* performances. They provide visual beauty to the whole performance with their colourful diversity and elaborateness; but most importantly, they are markers of character because, as often happened during the performance, some mediums ended up becoming possessed by more than one spirit. Costume, props and make-up were indicators of the identities of the spirits being represented. When, however, the speed of a spirit's arrival left the medium with insufficient time to effect a complete costume change, the assistants just placed a new costume onto the previous one to indicate the change of character, or added a *tsere* to effect the required character change, such as Siriddo receiving a stick or the European spirit being given sunglasses, a pen and notebook. At other times, it was left to the medium to signal the change through recognized character-specific movements or behaviour. Whichever means of signification was employed, the audience were able to immediately pick up what was happening or which spirit was present and responded accordingly.

Bori, as a ritual performance, operates mainly at the symbolic level – with elements such as costume, props, the special objects (*tsere*), being coded carriers of meaning. These items provide the basic means for the spectator-performer engagement to begin. Significantly, as in *Mmonwu*, no attempts are made in *Bori* to portray characters or situations realistically.

Music and dance

According to Besmer, 'horses, musicians and gods' are the key actors of the *Bori* cult. The musicians are professionals 'whose function is to preserve much of the oral tradition of the cult and to invoke the spirits with special songs during possession-trance performances' (1983: 1). The dancers must have music to accompany and inform their actions but, more importantly, the spirits require and demand it to announce and individuate their presence and power. Only through their personal music (*kirari* or praise chants and *waka* or induction music) are the spirits invoked, and it is through music that they possess their mediums. Most of the time, the possessing spirits are in dialogue with the musicians, who call and guide them during their presence. For instance, Sarkin Rafi: when the music intensified his legs stiffened, his hands were thrown to the side, chest puffed out and, although his words were inaudible, he was clearly saying things and answering the lead musician in response to his string of praise lines. And Rafi hit his chest hard, his own way of repeating and accepting all the praise names that he was being called. The music helped him to speak about himself, and it also reminded him of the kind of behaviour the audience expected of him.

It is also with the music that a spirit is sent back at the conclusion of their stay. The lead musician, who knows all the spirit songs and the sequence in which they are played, is responsible for ensuring that the correct musical cues are given and each spirit's praise song played correctly – he needs to call the spirits in turn, and recognize and respond accordingly to the few capricious ones who occasionally come unannounced. In recognition of this, all gifts presented during a performance are offered and left to the leader of the musicians, either directly by spectators/patrons or by the mediums who pass gifts they have received on to him. During the performance, some assistants were busy collecting from the foreheads of the mediums or picking off the ground all the money being given and putting them in a bowl placed directly in front of the leader of the musicians, which he distributed appropriately at the end of the performance. There is usually a previously agreed fees also, which musicians settle on with their hosts or the group that has invited them to perform. Good musicians are always in demand, and most cult groups tend to stick with one group of musicians. The music team at the Gidan Wakili performance have performed for the cult group for many years, and some had only played for this group.

Although central to *Bori* practice, music and musicians in Hausa Muslim society are not accorded high status, even though some musicians play at royal courts and enjoy a measure of social elevation through royal patronage. A hierarchy exists within the musical fraternity, with those who play for *Bori* being the lowest and most looked down upon. There are two main reasons for this. Firstly, music has no place in Islamic religious practice, musical instruments not being allowed to be played in mosques because devout Muslims are of the opinion that most traditional/native Hausa music is evil. The *goge* – a key instrument used in summoning and playing for *Bori* spirits – is strongly believed by Muslims to belong to the devil, and so it is hardly surprising that the spirits themselves in Islamic view are devils. The second reason for the low status of *Bori* musicians is that non-initiates who participate in *Bori* performances are seen to be 'keeping bad company' and *Bori* cult devotees are perceived and treated as deviants, and so the musicians share this stigma. In a predominantly Muslim cultural context, 'it is bad enough to be a musician, but inexcusable to practice one's craft in support' of a pagan cult (Besmer, 1983: 34). But that said, musicians are highly skilled artists, and their role in *Bori* is very demanding because of the volume of oral material that they have to learn and reproduce, while remaining flexible enough to improvise creatively in relation to whatever happens during a performance.

The music used is of two major types: either purely instrumental or both vocal and instrumental. Each type implies a specific kind of activity or situation: vocal music is used to honour or request the presence of a spirit and also to inform and entertain the audience. Through the praise epithet much information about a spirit is presented to the audience – genealogy, deeds, likes and dislikes, patterns of behaviour and so on. Each piece of vocal music is either a *kirari* or *waka*. The *kirari* describes the spirit and the *waka* is an invitation for it to possess a medium. The content of the first part and the lyrical pattern of these praise-chants are usually rigidly fixed as part of the orature of the *Bori* cult, and they hardly change from generation to generation. But the anecdotes and the actual call for the spirit to possess a medium depend very much on the style and discretion of the particular ensemble leader, and on the context and tempo of the performance. Purely instrumental music is used mainly for giving induction cues.

The effectiveness of the instrumental music in inducing possession does not depend on words, but rather on the melody and rhythm. This means that music plays a deep and essential role in *Bori* performances by providing the rhythmically powerful induction cues without which the mediums can not become possessed. It is the culturally defined and coded musical accompaniment which elicits patterns of behaviour and actions to match and answer the expectations of the audience. Once the cues are given the mediums are expected, and have been trained and primed to respond accordingly.

Detached observers at *Bori* events and those who have only heard or read descriptions of the cult and its performances, sometimes question whether or not possession or trance really takes place, or whether the mediums merely fake it. But, like all ritual performances, a *Bori* performance can be apprehended at two levels. At the Wakili performance, those who, like the cult members, believed in the ideas behind the ritual were in no doubt that the spirits were present. But for a few others, who did not share in the sustaining belief, the mediums were merely simulating possession by reproducing behaviour and actions previously learned and expected of them. Both modes of apprehension are valid, and rather than seeking to determine the truth or falsity of what happened, this study is more interested in investigating the areas of convergence between the two modes. The two main areas of convergence are the theatricality and the visual impact of the performance. Theatrically, the performance was good, and individual acting abilities were of a high standard: what one witnessed were undeniable 'transformations' of the mediums into specific spirit characters who the informed spectators had no difficulty identifying and interacting with. But just a theatrical analysis of what happened does not do justice to the unique experience of watching these performers or 'horses of the spirits' energize an 'empty space' with the presence of the other worldly. Months after watching the performance and seeing the video recording of it many times, one is reluctant to dismiss the belief and intense experience of a whole community as just theatrical make-believe.

Central to this experience was the pervasive and almost hypnotic power of music. Its rhythmic structure and sound patterns had a deep psychological effect on the mediums. The combination of the verbal and the purely sonic aspects of *Bori* music helped to push and guide the mediums into altered states of consciousness. It had a seductive repetitive pattern which can be explained psychologically. Besmer's conclusion that the aim of the induction music and cues is to achieve a state of dissociation in the mediums through a process of sensory overload supports this view. Each piece of induction music or praise-chant is fixed and conforms to a set rhythmic pattern and the power of the music to achieve the altered state of being comes from the fixed repetitive pulse. Induction was preceded by a relatively slow piece of music with a pulse of around 110–120 beats per minute. This set up the basic pattern for auditory overloading to happen. The piece which initiated dissociation had two phases: the first had a quick and increasing tempo with a single rising pulse of between 160 and 200 beats per minute and the second introduced a much faster and more complex pulse of more than 200 beats per minute. As the tempo of the music increased, so did the volume and density of the sound. This ensured that overloading occurred, both in the number of musical cues being given and their acoustic strength since the musical phrases at the fastest tempo occurred at short intervals and at the highest intensity (see Besmer, 1983: 141).

As the music reached its highest level of intensity, it became increasingly difficult for the waiting mediums to distinguish between the double (*garaya*) and triple (*buta*) rhythmic patterns within each musical phrase. The speed of the cues from the *garaya* and the intensity of the sound produced by the *buta* played very close to their ears were complemented by the loud and excited exclamations and exhortations of the energetically circling Wakili, the microphone clutching *maroka* and some spectators, to finally push the mediums into trance.

On Day Two, for instance, as the mediums came in to sit on the mat, the general music of the day before was repeated, including Sarkin Makada's music (Chief of the Drummers) with which all performances open. And when they had all sat down, the music turned to specific praise songs of the spirits who were expected. Gradually, the rhythmic pattern changed to a more intense and quicker beat. This produced an immediate effect on some of the waiting mediums – most became very still, bodies tense, eyes either closed or gazing vacantly round the arena, but without seeming to notice anything, and one or two looked apprehensive. Again, the rhythm moved up to a significantly higher number of beats per second, resulting in involuntary twitches and rocking of the body, foaming at the mouth, and glazed eyes. Then the music returned to and stayed on individual *kirari* and *waka*, with beats up again to a much higher and more complex rhythmic configuration of sounds, the *garaya*, in particular, took on a compelling urgency in the way its sound sliced the air.

Sarkin Rafi was the first, and as soon as his *waka* began, his medium started rolling his head from side to side, mouth frothing copiously, prompting the lead musician to motion three of the *buta* players to move closer to the mat. The three went straight and played very close to the medium's ears, the latter was then rocking and gripping the mat very tightly to keep himself on the ground. It was as if a powerful force was trying to lift him off it. They stayed close to him until one leg shot out from under him and hands stretched to the side, and suddenly he hit his chest three times to announce that he was Rafi. The music slowed down a bit to enable the lead musician to welcome him with more lines, punctuated with shouts of '*Sanu, sanu da zua*' ('Welcome, welcome for coming'). Then Kuturu's music was played, and again the *buta* players moved to his medium, and the intensity, quick tempo and the deafening closeness of the shakers helped quicken possession for the medium. This went on until all the mediums to be possessed for the day's performance had been induced, and the *buta* players returned to their positions. The music finally returned to the slower and more even beat which had preceded induction.

Overall, music was used extensively to prepare everybody for the performance – the entire first day and up to two hours of the second were devoted entirely to music and dance by all the cult members, and some members of the audience who are allowed to take part in the free dance programmes of the opening and closing.

Performer–spectator relationship

The ritual basis of *Bori* practice and performances to a large extent colour and inform the relationship between spectator and performer. Whichever type of performance, spectators are bound to have an ambivalent relationship with the performers and the performance. In general, for the average Hausa audience member, it is impossible to push aside the idea that *Bori* ritual provides a degree of explanation for illnesses and at the same time a mechanism for achieving a measure of control and adjustment to these illnesses. The spirits when they are appeased through being performed provide cure.

But, *Bori* performances are also great entertainment for those who watch. The violent *jifa* falls are met with great approbation, and the antics of those possessed by the spirits are often greeted with whoops of laughter. The music is loud and constant, and the crowd chatters and individuals talk with one another. It is by no means a solemn, sacred ceremony enacted in hushed tones. The audience has a paradoxical relationship with both performer and performance. Viewed as a ritual, the spectator is essentially a participant who shares the underpinning beliefs with the performer/medium. Interaction with the spirits/performers is conducted with utmost respect and decorum born out of the firm belief that the spirits have the power to and are expected to take away problems of the human community. A good illustration of this was the number of people, including members of the audience, who approached Sarkin Rafi or Kuturu to be touched and cured by them. Others were interested and eager to touch or be touched by Dan Mama when he threw himself among the women. But what these interactions suggested, from the standpoint of the researcher and sceptic, was an actively engaged audience who do so because of the total harmony between performer and audience arising from a shared perception of the world of the performance. The spectators were able to take part without any inhibition – they could identify with the performer who is, in all other respects, like them. There was no distance, separation or sense of specialization as in other theatres in which one person performed and the other person merely watched or in which performer and spectator belonged to two different orders of life (Okpewho, 1990: 160).

The audience is an integral part of *Bori* performances, especially the *wasan bori* (public or playful *Bori*). The *girka* or other forms of private performances are different because they, in the nature of rituals, do not have or admit of audiences. Everyone involved in a *girka* ceremony is a participant – as ritual guide, initiate, ritual assistant, musician, supporter or sponsor and so on. Everyone has the same goal in mind, and thus no separate agendas exist; neither is there any differentiation in roles, even though there are clear functions as either a performer or a participating supporter. Although there may be a multiplicity of functions, the purpose of the ritual is always the same for everyone – and in *Bori*, this purpose is to make a sick person better or to induct a new member. Specialization, in a professional sense, is responsible for the separation between performer and spectator in Western and other theatres, and thus far there seems to be an active resistance to specialization in indigenous performances in Africa. What also encourages the active participation of spectators in *Bori* and other African performances is their structural open-endedness and the absence sometimes of a finite individualized narrative, unlike in in other theatres.

As in the masquerade performances of the Igbo, the *Bori* performer depends very much on the audience for any performance to take place. During the performance in Zaria, although seemingly possessed by the spirits or in some instances deeply in trance, the mediums had some awareness of the presence of the spectators. This of course may give credence to the sceptical view that possession is simply shamming and nothing more than a display of learned skill in impersonation and improvisation. However, spectators or participants were intimately involved and interacted with the spirits; performatively as did the mother and child in the Sarkin Rafi scene and appreciatively by either shouting out approbation or by giving gifts to whichever performer they thought highly of or enjoyed most. Audience support for the show was manifested in this way: as an on the spot validation of a good performance rather than a pre-booked endorsement of a future enjoyment followed by a distanced post-performance analysis.

This is not to suggest that in *Bori* or other African performances, a post-performance analytical framework or activity does not exist or take place. It did after *Enemma* and also after the *Koteba* performance in Markala. The *Bori* members reviewed the performance after we had left and again when I returned nine months later to view the tapes with them. They talked about aspects of the performance which were good and also those that were not. This is a performance style in which there is no deferred reaction or feedback for the performers to sit back and analyse after the performance. Instead, they get an immediate response to take on board and use to instantly improve their performance if it is poor, or to bask in and do more if good. This is the general principle on which most African indigenous oral performances are based. The implication, for both spectator and performer, is that the performer has to get the audience on board since the latter's response and contributions are essential in order for a performance to take place. This is a demanding and risky form of performance because there is no guarantee for the organizers and the performers of a ready-made performance before contact with the spectators.

So, the famed audience participation of African theatre and performance is in reality double-edged because it makes huge demands on the artistic, emotional and economic resources of both spectators and performers. On the one hand, it makes artistic demands on and ensures aesthetic excellence from both parties. But, on the other, especially for the performers and artists, there is no hiding place because judgement is instantaneous. A poor performer is told straight to the face that he or she is no good. The performer equally tells an uncooperative audience so. Performers, both masquerades and *Bori* mediums, have been known to ignore, avoid, or shame uncooperative spectators or segments of them. The Hausa trader in the *Ochammili* masquerade performance in 1994 is a case in point. Having approached us and offered a choice of sweets, cigarettes and kola nuts, he stopped performing because we had ignored him by not buying anything from him. He literally stopped playing until we were willing to play ourselves. During the *Bori* performance, after demonstrating his magical sword skills on himself, Barade asked for audience volunteers and when nobody came forward he showed his disappointment and disapproval by a rude dismissive wave of his left hand before he began to demonstrate on a willing cult member. He kept teasing and reminding the spectators of their cowardice by occasionally slashing or swinging his sword in their direction.

Social, political and entertainment functions

Bori has always had a function in the societies in which it is performed, especially for its adherents for whom this function goes well beyond the entertainment which it obviously provides for its ever-increasing number of audiences. *Bori* always has a therapeutic function, not only for the members, but also for the numerous participants and spectators who come to be helped by the spirits during performances. For the cult members and also for afflicted individuals an,

initiation into the cult through *girka* is the pathway to knowledge
of the spirits as well as the most dramatic form of medical treatment . . . . (Wall: 240)

Most *girka* ceremonies are curing rituals and becoming a member of the
cult is only an incidental outcome to a patient getting well. Even the
specially arranged performance that I watched was still expected to help
bring about cure for some of the mental patients being treated by Wakili.
In addition to its direct therapeutic function, *bori* experts use their specialist
knowledge to give advice, foretell the future, and generally contribute to
the emotional and physical well-being of their clients and society.

At the socio-political level, *Bori* contributed immensely to Hausa autochthonous culture and continues to contribute to contemporary society. *Bori*
also performs a satiric function as mediums use their specialist knowledge
and privilege when possessed to make social commentary. When people do
wrong, they are usually frightened that they could be exposed by possessed
mediums, and in this regard, *Bori* mediums are like the Igbo masquerade
characters who are believed to be all-seeing and all-knowing. Mediums
also use possession to challenge authority by taking a stand on social and
political issues.

In the context of the larger Hausa society, *Bori* is represented as an evil
that needed to be eradicated or at least subdued in order for the new Islamic
order to take root, and in order also for the health and well-being of the
community to be ensured. This view of *Bori* is still very strong today; for
example, one of my research assistants showed a great deal of unease about
the possibility of being perceived by relatives, friends and fellow Muslims
as associating with members of a discredited cult. I had to reassure him
that I was going to edit him out of all the tapes. The main import of this is
that for most devout Muslims, any performance of *Bori* or association with
people who hold the belief is a threat to and a betrayal of Islamic principles
and beliefs. But more importantly, however, any performance of *Bori* is
also an assertion of an enduring pre-Islamic Hausa cultural identity. In this
respect, every *Bori* event is a political as well as a cultural act. Little wonder
that cult practices and members are often targets of Muslim extremists and
fundamentalists – an ever present and recurring phenomenon in most parts
of Islamic Northern Nigeria.

At the time of my visit for this research, for instance, both groups
had just been forced out of the city of Zaria, being perceived as having
a bad influence on the religious and social morality of the city and its
Muslim inhabitants. As part of controlling and monitoring *Bori* activities,
groups must now obtain local authority permits in order to perform. The
Gidan Wakili group pointed out that even from their location of exile

they had to obtain a licence to organize any public or private ceremonies. One can understand the reason why the authorities are doing this. While they cannot influence the content of any performance through formally censoring material, they can significantly curb the satiric power of *Bori* by withholding permission to perform altogether. The can also control the number of people who are able to see the performances if they are located in distant villages. Some of these villages are quite small; sometimes they consist of a few families or compounds. Performances in the urban centres, on the other hand, attract crowds of people; sometimes up three to four hundred watch a performance. The authorities are quite nervous about criticisms of the society or of people in power by *Bori* mediums, because purporting to come from the spirits they are incontrovertible in the eyes of the people and therefore very potent.

At a third level, *Bori* performances can be seen as instruments and contexts for marginalized and oppressed groups in Hausa society – such as indigenous non-Muslim groups, the sick, homosexuals, transvestites and prostitutes – to express forms of social identities and status. The perception of some of these groups as either deviants or undesirables has not helped the image of *Bori* adherents, for it reinforces the pagan, evil, unclean and amoral typing of the cult by the dominant Islamic culture. In the immediate post-Jihad Hausa society women were another group who became oppressed and marginalized by the men – fathers, husbands, brothers and uncles often determined a woman's future life for her. For such groups, having a cultural practice with which the dominant elite or culture exists in such an ambivalent relationship gives them a safe space in which to speak and an effective instrument with which to periodically challenge their oppressors and their marginalization. Female mediums, in particular, are able to challenge male power and dominance by getting their husbands and men folk to do their bidding under the pretence that the orders were those of the spirits. *Bori* provides both an emotional and therapeutic outlet for the politically, socially and sexually repressed groups in Hausa society. The Wakili group included representatives from virtually all these segments of society and within the cult they find a home in which they can be themselves. Their *Bori* activities, including performances, give meaning and direction to the lives of members of the group.

Because the belief in the existence and power of the spirits is still very strong, even among the very devout Muslims, the attitude of the Muslim leaders to *Bori* is ambivalent, especially among the highly respected *mallams*. It is both feared and tolerated. The eclectic incorporation of Muslim spirits into *Bori's* pantheon means that mediums when possessed by these spirits have considerable power over the human spectators. Wives, daughters and mistresses have used this position to impose their wills on autocratic husbands, fathers and male friends. *Bori* mediums have also been known to admonish political leaders for wrongdoing. The Wakili group, although this particular performance was ostensibly apolitical, have in the past been used by political parties to try and convince voters that their programmes had been endorsed by the spirits, and sometimes to destroy the reputations and political careers of opponents. This is a measure of the potential or perceived power of *Bori* on the imagination of the population. Even some devout Muslims and their leaders have been known to consult *Bori* soothsayers and medical gurus in moments of difficulties, and are usually prepared to do what the 'spirits' invoked on their behalf demands of them.

For as long as there is belief in the power of the spirits to influence life on earth – to cause diseases, bring good or bad luck, or tell the future – *Bori* will continue to perform the inter-linked functions outlined above within Hausa society. It is not uncommon to see or hear people speak disparagingly about the cult and its practices, but these same people will nonetheless flock to *Bori* compounds or venues to watch and enjoy the performances, and some will even consult and give gifts to the spirits. During our second visit, Lawal, the assistant, who did not want his pictures from our first visit seen, was not averse to consulting Wakili for what he claimed were some personal medical problems. This is a sign that *Bori* still has a future in Hausa society, not everyone would want them to perform, but when they do there will always be an audience eager to welcome, interact with and be entertained by the spirits. This is in marked contrast to *Jaliya* which is a prestigious performance in Mande culture in which spectators are keen to be singled out and praised by the *jali* during a performance. To be a able to have a personal *griot* is highly regarded and something to be proud of.

4 *Jaliya*: The art of Mandinka griots and griottes

Introduction: Mande cultural history

Mande refers to a large collection of West African ethnic groups who can be found in Mali, Senegal, the Gambia, Sierra Leone, Burkina Faso, the Ivory Coast, Ghana, Guinea, Guinea Bissau and Liberia. Mali is still regarded as the centre of its culture and is the spiritual and political home of Mande *griots* (bards, raconteurs or oral historians). Kangaba is the cultural centre to which *griots* from all over Mande return every seven years for the *Kamabolom*, a celebration and reaffirmation of their Mande cultural identity through the art of the *griot*. While *griotism* is found in the whole of Mande diaspora, I have chosen to look at the art form as practised among the Mandinka, who are now mainly distributed in an arc of some eight hundred miles, extending from the mouth of the Gambia River in Gambia and Senegal to the interior of the Ivory Coast (Atkins, 1972: 6).

The Mandinka word for a *griot* is *jali* (sing.) and *jalolu* (pl.), and I will be using these vernacular terms in the chapter because of their gender neutrality. A *griot* is a *jalikeo*, while a *griotte* (female) is a *jalimuso*. *Jaliya* is the art of the *griot*, while *jalikan* is the language of *jaliya*. To understand the place and role of the *jali* in Mandinka culture, one needs knowledge of the social structure of Mandinka society, and also the nature of the relationship and division of labour between the social groups. There are three status groups in Mandinka society: *forolu* (nobles), *nyamalolu* (artisans) and *jongolu* (slaves). Within the *nyamalolu*, there are further divisions into *numolu* (the blacksmiths), *jalolu* (*griots*/bards), *karankolu* (leather workers), and *kulolu* (wood workers). This social structure is mainly based on the principle of gift or service exchange between the groups. Knowledge of this helps our understanding of the kind of relationship or behaviour expected when people from different groups meet. It also explains the fact that a *jali* expects some form of remuneration from a *batufa* (a patron) for her or his performance. The latter, in most instances, comes from the other social groups. The prevalence of endogamy within the *jalolu* status group has resulted in a complex network of connections developing over time between *jali* families in Mandinka society. These connections also extend beyond Mandinka boundaries, and so it is not surprising to find the same patronymics and *jamung* across the various countries of the Mande diaspora. Major *jali* patronymics are: Kouyate (Kuyate), Kanoute (Kanute), Kante, Jobate or Jabate (Diabate), Cissoko (Sissoko), Sumano, Sousou (Susu). Of these, the Kouyates have pride of place – only they can be *griots* to other *griots* as was shown during the *jaliya balundo*, when all other *jalolu* came with their own Kouyate *jali*. Only the Kouyates expect gifts from other *griots*. This privilege stems from their being the descendants of Balafasseke Kouyate, the famed *jali* of Sundiata, the founder-ruler of ancient Mali Empire.

The existence and usage of *kontongo* (patronymic greetings or praises) and *jamung* (chants/lines) in Mandinka culture have advantages for the *jalolu* in their performances. Each family has a *jamung*, a set of praise lines that recount and extol the heroic deeds and past histories of long gone ancestors. *Jalolu* manipulate these praise lines in their encounters and dealing with established patrons, with potential ones, and even with complete strangers. Once an individual's patronymic is known by the *jali*, it is easy to recite or sing the appropriate *jamung*. It is also easy because most of these illustrious ancestors are part of a complex web of history whose narratives involve wars, battles and great encounters with supernatural forces in which the ancestors featured. Reciting the grand Mande epics is always sure to somehow include one of the patron's great ancestors and invariably the patron himself if he or she is of Mandinka or Mande ancestry.

Jaliya is a highly respected and appreciated performance form in Mandinka culture for a number of reasons. The first and main reason is that it is a very entertaining and socio-politically relevant art form through which the Mandinka keep their history and culture alive. The second is its affective power (*nyama*), which resides in the perceived sacred power of words. For the Mandinka (Mande), to speak is to control and release this latent power in words. Thus the *jali*, the acclaimed wordsmith, although of lower status is highly feared and respected for his or her ability to manipulate the *nyama* in words for dramatic, emotional, political or economic effect. The *jali* is like a 'holy' actor who negotiates between the sacred and the profane, in the same way that he or she stands at the threshold of the past and the present. But *Jaliya* is unlike any other art form of Africa in its reliance on words, most other African traditional performances being non-verbal. But unlike other word-based performances around the world, it is not dialogic. The *jali*'s engagement with an audience is not about exchange of information through words, rather the flow of words is in one direction only – *jali* to patron or to another *jali*. What the *jali* gets in return from the audience is a gift of money, clothes, jewels and so on, and from fellow *jalolu*, an amplifying conduit for their word to a target audience. Over a period of six months in 2004 I observed *Jaliya* performances in and around Dakar, Senegal, at weddings, naming ceremonies, wrestling matches, and at a Dakar *Jaliya Balundo*. My analysis will be based on the *balundo* because it offers the chance to examine a group of *jalolu* performing together in a varied programme in which many facets of *Jaliya* were displayed.

Jaliya Balundo performance in Dakar

The performance took place at the Municipal Council Hall in Sacre Coeur, Dakar on Saturday 13 March 2004. It began in the afternoon and lasted well into the evening, finishing at about eight o'clock. There were breaks for food and drinks. *Jaliya Balundo* is a yearly gathering of Mandinka *griots* and *griottes* living in and around Dakar. It was a special event because it was an occasion for *jalolu* to perform to and for themselves. Certain rules and etiquette applied, such as who could sing to who, how and where individuals could stand in relation to others on stage during a performance, who was or was not expected to give money to a *jali* when they are performing. These codes of behaviour are very different from when *jalolu* perform to other status groups, when roles and responsibilities are well defined. A typical *jali*'s performance consists mainly of singing, reciting, dancing, echoing or 'broadcasting' (when the *jali* acts as a mouthpiece or amplifier to another person as the *maroka* is in *Bori*), call and response sessions with other *jalolu*, or brief exchanges (again with other *jalolu* or with members of the audience occasionally).

We arrived at the performance venue at about one o'clock in the afternoon. All around were pockets of people drinking and chatting to one another. A middle-aged man dressed in a shiny dark green *boubou* (a voluminous two or three-piece African dress worn by both sexes) and a small round cap of the same material, met us at the door. He demanded to know who we were, and when told that we wanted to watch and record the festival, smiled and informed us that we needed to give some present to the performers 'to make them happy'. Having been forewarned by our guides, we gave him one hundred and fifty thousand francs (approximately one hundred and fifty pounds sterling) and were welcomed warmly into the hall.

The hall was rectangular with two main exit/entrance doors at opposite ends to the left side of the auditorium and performance space. Another door led from the auditorium to a blocked off area at the back which were storerooms and toilets. Running parallel to the auditorium was a long wide corridor which connected the two main entrances. Three fairly long steps descended from the corridor into the auditorium and performance space. The hall was well decorated, with exquisite murals in bright colours painted on the four walls. The performance space itself (with a raised stage for the musicians/instrumentalists) was far centre-right or straight centre, depending through which door one had entered. The audience space began right from the edge of the performance space with rows of chairs facing the stage. As the first wave of audience members began to arrive, the band was already on stage tuning their instruments and testing their other electrical appliances, such as loudspeakers, microphones, and electric guitars (**Figs 4.1 and 4.2**).

The instruments were: one *tamou* or 'talking' drum played by Baka Cissoko, a twenty-one piece *balafon* played by Adama Cissoko, two *kora* played by Soriba Kanoute and Jabel Cissoko, two electric guitars (one was played by Morou Sumano), two *djembe* drums (one was played by Jibi Kanoute) and one *dun dun* drum (this was not used much all evening). The *tamou* is a two-headed cylindrical wooden pressure drum. The heads are covered with fish-skin or other membrane; cords that run the length of the drum's body and wrapped around two wooden hoops are squeezed to change the instrument's pitch. A curved stick with a leather-covered round tip is used for playing the instrument. The *balafon* is a percussive and melodic instrument made from seventeen to twenty-one rectangular wooden slats arranged in an array from low to high notes. Two rows of calabashes, arranged in an array from small to large and fixed below the slats, serve as amplifiers to the *balafon*. It is played with two tuned sticks of approximately ten to twelve inches long. The *kora* is a harp-like instrument, similar to a lute or guitar but much bigger. Its body is made from calabash gourd cut in half and partially covered with cow skin. A traditional *kora* has twenty-one playing strings plucked by thumb and forefinger of each hand; the remaining fingers grip the vertical hand posts just above the calabash gourd. The *djembe*, a goblet-shaped wooden drum open at the base, has a single head whose tip is stretched over with goat or antelope skin and secured by two metallic rings. A row of strings are attached to the tips and secured at the neck of the goblet by a third metal string and used for tuning the drum. The *djembe* can produce a range of sounds, from deep and resonant bass to sharp and short beats. The *dun dun* is a two-headed medium-sized wooden drum named because of the dull heavy bass that it produces.

By the time we entered the hall, Fanta Mbacke Kouyate, an elegantly dressed *jalimuso*, was already on stage, and ready to begin. She wore a *woramboo* (a large gown) made from shiny dark brown damask with tiny white spots and small orange circles running in alternating lines all over,

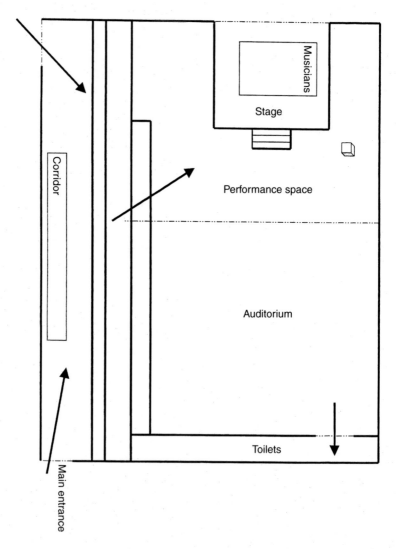

Figure 4.1 Diagram of municipal hall/*Balundo* stage.

and on her left shoulder an orange chiffon scarf. A shiny dark brown head-tie designed in folds rising to about eighteen inches completed her costume. Her make-up consisted of heavy mascara, shiny lip-gloss, and added eyelashes which gave her face a mask-like appearance. She also wore large gold earrings and large rings on three fingers of her left hand (**Fig. 4.3**). Other *jalolu* and their guests were milling around, greeting

Figure 4.2 Stage with musicians.

Figure 4.3 Fanta Mbacke Kouyate (a Mandinka *Jalimuso*).

friends or getting themselves ready while waiting for more guests to arrive
and the performance proper to begin. Apparently, they were also waiting
for Mandogo Jobate, the guest of honour, to arrive and take his reserved
seat in the front row.

When it eventually began, the evening's performance alternated between
the four main styles of *jaliya* performance, with climactic moments at
various points during the evening that always brought many *jalolu* to their
feet and sometimes into the performance space to dance, clap, cheer, offer
gifts, and perform other acts of encouragement to whoever was performing
at the time. The hall began to fill up, and as more audience members
arrived, the musicians began to play in earnest. The first indication that
the performance had begun was Fanta Mbacke Kouyate's powerful voice
piercing the air as she sang a welcome to her friend and neighbour, Oumou
Sinare, who at that moment had entered and was standing at the right
entrance door:

> Oumou Sinare has come!
> Your traffic blocker has come!
> I am pleased about the clothes
> you are wearing,
> Ah!
> Mother of Baby Jolie, nice baby
> You are welcome
> You can go and take your seat

Fanta's style for this opening song was a mixture of singing and recital.
Although the song was fast tempo, the voice was not high pitched, but
was rather quite soft and endearing, to reflect the affectionate friendship
between her and the patron she was singing to. The voice went up each
time she called her friend's name or the name of her child, Jolie. She did
not dance, but used hand and facial gestures to enhance her delivery. She
held the microphone in her right hand, and with the left she pointed many
times, above the heads of the seated spectators, in the direction of Oumou
Sinare and then back to herself, as if to illustrate this close bond between
them. Having finished her song, Fanta returned to her chair at the foot
of the stage, while Oumou Sinare came down the steps to take her seat in
the auditorium.

Meanwhile, the band and Baka Cissoko carried on playing a melodious
'highlife/mbalax' tune, which they had struck up during Fanta's song. It
had a basic one-two-three : one-two (1-2-3 : 1-2) beat provided by the
two *djembe* drums and the *balafon*, and a shorter one-two : one (1-2 : 1)
beat from the *dun dun* drum. The two *koras* and the single electric guitar

wove in and out of these two beats with a rich inter-linking melody. This remained the background music for most of the evening – a slow flowing beat, which the *jalolu* spoke against or with, their words slicing through or gliding along with it. All through the opening song, Baka punctuated and supported Fanta on his *tamou*, by intermittently playing little bursts in between her lines.

For the next item, Baka delivered a recited performance directed at an individual in the audience who, it seemed, had refused to give him any money even though he had sung his family *jamung*. Baka's intention was obvious as he tried to shame the reluctant patron by broadcasting his stinginess to the gathering. The latter, however, did not seem to be bothered, even when Baka threatened to keep calling attention to him all evening. It was, however, a very joking confrontation because Baka and this audience member happen to be very close friends, and this greatly amused the spectators. Baka infused a lot of comedy and humour into his performance through his exuberance, facial and hand gestures, and more than any of the other performers, he brought titters of laughter from the audience each time he took the stage. His solo was followed by an instrumental interlude, as more people arrived. The hall was nearly full by this time and the atmosphere was one of excited anticipation. Then Baka took the stage again, interspersing his recital with an occasional quick one-two-three : one-two-three (1-2-3 : 1-2-3) beat on his talking drum. He turned now to Madi Kanoute, the man in the shiny green *boubou*, who as it turned out was the organizer of the evening's event:

Hello, hello!
My fellow Mandinka, I greet you on this occasion
Hello *jalolu*
Madi is coming!
If you don't know, I will tell you
That his real name is Habeleh Kanoute!

His short recital was followed by another instrumental interlude. By this time, those *griot* delegations and guests who had been congregating and having some refreshments in nearby compounds and open spaces around the hall began coming into the hall. Fanta Mbacke's opening song must have carried, to alert them that the performance had begun.

The first group to enter the hall was a team of about six colourfully dressed women led by Fanta Sakiliba. Bundaw Kouyate, her personal *jalimuso*, was by her side. As soon as the group stepped into the doorway, Bundaw sang a short introductory song to announce the arrival of her *batufa* (patron). It was delivered in a flat matter-of-fact voice and tempo, but it still carried powerfully across the hall and made those already inside turn towards the door to see who it was. This drew a response from Fanta Mbacke who climbed up the steps to meet them. She welcomed Fanta Sakiliba with a combination of recited and sung praise lines. In the song she gave some biographical information:

> Hey, yeh, Fanta Sakiliba
> Oh, oh Fanta Sakiliba
> The gathering has been good to you
> You do good things for people
> My good neighbour, Fanta Sakiliba!
> You are welcome!
> Hey, hey,
> *Jalimusolu*, pay attention!
> Fanta Sakiliba has come
> I will praise you, I will sing to you
> Cherino Cissoko's daughter!
> You are welcome

While Fanta sang, the group that had just entered stood on the upper steps rummaging in their handbags for money to give her for her singing; that done, they went into the auditorium to find seats for themselves.

Fanta herself returned to her seat, but was up almost immediately as somebody in the auditorium had caught her attention and immediately became the subject of her next song:

> Yankuba Koulibali,
> Koulibali, I will sing to you
> You of the Jagili tribe, you of the Jagili tribe
> You of the Jagili tribe, you of the Jagili tribe
> The son of Sofi Trawale, of the Jagili tribe
> Of the Jagili tribe (**three times**)
> I will sing to you
> See how he is sitting!
> Koulibali!

Fanta Mbacke's style in the third song was quite different from the first two. Firstly, the background rhythm with and against which she now sang was different. Secondly, the intimate tone and free improvisatory style gave way to a standard beat for the Koulibali *jamung*. Praise lines have standard tunes (*julo*) to which they are sung, and each rhythm or tune corresponds to a song (*donkilo*). But while the *julo* may be standardized or fixed, the *donkilo* is not. A talented *jali* is able to sing different lyrics or lines, especially improvised texts, using the same tune. Creativity and mastery of the art lies not in reciting these lines to the rhythm, but mainly in the ability to improvise new lyrics to the standard rhythms or tunes.

The Koulibali *donkilo* consisted of two short opening lines in which she called out his name and her intention to sing to him. She then moved to the next two longer lines in which she expanded on his genealogy – 'You of the Jagili tribe' was repeated four times with each line drawn out slightly longer than the one preceding it. The lines about his father and his tribal origin were further drawn out, and the 'of the Jagili tribe' was sung three times. She then returned to the shorter, 'I will sing to you', and, with a gesture in the direction of Yankuba Koulibali and a slight lowering of her voice, she invited the audience to 'See how he is sitting'. The final line 'Koulibali' was really drawn out as she turned to go back to her chair.

There followed a short scene between Fanta Mbacke and Baka Cissoko, in which Baka elaborated on the good qualities of Yankuba Koulibali:

Baka: Fanta!
Fanta: Nnam
Baka: You see the song you sang for this man
       It is true
       He is a good man.
Fanta: Nnam
Baka: I know that
       His father and his mother also are good people
       He does good things for the sake of Allah
       And for the sake of the Prophet...

The scene was brought to an end by the arrival of another group at the entrance to the hall, at which Fanta broke off from Baka to send an animated greeting to the new group led by Mahamba Sakiliba. This group's response was to break into a dance which took them forward to the steps where they waited while Fanta concluded her song. Mahamba descended the steps to offer her some money in appreciation. Fanta had praised her as the wife of Mandogo Jobate, the leader of the Mandinka *griots* in Dakar. There was a hint of irony in this since it sharply contrasted with the vilification of Mandogo later in the evening by some of the *griots*, including Fanta Mbacke herself.

Madi Kanoute, the event organizer, took the stage next. His performance was mainly direct speaking with very expressive body and facial gestures, occasionally punctuated with dancing and clapping. Madi's style, in contrast to Fanta Mbacke's or Baka's, was conversational, except that this was a monologue directed at the audience. In this, he adopted different personas, attitudes and voices – a public speaker trying to persuade the audience to see his point of view; Madi, the event organizer, admonishing and imploring people to behave and make his event successful; a *jali* who was both himself and performer. He modulated his voice appropriately – from the serious to the playful, and from the matter-of-fact to the highly emotional. And as if on cue, at Madi's last word the orchestra changed the background music to a high energy cadence for Mamadou Cissoko's song, at which Madi broke into dance – head tilted to one side, face smiling, hands extended to the sides and coming together in a soft rhythmic clap. The clap corresponded to the rhythmic arching and relaxing of the upper body. Although, unlike Fanta and the others, Madi did not sing, his appearances were quite as captivating and powerful. His speeches were marked by the measured cadence and voice modulations which he employed for effect; his hand and facial gestures were copious, with his index fingers constantly used for emphasis. His whole body became remarkably alive and his shiny dark green *boubou* appeared even more colourful whenever he performed. In fact, he seemed able to transform himself from the amiable and ever smiling Madi who had welcomed us when we arrived, to this serious faced, finger-wagging impresario asking the spectators and performers alike to behave themselves. He effortlessly slipped in and out of these personas throughout the evening.

While Madi was performing, Fanta went back to her chair where Fanta Sakiliba joined her. As soon as Madi had finished, she broke into another song to welcome another group just arrived at the door. Her role was that of a link between different performers or acts, as well as performing with other *jalolu* from time to time in the course of the evening. Fanta Sakiliba, resplendent in a sky blue *woramboo*, a headscarf and a shawl, was the next to take the stage. She had light shades of blue mascara, gold earrings and a necklace to match the costume. At first, she spoke in a low conversational voice and tone while Fanta acted as an amplifying mouthpiece by repeating everything the former said. This went on for a while before she suddenly burst into a song which got a good number of other *jalolu* to their feet, reaching into their pockets and handbags to shower her with money. This act ended with Fanta Mbacke doing a prolonged solo in which she kept singling out individuals for praise.

Madi Kanoute came back again, looking more serious than ever. He took the microphone from Fanta and staring straight at the audience as if to intimidate them, he began:

> Take your seats everybody!
> *Ibisimilahi* (You are welcome)
> Anything you need, I'll give you!

Don't talk to anyone
Anything you need I'll give you
If you ask I'll give you
That is it
Salam Aleikun
Ibisimilahi
Fanta Mbacke, the microphone!
I want you to sing
And anything you want!
Just ask me
And I'll give you
Everything is ready.
Sing!

He again ended with his dance and hand clapping routine to the beat, which had been playing softly in the background. And Fanta taking the microphone from Madi invited Mamadou Cissoko:

Mamadou, come here and take the mike and sing.
Sing for the *jalolu* so that we can become excited.
Come and sing
Sing to get the *jalolu* going!

Mamadou took the microphone, and pumping a clenched left hand in the air began his performance. His song was a praise dedication to his *batufa*, Cherino Saho:

Suh, suh, suh!
I am liked by people
And anybody who is liked by people
It is due to the will of God
Cherino Saho has gone to Paris
And he has been lucky in Paris
He was also lucky in Senegal
Senegal had also been good to him
And he has been good to me

Suh, suh, suh!
Kulufang's son, Mamadou!
Confidence in a person
Nobody can destroy that
If he has done something
The great God has done it
If he has done something

It is this great God who has done it
If this great God has done something
Nobody can destroy it

To be a good *jali* is due to the individual
Madi, your *Jaliya* depends on yourself
Nobody can destroy it
Yeh, ya yeh!
There is an end to this worldly life
Cherino Saho!
Being abroad has been a success for you!
The son of Ndongo Ceesay!
I am greeting you!
I am in your debt
Until the day the great God will do his will to us
Kulufang's son, Mamadou, is praising you!
(Make the music lower)

The last line was directed to the orchestra to indicate that he was coming
to the end of his song.

Madi had responded to this song by initiating a gliding dance in which
his hands were spread out wide on both sides to make big wings with his
boubou. His legs and arms resembled a bat flapping its wings in flight, but
bringing the tips (palms) to clap at the end of each flap. Madi's clapping
and Mamadou's fist pumps were invitations to other *jalolu* to join in the
dance. Nding Nding Kanoute (Madi Kanoute's aunt) was the first to rise
and she went straight to give Mamadou a hug, lift his left hand up in
the air a few times, and then she stepped back to begin the same dance
movement as Madi and Mamadou. But instead of making a wing, her
left hand was across her chest and her right slightly in front holding a
black handbag. Other *jalimusolu* joined her, and all fourteen of them were
doing the same movement on one spot, but with individual variations.
They formed a semi-circle in front of Mamadou. One of the dancers, after
a while, went round to raise the left hand of each dancer in turn – a sign
of appreciation and encouragement to the performer. She was followed by
Madi, who, instead of raising their hands, gave money to each performer,
including the musicians. Madi paid a special attention to Mamadou whose
performance had succeeded in galvanizing the entire hall into dancing,
singing or clapping to his song and the music. Mamadou received the
most money from Madi and from other *jalolu*, some passing what they
had received from Madi over to him (**Fig. 4.4**).

Gift or service exchange is a central feature of Manding culture, and it
is a crucial element of the *jali-batufa* relationship. The *jali* strives in his

Figure 4.4 Madi Kanoute gives money to Mamadou Cissoko.

or her performance to move the listener to a spontaneous act of giving, and the level of generosity in the giving is a measure of the success of the *jali*'s performance. Spontaneous gifts of money were frequent during the performance. For example, when Fanta Mbacke spotted Yankuba Koulibali seated in the third row, she got up from her chair and, with her left arm stretched out in his direction, began her song to him. At first he just tilted his head to one side and smiled. But gradually as the praise lines grew, he sat up, hands folded across his chest. The smile had gone, replaced by a fixed expression, eyes on the floor and mouth slightly open. His chest heaved as he took deep breaths. It was as if the song had expanded his physical presence. He remained in this pose for a while, and then slowly got up and, drawing a hefty wad of franc notes from the chest pocket of his *boubou*, strode forward and began a slow stepping dance with the notes held high in his left hand. Revelling in the adulation and honour of his family *jamung* and Fanta Mbacke's stirring performance, he began pasting the money on her forehead and sometimes just letting the notes rain down on her. Yankuba emptied his pockets completely and showed the audience that he had nothing left by turning his pockets out and leaving the flaps to dangle, while he danced as if it did not matter. It was an electrifying moment as performer and spectator became one; when the praising and the giving became inseparable from one another. His friends and members of his family joined him in the dance, and they too showered Fanta with a confetti of franc notes. They must have given her up to one hundred thousand francs (approximately one hundred pounds). For the *jalimuso*, it was a successful outcome for her performance.

Other people singled out for praise reacted, some by dancing vigorously, others by frantically fumbling in their pockets or handbags for money to shower her as she had showered them with words. The aim of each encounter was to make the person being praised the centre of attention, and the more the *jali* was able to keep the individual the focus of attention, the more the individual gave. The Mandogo Jobate scene proved this point. The combined barrage of words and songs from Fanta, Bundaw and Madi Kante drew the expected reaction from Mandogo and Grimo – they both emptied their pockets, made promises of more and better treatment of the *jalolu* in future. Watching Mandogo as he sat in his chair it was evident that the verbal attacks were having a psychological effect on him, for even though he appeared outwardly calm, the little twitches of his fingers and legs told a different story. The spectators could sense what was going to happen and who was going to win the battle. In the end the *jalolu* won when Grimo, on his brother's behalf, pleaded for them to stop. In response to the question of what he aims for in a performance and how he assesses whether or not that aim has been achieved, El Hajj Mansour Mbaye (13 March 2004), said that he strives to transport his listeners or clients to the time of their ancestors, to use his singing and recitation to make the audience member forget where he or she is, to help them recapture and relive the heroic deeds of their ancestors through singing or reciting the family *jamung*, and to make them so thankful that they've been elevated into heroes themselves that they are willing to give their last franc in appreciation and gratitude.

When Mamadou finished his song, Fanta and Bundaw did a song together while all the *griots* and *griottes* were still dancing and exchanging gifts and handshakes with one another. It was in the middle of this duet that Mandogo Jobate and his brother, Grimo, entered the hall to take their reserved seats. Mandogo, being the overall leader of the Mandinka *griots* in and around Dakar, was one of the patrons for the *jaliya balundo* and hence was given pride of place in the seating. The other patron was Mariam Faye, a very wealthy woman who lives in Dakar and had been chosen to preside over the second section of the evening's programme. Mandogo's arrival was a cause for celebration and a special display, duly supplied by the combined talents and performing styles of Madi Kanoute, Fanta Mbacke, and Souware Kouyate, Mandogo's personal *jalimuso*. Souware and Fanta sang their welcome in very excited and impassioned voices, while Madi recited and gestured in his characteristic flat and mock-serious manner:

Souware:	People, get out of the way!
	For the man of men has come
	Mandogo Jobate has come!
Fanta:	Clear the way for Mandogo Jobate!
	Mandogo Jobate has come!
	Grimo Jobate has come!
	Insa Sakiliba's sons have come!
	Luntanding Jobate's son has come!
	The great man Mandogo Jobate has come!
	The good man has come
	Clear the way so they can take their seats
Madi:	Fanta!
Fanta:	Nnam
Madi:	Everybody, sit down!
Fanta:	He said, everybody, sit down in their individual places
Madi:	I am coming to Mandogo Jobate!
Fanta:	He said, he is coming to Mandogo Jobate
Madi:	My good relatives have come!
Fanta:	He said, his good relatives have come
Madi:	My elder brother has come!
Fanta:	He said, his elder brother has come
Madi:	You are welcome
Fanta:	He said, you are welcome
Madi:	If I spend a million in your affair, I can't repay you
Fanta:	Oh God, Oh God, Oh God!
Madi:	Last year I had this occasion and you were present with your younger brother
Fanta:	He said, last year he had organized this occasion and you and your brother were present.
Madi:	With the goodwill of your mother, Insa Sakiliba
Fanta:	He said, with the goodwill of your mother, Insa Sakiliba
Madi:	What Mandogo and his brother do not want, me too I don't like it
Fanta:	He said that what Mandogo and his brother do not want, he too does not like it
Madi:	What I don't like, Mandogo doesn't like it too
Fanta:	He said that what he doesn't like, Mandogo doesn't like it either
Madi:	If Mandogo has a programme here in Dakar, I will pay him!
Fanta:	Oh, God! Oh, God! Oh, God!

The audience clapped at this to show its appreciation of Fanta and Madi's display of an interesting element of *jaliya* – when a *jali* acts as interpreter and megaphone to a speaker in a public arena. The *jali* repeats what the speaker has said and occasionally adding his or her own embellishments to the speaker's words and expressions. And Fanta did exactly that in the scene above, and the audience enjoyed it more whenever she added anything to what Madi had said. When they finished, Souware Kouyate took the stage to sing for Mandogo. She was dressed in a pink *woramboo*, with dark red stars and yellow square patterns. She had a yellow shawl wound around her shoulders. Her performance was very animated, even though her voice lacked the sharpness and penetration of Fanta's. She had four backing singer/dancers, who wore different coloured *woramboos*. She sang the praises of Mandogo, his accomplishments, his generosity and those of his ancestors, whose *jalolu* her own ancestors had been. She recounted especially the generosity and greatness of Mandogo's father, Luntanding Jobate, and his mother, Insa Sakiliba, whose griotte, Bundaw Kouyate, was also in the hall. She also sang to his brother, Grimo. While she sang, the four backing women did an energetic dance, in which their movements suggested paddling a canoe, then changed to digging and hoeing the earth done in unison. The gusto of her performance, of course, brought both men to their feet to shower her with money. It also brought other *jalolu* and guests to their feet to acknowledge Mandogo and Grimo, whose hands they raised in salutation.

This act of praise, salutation and exultation of Mandogo was however brought to a halt by Bundaw Kouyate, who apparently was not impressed by Mandogo's supposed generosity. She stopped everybody with a sharp call, and immediately there was tension in the air as everything stopped, except for the background music which unnoticed had changed to a much slower one : one-two : one (1 : 1-2 : 1) beat:

Bundaw: Fanta!
Fanta: Nnam!
Bundaw: I want you to transmit my message to Mandogo.
             I will only sing for someone
             Who will give me a human being with his ears!
Fanta: Nnam!
Bundaw: In the time of your mother
             In the morning she gave me a bag of rice,
             She gave me oil, and she slaughtered a goat or sheep for me.
             In the afternoon, she gave me gold and silver to wear.
             And finally, she said to me, 'I'll give you a human being with
             his ears so that he can work for you'.
             I will not sing for someone
             Who gives only mere piece of paper!

Figure 4.5 Fanta sings to Mandogo Jobate.

Here she disdainfully brandished a handful of franc notes which she had received from Mandogo, his wife, Mahamba Sakiliba, and Grimo. She adopted the insulting or rebuking technique which *jalolu* employ some-times to shame their patrons into giving more. She compared Mandogo's paper money to the numerous items which were evidence of his parents' generosity. The audience had already sensed by her tone that some-thing dramatic was about to happen, they all seemed to know that the performance was changing gear and direction, from the initial jollity and camaraderie of the opening scenes to a sustained torrent of verbal assault. The power of the *jali*'s words to either, enlarge and elevate a person, or to belittle and cut them down was about to be enacted. Everyone's attention shifted to the unfolding drama between the *jalolu* and Mandogo Jobate. Bundaw Kouyate performed a few slow and graceful dance steps to the music before moving in again on her target (**Fig. 4.5**):

Bundaw: FANTA!
Fanta: Nnam!
Bundaw: When a *jalimuso* begins to sing the praises of dead
      ancestors,
      It means that those descendants who are living
      Are not living up to expectations.

	They are not living up to the family name and honour.
	Mandogo Jobate!
	What your mother has done.
	Are you not able to do it?
Fanta:	Nnam (laughs)
Bundaw:	Insa Sakiliba!
	Won't you answer me?
	Answer me, because what I have
	Is a mere piece of paper in my hand! (*brandishes the franc notes again*)
Fanta:	Nnam!
Bundaw:	They have given me a human being with his ears
	They have given me gold
	They have given me silver A horse, cattle
	Mandogo!
	What do you give me?
	You don't give anything!
	Other than mere piece of paper!
	Your great-great-grandfather was great
	Hey, you, Mandogo Jobate!
	Can you not fit the shoes of your father on your feet?
	Can you not do that?
	Can you not fit the shoes of your mother on your feet?
	Can you not do that?
	You can at least try and match what your parents did
	Fanta!
Fanta:	Nnam!
Bundaw:	Tell Mandogo,
	If he can not put on his father's and his mother's shoes on his feet
	He should show me the people who can put on their father's and their mother's shoes on their feet
	(*Fanta and the audience burst into laughter at this before Fanta turned to Mandogo to pass the message on.*)
Fanta:	Insa Sakiliba's son, Mandogo Jobate!
	Have you heard what the woman has said to you?
	The Jobates, they are business people
	The son of a businessman is a businessman
	Mandogo Jobate!
	Can't you respond to what the woman has said to you?
	Your father was wealthy
	Why can't you do as your father did?

Hey, you, Mandogo Jobate!
Your mother's last word in this life was
That she did not know if there was anyone
Who could match what she has done for the *jalolu*
Mandogo Jobate!
Your mother told you never to fail
To fulfil your obligations to your relatives
When people have done bad things to you
Do not repay them with bad things
Mandogo Jobate!
I am warning you
If anybody has done a good thing for you
You must pay them back with a good thing
I am warning you, Mandogo Jobate!
Never allow there to be something... (*inaudible*)
You should not ignore to repay good things done to you
That good thing they've done for you
It is a loan you have to repay
Mandogo Jobate!

There was a brief musical interlude here while Fanta did a brief dance
while adjusting her gown and scarf, to let her last words sink in. Mandogo
and Grimo sat still and waited, as if they knew it was not over yet.
Another *jali*, Madi Kante, took the second mike and joined Fanta in
the centre for another amplification scene. Fanta was about to return to
telling Mandogo off, when Madi Kante cut in with questions to Fanta.
He pretended he could not bring himself to speak directly to Mandogo:

Madi Kante: Hey, Fanta!
Fanta: Nnam
Madi Kante: His father never refused the *jalolu*
When they demanded from him
Why is Mandogo refusing to face the *jalolu*?
Hey, Fanta!
Fanta: Nnam
Madi Kante: Tell Mandogo
His father did not refuse when people asked of him
Why is he refusing?
Fanta!
Ask Mandogo if he is a child out of marriage!
Ask him if he is a true son of his father!

Fanta and the audience broke into laughter at what was perceived as an insult to Mandogo. He had to respond and so Fanta went down on her knees saying she would not get up until she got a response. What followed was an impassioned plea to Mandogo and Grimo Jobate, with her voice really rising and the words delivered faster than previously:

Fanta: Grimo Jobate! . . .
        Mandogo Jobate!
        I am asking you
        What this man has said, is it true?
        Is it true that you are an illegitimate son?
        You have to show these people here, in this place
        That what the men said is not true

        Mandogo Jobate! (*kneeling really close to him and his brother now*)
        Before I will get up from here
        You must tell me whether what the man said is true or not
        Mandogo Jobate!
        What I asked you, you have not given me a reply

Mandogo still did not move, he just kept his gaze fixed on the stage wall behind the musicians. But Grimo all the while was offering more money and begging Fanta to tone it down and to get up from her kneeling position. Grimo called Madi Kanoute over and whispered in his ear, after which he brought out more money from his pocket to offer to Fanta and Madi Kante. Madi Kanoute's rescue effort seemed to work. He began clapping and eventually managed to get the audience to join in and this succeeded in deterring further assaults on Mandogo, who kept his cool in the face of such onslaught and humiliation from the three performers. However, Fanta carried on with her singing until Grimo got up to offer more money to Madi Kanoute to give to the still furious *griots* and *griottes*. Grimo implored them – through Madi Kante who acted as his interpreter and megaphone – to forgive him and his brother and spare them further humiliation:

Grimo/Madi Kante: Fanta!
                  Tell the *jalolu* to forgive Mandogo and me
                  Because the days of our father and our mother
                  Are not the same as ours
                  They are in the past
                  We can give paper money now

But we can not give a human being with his ears (*Pause*)
Tell the jali, Madi Kante (*Madi Kante is telling this to himself*)
The things our fathers could do in those days
We can not do them now
We can not, Mandogo and I
We can not give a human being with his ears!
But I will give two hundred thousand cfa (francs)
And Mandogo will give one hundred thousand cfa
Give it to Madi Kante, let him use it to return to the region
Let him forgive us.
Let the *jalolu* forgive us.

Fanta (sings): Let the *jalolu* come out and dance!
What Mandogo Jobate, and Grimo Jobate
Have given to Madi Kante is mere breakfast, it is nothing
So, let the *jalolu* come out and dance.
When someone does such a plaything, such a small thing
You have to...(*inaudible*)
Let the *jalolu* come out and dance!

The rest of her song was swallowed up by the swelling voices of other *jalolu* getting up to join in the singing and dancing to mark the end of this very tense and dramatic episode in the evening's performance.

It also marked the end of the first section of the evening's programme. Mandogo, his wife, Mahamba Sakiliba, his brother, Grimo, and the rest of their entourage departed at this point to make way for the arrival of Mariam Faye, for the second part of the evening's show. What this scene had illustrated was the power of the *jali* to enhance or destroy reputations. It was also significant that it ended without resolving the issues it raised, thus suggesting future confrontations of this kind. It also highlighted the power relation between *jali* and *batufa*. Mandogo is a very good *jali* himself, but in the context of the *balundo* performance, he could not speak back to defend himself because the attack came from one of his family's *jalimuso* – Bundaw Kouyate being his dead mother's personal *jalimuso*. Thus she could criticize Mandogo who, for the evening, was assuming a noble's or patron's status and so was not allowed to raise his voice in public: it is considered undignified for nobles to do so. The *jali's* voice, on the other hand, belongs in the public space, and Bundaw and the others showed by their attacks that they had been trained to 'shamelessly' but creatively use it to achieve desired ends.

Jaliya: The art of the *griot*

Most *jalolu* are born into their profession, but that does not mean that every person born into a *jali* family ends up practicing *jaliya* for a living or that every member of a *jali* family can perform or wants to become a performer. But other members of Mandinka society expect every *jali*-born to be able to perform and people born into *jali* families see themselves as *jalolu*, even when they've chosen not to pursue a career in *jaliya*. In the *balundo* performance in Dakar, most of people present were *jalolu* by birth, but not everybody chose to perform or was able to perform.

Being a *jali* involves many things, but the renowned Malian *griot*, Mansa Makan Diabate, sees it as being '*la memoire sociale de la societe Manding*' (1984: 118). *Griots* have been studied extensively in the past as oral historians, diplomats, mediators, or as guardians of the word and communal memory. They are also storytellers, genealogists, panegyrists, moralists, entertainers, singers, and instrumentalists. A widely held belief in Mande society is that what *jalolu* do not know has not yet happened, and so they are also seen as guardians of communal and individual secrets. Obviously, *Jaliya* is a very complex art form and requires innate talent, complemented by skill developed and perfected over an extended period of training.

Jaliya primarily is the use of words, music and dance to initiate a performance engagement with an audience. This art is, like the *Mmonwu*, spectator-directed and dependent. The *jali* will have no performance if the spectator or intended patron is not captivated, held spellbound by, or does not respond to the overwhelming wash of praise lines or narrative which he or she weaves about and around them.

Jalolu adopt specific performance styles, and most *jalikeo* are known by the kind of instrument they play, or others play for them to sing or recite to. Traditionally, only *jalikeo* play instruments, while *jalimusolu* mainly sing and occasionally play the *neo* (a small handheld instrument) or gourd rattles or calabash drums. The main instruments played by *jalikeo* are: *nkoni* or *kontingo* (a narrow boat-shaped four-stringed lute), *kora*, *balafon*, *djembe*, *tamou*, and *dun dun*. In a *griot* family, a male member may choose to master any one instrument, and so one family can boast a full complement of instrumentalists. The orchestra at the *balundo* came from mainly two families – Cissoko and Kanoute. As is increasingly happening, families are forming teams or performing groups.

There are mainly two kinds of *Jaliya* performances. The first are the special occasions when the *jali* is invited by a *batufa* to grace private or family ceremonies, such as weddings, naming a new child, initiations, circumcisions, and funerals. The second type is the public or open events such as *griot* association meetings or *boloms*, sports events, and political rallies. Aesthetically though, there is no difference between the two types of performances since the main ingredients in both are the standardized tunes (*julo*) which correspond to specific songs (*donkilo*).

However, very good performers are able to sing different songs to the same tunes. Nding Nding Kanoute's impromptu composition for me during our interview illustrated this adaptability as her new lyrics were sung to a standard praise tune that I had heard at the performance the day before. Two standard tunes were used at the *balundo* and while the songs and lyrics changed the tunes remained fixed. For the *jali*, it is not the content of the performance that is important, rather it is the manner in which she or he performs that is crucial. A performance is made up of standard tunes and praise lines which are mere handy material learnt over time, but which the *jali* constantly reshapes and manages to fit in with different performance contexts. In a commissioned performance, such as a marriage ceremony or a naming, the *jali*, while being aware of other and or potential patrons, will principally focus on the genealogy of his or her host, and it is more likely that it is the family's *jamung* which will make up the bulk of their performance text. Occasionally, the *jali* can acknowledge and solicit other guests at the ceremony. A free standing performance event such as the *jaliya balundo*, on the other hand, left the *jalolu* free to praise or perform for anyone who they noticed in the audience.

The second kind of performance is sometimes seen as more demanding and more difficult because it lacks an established structure and the possibility of learning the lines in advance. The element of uncertainty arising from not being very familiar with every patron whose praise they sang in public means that *jalolu* are forced to be creatively adaptive in how they use well-known tunes, songs and praise lines to address total strangers. Or, as was the case at the Dakar *balundo*, when things happened that had not been planned, the *jalolu* responded by improvising lines using standard tunes appropriate to the emotions, feelings, mood and ideas that they were dealing with. The verbal attack on Mandogo had not been planned before hand: Bundaw just felt like attacking him as he walked in and so did, with the other *jalolu* and the musicians joining in as appropriate. The many songs and recitals which emerged during the rebuke scene showed the adaptive and improvisatory skills of individual *jalolu* involved in the scene. Fanta Mbacke, as the *jali* singing and welcoming the groups, showed remarkable memory skill and adaptive ability, as she reeled off standard praise lines for each of the leading *jalolu* as they entered the hall. Even in the middle of a scene with Baka Cissoko and Madi Kanoute, she broke off to sing for Fanta Sakiliba, Mahamba Sakiliba, and then for Yankuba Koulibali, before returning to Baka and Madi. Ultimately, a measure of the success of a *jali's* performance is if it is able to make the gift-exchange, the basis of the *jali-batufa* (*griot*-patron) encounter and relationship, possible.

The making of a griot

Although usually born into the profession, *jalolu* still have to train intensely for a long period of time to develop their performing skills. A lot of hard work in training, and continued practising afterwards, are necessary for developing and maintaining the skill.

The most popular and most used method of transmitting the craft and skills of *Jaliya* from generation to generation is informal in which a father, mother, uncle or aunt teaches their children. Nding Nding Kanoute recollects her first steps on the road to becoming a *jalimuso*:

> I was always beside my parents when they performed. I watched them, and saw how they did things. And I began to copy them. After a while they started to encourage me to perform in front of them so that they could help correct and improve my performance. If I made a mistake, they'd say: This and this was not good. You should do this and that to make it better . . . to make it perfect. (Interview, 15 March 2004)

She never underwent formal training. Nor did any of the other performers at the *balundo*. They all were, like her, trained by their own parents. Training, generally, is gender-based – that is, mothers train their daughters, while fathers train their sons. Nding Nding felt quite privileged to have had both parents involved in her tutelage, and she believes that this had made her a better and more versatile performer – she can sing, recite, dance and play a few instruments.

But formal training is increasingly becoming an option, especially in the training of *jalidingo* – a male trainee. There are now special schools and cultural centres, and according to expert opinions, the best is at Kela, about thirty-six kilometres from Bamako in Mali. Instruction of apprentice *griots* is entrusted to the *Kumatigi* – the Master of the Word – the highest rank among *griots*. This is regarded as the highest and best 'certification' any individual can get, and so pupils come from all over the Mande diaspora to be trained at Kela by the *Kumatigi*.

By the age of fourteen, some male *jalidingo* graduate to become their fathers' instrumentalists. By this age they each would have learned how to play an instrument, very often the *nkoni*, or the *balafon*, or the *kora*, depending on which instrument the father specialized in or prefers to use. By the age of twenty-one, the trainee is supposed to become free of supervision and is free to travel and come into contact with other *griots* with whom he exchanges experiences. For those who choose to go to the centres of oral arts, such as at Kela, this happens at this stage. At the school, the learner-*griots* are not allowed to sing, rather they learn to listen, and are taught the philosophy and ethics of *jaliya*. These schools not only teach *jaliya*, but also serve as repositories and conservatories of Mande cultural heritage. *Jaliya* is central to the notion and maintenance of *Mandinkaya* – Mandinkaness – because it is through the performances that this is evoked and sustained. So, to be a good *jali* is to be a master and custodian of Mandinka social and cultural history. Once through a school, the *jalikeo* is now fully qualified and very highly respected in the profession.

Part of training concentrates on helping the pupil to get rid of feelings of shame since it is believed that to be a successful *jali* requires being able not to be ashamed or awed about performing in public. Barbara Hoffman says that the *jalidingo* learns 'to be ashamed of being ashamed' (1995: 37), a view supported by Nding Nding Kanoute:

> To be able to dance and speak, pretend anger or joy, and wear colourful clothes and equally loud make-up, and to be able to do all these things in front of other people – this is what makes you a *jali*. And you are taught and encouraged from childhood to be all these things. (Interview, 15 March 2004)

Even when feelings of shame remain, a good performance requires the *jali* to give the appearance of shamelessness in their use of language and behaviour, as well as in dress and make-up (only *jalimusolu* use make-up).

Training is not about learning, memorizing and reciting well-known texts or praise lines but about learning correct behaviour and good speech. A significant period of training is devoted to the mastery of social practices and etiquette. The *jali* should be an expert in the art of social intercourse and thus is able to carry out the role of mediator and intermediary between different social groupings and persons. Training in memory (considered useful for *Jaliya*) is acquired informally in early childhood when praise lines and tunes are learned and tested. Once learned, however, what is important and used as a measure of artistry is correct usage and not accurate recitation.

The three important elements of *jalikan*, which the apprentice is expected to acquire during training, are therefore: good speech, social memory and the ability to construct appropriate metaphors. Of the three, good speech receives more attention and the apprentice learns how to pronounce correctly and clearly. However, good speech alone is not enough to make a good performance since, in addition to it, the *jali* must have a passion for knowledge about social relations and the history and conventions underpinning these relations. Knowledge of appropriate behaviour between the different social groups in Mandinka society is a vital ingredient of the *jali*'s performance armoury. And mastery of these skills comes from practice, in particular that of repeating and retelling of stories and events, of reciting praise lines, sometimes to oneself. The skills to construct or select appropriate metaphors and develop other speech nuances which characterize most *jali* performances, are acquired much later. Experimentation and sustained usage is also necessary after training to ensure that this important skill is acquired and honed. All three elements are constantly and rigorously tested and critiqued during training until the apprentice is deemed to have mastered them.

Staging and performance techniques

Unlike the other African performances studied in this book, *Jaliya* is the most economical in terms of staging techniques and requirements. Most often a *Jaliya* performance is characterized by the personality of the *jali*, which suggests that ultimately the *jali* is the performance. He or she may be dependent on space and stage arrangement in the same way that the masquerade performer or the *Bori* medium or the *Koteba* performers are, but the *jali* does not require a big or an elaborate performance space because, unlike the others, she or he can perform in whatever space is available – private rooms, tiny compounds, halls and sports arenas. The *jali* does not require a complex staging arrangement – thriving better in non-defined spaces where only his or her words and music and the manner of their delivery are the most significant things. But there can be elaborate *Jaliya* performances, such as the *balundo* in Dakar, which had an elevated stage for the orchestra, plus a complex array of electronic and audio support. The *balundo* also required a big enough performance space and auditorium to accommodate the large number of *jalolu* who sometimes had to perform together. A *jaliya* performance can range from the most austere one-man or one-woman shows performed at naming ceremonies and weddings, to big shows such as the *balundo* or the once in seven years *Kamabolom* usually held in Kela, in which hundreds of Mande *griots* and *griottes* gather to celebrate their shared Mande cultural heritage.

The setting for the *balundo*, the Municipal Hall in Sacre Couer, Dakar, was chosen because of the urban setting of the event. Traditionally, this would have been in an open space in the town or village centre, or the leader's compound or any other communal space chosen by the group. For this occasion, the hall provided a relatively big space, broadly divided into three active performing areas (**see Fig. 4.1**). Area One was the elevated stage, which measured approximately twelve feet by fourteen feet and was used mainly by the musicians. Area Two was the rectangular shaped performing space between the elevated stage and front row seats of the auditorium. This space was on the same level and merged with the audience space. It ran the whole width of the hall and would have measured approximately twenty-eight feet by twenty-two feet. About twenty rows of seats had been set up in the auditorium to take in about one hundred and twenty people sitting, and probably another thirty standing around the sitting area, or along the raised corridor running from one end of the hall to the other. Even though there were seats, spectators and guests constantly moved around the hall, as they either greeted friends or went up to offer gifts to performers, or when they went to join in the singing and dancing. Although not the ideal staging space by the standards of African traditional performances, but considering the time of the year and the urban location of the event, the hall was the best available space. There was enough space for groups of people to dance or move about and the orchestra had instruments that needed to be connected to electric sockets. Thankfully, it did not rain on the day so the moveable roof-cover remained open, giving a slight feel of an open-air theatre show. There was no specific scenery, but the permanent murals painted on the walls enhanced the visual effect by providing a supporting background for the performance. In spite of the elevated stage, fluidity of movement was maintained between the three areas. The bright sunshine coming in through the open roof and the large windows on both sides of the hall provided lighting for the performance, and even when evening was coming there was no need to put on the hall lights, so the performance carried on with natural lighting until around 7 p.m. when the hall lights came on. By then, the performance was coming to an end and some spectators had already started leaving the hall to continue with their merriment outside.

Right from the opening scene when Fanta Mbacke sang to welcome Oumou Sinare into the hall, it was clear that there was a pre-planned programme and that each performer knew their cues, which were usually provided by the band. The group had part-rehearsed the programme for about three hours on the previous day so as to get the running order sorted out and for the musicians to set the cues. But the actual songs and the spoken sections were not rehearsed as this would have been counter to the spirit of the performance. There was no plot or storyline, even though there was a performance structure, but this was not fixed either as allowances were made for the unexpected, such as the *jalolu*-Mandogo confrontation. *Jaliya* demands of the jali a readiness to improvise and fit in new material and situations into fixed musical structures. The performances alternated between the *donkili* (a sung welcome or praise) and the *saatari* (a recited, often discursive piece). The *saatari* is the mode adopted for echoing or amplification and sections of dialogue, such as between Fanta Mbacke and Bundaw or between Fanta and Madi Kante. Most of the *griottes* used the *donkili* style, while the *griots* used the *saatari*, except for Mamadou Cissoko who sang to a highlife beat. But in general, *jalolu* alternate between the two in performance.

The relationship between the band and the performers at the *balundo* was evidence of the improvisatory nature of *jaliya*. While the band played three fairly consistent rhythms with slight variations throughout the evening, it was up to each *jali*, to weave his or her words and movements in and out of, in tune with, or against these rhythms. This was more obvious each time an unexpected incident occurred, such as the move from praising Mandogo to the torrent of verbal attack that he received from Bundaw Kouyate, Fanta Kouyate and Madi Kante. The same rhythm played softly in the background throughout the scene and only changed to a dance beat for Fanta's final song as Mandogo and Grimo left with their entourage, escorted by a mass of colourful dancing *woramboos* and *boubous*.

But what really distinguishes a good performer from an average one is the *jali's* ability to alternate between the standardized family *jamung* and new or improvised lines based on recent events or the immediate context. Why this is important is because, in principle, the aim of a *griot's* or *griotte's* singing or reciting of a *jamung* to a descendant of the hero from the epics or from the past is that through his or her performance, the *jali* is able to bring the past into the present and through this juxtaposition to move both into the future. So, by reciting an individual's recent personal achievement or underachievement (as in Mandogo's case) alongside the achievements of the great heroes or ancestors from the past, the two times are made contemporaneous with each other. The *griots'* ability to erase the boundaries between different time frames derives from their ability to manipulate the *nyama* inherent in words. This can be an intense emotional experience for the person being praised and it has been known to make people to virtually 'lose their heads' and give everything they have got, and sometimes more than they actually have, as Yankuba Koulibali and Grimo Jobate did. At the peak of his or her delivery, the *jali* is able to electrify the whole atmosphere around and in which she or he is performing, with the result that the words, the speaker, the spoken about, and the containing space and music merge into one. It as such moments that one experiences a feeling of 'flow'; there were such moments during the performance when time seemed not to matter and everyone held their breadth.

Texts and contexts in *Jaliya*

There are three types of texts in *Jaliya*. The first are the well-known founding epics, legends and tales that tell of past Mande heroes, such as Sundiata, Sumangourou, the Sousou king and Sundiata's great rival, Bala-fasseke Kouyate, and other well-known warriors and founding ancestors. The second are the standard *jamung* of various families through which their respective ancestries are traced and recounted. The third are the usually ephemeral texts as 'written' and delivered by the *jalolu* during perform-ance. This performance text is usually based on materials from the standard texts and the improvised responses of *jalolu* to their respective performance contexts. Ultimately, the context of a performance determines the theme or themes, and even when the content is the same, each context shapes and colours the theme.

The chants and recitations at the *balundo* reflected in their pitch, intensity and purpose, the context in which they were being performed – a celebration of Mandinka cultural heritage and identity. Secondly, it was unique because it played with the Mandinka sense of division of labour between the social groups. During the performance, there were *jalolu* playing the roles of *jalolu*, and there were also those who performed the role of *batufa* (patron). The latter is a role customarily played by members of other social groups, but especially the nobles. But even within this situ-ation, it was also clear that only the Kouyates could be *jalolu* to other *jalolu*. Only they could praise and expect gifts from other *griots*.

The *balundo* performance illustrated two kinds of *jali-batufa* encounter. The *jali* often uses two strategies to get the *batufa* to do what is expected of them. First, he or she can praise the *batufa* by extolling her or his patronymic and by implication elevating her or him to the status of a hero, on equal footing with the great heroes of the past. This was evident in the welcome praises for Mandogo and Grimo when they arrived for the performance. As intended, this succeeded in moving Mandogo, Grimo and members of their entourage to shower the singers with money before making their way to their seats. But the same great past and ancestry were used against Mandogo later on by Bundaw Kouyate.

She, Fanta Kouyate and Madi Kante, kept recalling the great deeds of Mandogo's ancestors as a way of highlighting and belittling his own efforts and thus shaming him into improving his attitude and generosity to the *jalolu*. This possibility of both praise and rebuke based on the same text could only happen because of the context, the *balundo*, which is a celebration of Manding culture. The concept of *Mandinkaya* – Mandinkaness – is based on the interconnections between the past, the present and the future. The insults and rebuke to Mandogo, when they came, equally fitted perfectly into the context of the *balundo* since Mandogo became a target because he was deemed, by not upholding his family name and honour, to be threatening the survival of *Mandinkaya*.

Praises as delivered by *jalolu* are not simply announcements of individual and family qualities, but also of duties and responsibilities (Hale, 1998: 48). Although Mandogo's perceived failure in his duties and responsibilities were shamelessly exaggerated by Bundaw Kouyate and Madi Kante, but that is what *jalolu* are good at and known for; they are masters and mistresses of the feigned outrage and anger, of hyperbole and extreme emotions. For the *jalolu*, there are no in-betweens, they move their audience constantly between two extreme poles of feelings. If they praise you, you give them something to acknowledge their effort, and if they insult or berate you, you hastily give them also to shut them up or make them change their tune. Thematically, therefore, the *balundo* performance explored through various means the idea of duty and responsibility. Mandogo, in the eyes of the *jalolu*, had failed to perform his duty to them as his parents and ancestors had done before him, and so he got a humiliating public tongue lashing from them for it. But those, like Cherino Saho and Madam Faye, who fulfil their social and family obligations, the *jalolu* were fulsome in their praise and honour.

Audience–performer relationship

For the *jali*, every member of the audience is a potential patron, and thus is wooed in order to get them to give generously. A *jali*'s performance is spectator-orientated because it is for and with the spectator that she or he constructs and executes his performance. Although, in principle, a lot of the words that *jalolu* use are passed down from generation to generation – from father to son, from mother to daughter and from master to pupil – the reality is that each performance is a new creation and reinterpretation of pre-existing texts. The texts, though well known and highly respected, are not sacrosanct. What a *jali* chooses to include or omit from the story or text he or she is working from depends, to a large extent, on the context, and especially on the audience. Even well known texts, such as the Sundiata epic, are never faithful retellings of the past but reinterpretations of that past in the light of the present. That present has a lot to do with the audience for whom the epic or history is being reinterpreted. Thus, for the *jalolu*, these texts are merely performance tools, and the praise lines serve as a catch-all introductory overture which enables a *jali* to weave an all-inclusive and magical world in which all members of the audience share a common history and a common ancestry. The *jali* in his or her relationship with the audience strives to achieve what the Mande call a feeling of *badenya* – mother-childness. *Badenya* is the ultimate signifier of harmony, solidarity, loyalty, compassion and protectiveness between people. Even though Mande culture is patrilineal, relationships on the mother's side are perceived to be much stronger than relationships on the father's side. Children of the same mother have *badenya*, and they bond more than children of the same father, who have *fadenya*. The latter, in fact, is felt to be very competitive and full of tension, whereas the former is full of love and oneness. The *jali* hopes to envelop his audience in *badenya*, this feeling of belonging to and originating from a common source which is captured and celebrated in the founding epics and stories.

To achieve this, the *jali* does not need to know every member of the audience in order to include them in this performance envelope. The epics and praise lines in themselves can make each individual feel special and singled out for praise. The reason for this is quite simple, as Jansen writes:

> When a *griot* meets a stranger or visitor . . . he will greet them by referring to his or her patronymic (*jamu*) and by reciting or singing praise lines. The stranger or visitor, overwhelmed by the respect paid him by the *griot*, and not being a specialist in oral tradition, is given the impression that 'this *griot* knows all my ancestors', as these praise lines contain the names of many kings and many expressions which are difficult to understand. (2000: 58)

For individuals of Mande origin, there are a limited number of patronymics celebrated in the founding narratives of Mande history. It would therefore be unlikely for an individual not to have one ancestor mentioned in the course of a song or recitation. *Jalolu* are also quick learners and can instantly ask and get information about a potential patron, which they immediately incorporate into their performance. I was included in one or two songs by Nding Nding – and she later composed some praise lines based on information about me which she got out of Cheikh Seydi, my Mandinka assistant. She surprised me by opening one of our interview sessions with this praise song, and I have since been 'officially' adopted as one of her patrons.

The *jalolu* constantly seek and respond to the reactions of the audience – this reaction can be individual or collective as was demonstrated during the Dakar performance. A *jali*'s performance can be perceived as being simultaneously individual and collective. The audience listens as a group to the *jali* as he or she sings or recites or plays his instrument, but when he or she singles out an individual for praise or rebuke, it becomes, at one level, just between that individual and the *jali*, with other audience members merely looking in or on. The world which the *jali* creates, as he or she recites or sings the individual's praise lines, places the individual in an exclusive cocoon of emotional glory that can be theirs alone. Yet, the onlookers are not totally excluded because of the network of connections between people in Mandinka society, and because of the *badenya* created by the *jali*'s artistry. For example, during the attacks on Mandogo, even though the *jalolu* were directing all their words at him alone, it was his brother, Grimo, and his cousin and close friend, Madi Kanoute, who intervened to pacify the *jalolu*. Other spectators chipped in with monetary gifts while still enjoying the performance by dancing or laughing and clapping when the *jalolu* said funny or outrageous things, such as accusing Mandogo of being illegitimate or not being able to give Bundaw 'a human being with his ears'.

As in all African performances, a *jali* is as good and as successful as the audience makes them. The *jali*'s principal aim is to arouse intense emotions in the audience, and in doing so to get them to show their appreciation of this excitation by giving of themselves through joining in the song and dance, and ultimately offering generous gifts. *Jalolu* are always conscious of this and so select and arrange their material accordingly. For instance, during the *balundo* when the teams of *jalolu* had arrived, Madi Kanoute handed the microphone over to Fanta Mbacke, and she in turn invited Mamadou Cissoko to sing to get the audience and the assembled *jalolu* excited. Mamadou duly obliged by singing a very catchy and danceable song which got almost half of the hall to their feet in a shared dance of belonging and togetherness. The fact that so many people got up to join in the dance greatly enhanced Mamadou's performance, because it elevated his singing and dancing. The audience does not wait politely, as they do in Western theatre, for the *jali* (performer) to finish in order to show appreciation. In fact, the audience's response is supposed to be a barometer of the *jali*'s ability or inability. Thus you are expected to offer the *jali* some reward to encourage them to praise you some more or to make them stop rebuking you. Either way, the *jali* will not stop until the audience has responded in some way – as the audience member found to his embarrassment when Baka Cissoko kept reminding him and the whole audience that he had not been rewarded for both the praise and rebuke he had heaped on the man. In the end, the reluctant patron was shamed into offering some money to Baka. It is also the case that if the *jali*'s performance is poor, the audience wastes no time in showing its disapproval: by not giving her or him anything, by ignoring them completely or if the performer is really bad, by walking away from their performance.

Between the *jali* and his audience there is a close and fluid physical relationship. Even with the almost proscenium arrangement of the municipal hall, this relationship was maintained throughout the evening, with constant movement between the auditorium and the designated perform-ance spaces. Fanta Mbacke, for instance, kept moving forwards and back-wards, and sometimes climbing the steps as she sang to welcome groups as they arrived. These movements took her into and out of the audience space. The other *jalolu* sometimes threaded their way in between rows of seats as they identified and sang or recited for any particular member of the audience. The audience, for its part, was not restricted to the seats. Individuals moved around very much, and some, if they felt like doing so, joined the *jalolu* on stage, to dance, give them gifts, or merely raise the performers' hands in appreciation. It was a completely flexible staging arrangement, although hampered slightly by the fixed spatial envelope in which it was placed. Such a performance does not call for the restrictive walls of a building; its natural setting is the open air, the unrestricted compounds of patrons, the village common, the wrestling arena or, as is increasingly becoming the case, the sports stadiums and streets of urban environments. But good *jalolu* will always find a way to breach the barriers between them and their public because the essence and validation of their performance is in their ability to get their listeners to do something in response to their words: either to dance or give gifts.

A theatre of many functions

One key role of the *jali* in Mandinka society is as keeper of genealogies, one who transmits communal memory and history from generation to genera-tion. A superficial perception exists, however, of the jali as just a storyteller or a narrator of epics, one who sometimes plays an instrument to support his singing. But a *jali* is much more than a storyteller or praise-singer, as he or she performs many other important roles in their communities. As well as being historian, genealogist, and custodian of communal memory, the *jali* is an adviser, a spokesperson, musician, composer, diplomat, medi-ator, interpreter and translator, teacher, exhorter, warrior, witness, and master/mistress of ceremonies, or participant in a variety of traditional ceremonies. One can analyse these roles individually to see how the *jali* performs them, but as the roles tend to combine or overlap in a lot of contexts, it will be better to look again at the *jaliya balundo* in order to identify instances when the *jalolu* performed these roles.

The *balundo*, although ostensibly celebrating and affirming Mandinka cultural heritage and identity, was also a celebration of *Jaliya*. The overall ambience of the performance was one of harmony, of oneness, of *Mandinkaya*. Its underlying theme therefore was one of unity, of *badenya*, of sharing a common bond, of friendship, cooperation and mutual support.

Individual scenes or moments were explorations of aspects of this composite theme. The event was intended to help both old and young Mandinka not to forget who they are, and it also enabled participants to collectively negotiate the tensions and conflicts between themselves. The displeasure with and disapproval of Mandogo Jobate's behaviour by Bundaw Kouyate were aired in song and recitation with the guilty party present, with the chance to put things right. As Nding Nding Kanoute pointed out, whoever shared the stage with you, and whoever shared the *balundo* space with you, is never likely to do anything behind your back to hurt you.

The performance also revealed other roles, which the *jali* performs in Mandinka society. In the songs, the *jalolu* acted as praise-singers, genealogists and historians of Mandinka social and cultural history. In their texts, they revealed so much about the subjects of the songs and recitations. Mamadou Cissoko's song, for instance, revealed who his benefactor was, where he lived and worked, the level of his success in Europe, and the things he had done for the *jali*. As the song progressed, more information was given about both Cherino Saho, the subject of the praise, and Mamadou, the *jali*. We learnt who Cherino's father was, the great things he had done and achieved, and we also learnt who Mamadou's father was. The song also explored and asserted, in a general way, key tenets of Mandinka philosophy of life and beliefs. Individuals and their attributes and circumstances are the handiwork of God, and these can never be taken away from them. However, each individual can improve on what God has given them at birth. The spectators are meant to learn from these philosophical statements and accept individual merits and successes. They are also meant to learn to work hard to be successful themselves, instead of envying others their good fortune and successes.

During the performance, there were instances when *jalolu* acted as mediators between other warring *jalolu*, and sometimes they acted as translators or interpreters, such as when Madi Kante was interpreting and amplifying Grimo Jobate's plea to the *jalolu* to forgive him and his brother for their perceived inability to behave appropriately towards them, and to Bundaw Kouyate in particular. In Mande culture, the art of mediation is highly valued, and parties or individuals often employ a *jali* to perform this for them. Because of their acknowledged command of language, as well as a deep knowledge of social history and etiquette, the *jali* is often able to diffuse tensions between people through knowing the right words to use to create harmony and a feeling of oneness between the warring sides. The *jali* is a bringer of peace and harmony between people. *Jalolu* also act as spokespersons and go-betweens in matters such as courtship and marriage negotiations, and at initiations and circumcision ceremonies. Mande society, divided as it is, based on craft or professional belonging, observes a very strict regime of division of labour. Nobles and other free-born are farmers and warriors, the blacksmiths work in iron and produce weapons, farm implements and other items for use by the other groups, the leather workers produce leather items such as shoes and sandals, bags, leather coats and mats, the woodworkers produce chairs, beds, horse and donkey-drawn carts and so on, while the *jalolu* are expert wordsmiths who create and recreate the world through their perceived power to manipulate the *nyama* inherent in the spoken word. Their ability to deploy words for desired effects is well known. Because of this, tasks which involve speaking in public, public relations or sensitive negotiations are the preserve of the *jalolu*, and their services are often in demand. And although of low status, paradoxically their art elevates them in the eyes of Mandinka society. The same can not be said of the *Koteba* performers in the Chapter 5 who, although appreciated, are treated as no-good vagabonds or likeable rogues.

5   *Koteba (kote-tlon)*: Comedy and satire of the Bamana

Koteba is the indigenous performance tradition of the Bamana of Mali. *Koteba* literally means 'big snail' (*kote* means snail and *ba* is big) and is the generic name for all forms of Bamana indigenous performances. The metaphor of the snail is used because *Koteba*'s staging formation is made up of concentric circles of spectators, dancers and actors, singers and musicians which resemble the shape of the snail's shell starting with the larger circle at the bottom and rising to the smallest at the top. The circles of performers get smaller as one goes inward to the centre of the performance space. But the metaphor also has a deeper symbolism, since the *Koteba*, just like the snail, carries its world and experience around on its back. It contains within its orbit the entire Bamana world and experience. It is true to say that nothing escapes the panoramic lens of the *Koteba*.

In general, there are two types of *Koteba* – masquerades and marionettes performances, and satiric or farcical sketches. The first type usually takes place during the day and on specific occasions, while the second mainly takes place at night or in early evening, and can be staged at any time. One other major difference is that the masquerade or marionette performances deal with mythical figures and ancestors, while the sketches deal with contemporary life and situations. The latter is more immediate and direct in approach, the masquerade performances seeming distant and not speaking directly to or about its audiences.

Koteba, sometimes called *Kote-tlon* or *Kote-komagnagan*, is deeply rooted in Bamana culture and society. In some areas the masquerade and marionette performances (*Koteba*) differ from the satiric sketches (*Kote-tlon*), whereas in others, such as Segou and Markala, all are referred to as just *Koteba*. For clarity, I will endeavour to use the term *koteba* throughout this work. Plays of the *Koteba* repertoire are generally comic and satiric and a performance, such as the presentation in Markala, is usually in two parts. The first is a danced sequence in which the performers introduce themselves to the audience. It is also used to warm the space and set the atmosphere. This part opens with a procession of the actors/characters who are going to feature in the evening's plays and includes a lot of singing, dancing, drumming, ringing of bells by the performers and singing and clapping of hands by the spectators. Usually one or two actors detach themselves to engage in a playful opening exchange with the spectators. The second part, which also includes singing and dancing, usually is made up of farces and satirical sketches based on many facets of life that include a wide range of characters from everyday life. Well-known physical, psychological, cultural or ethnic characteristics often define the characters, such as the Leper, the Polygamist, the Cuckold, the Unfaithful Wife, the Blind Man, the Stranger or Foreigner, the Con Man or Smooth Talker, the Been-to, the Corrupt Policeman, the Boastful Coward, the Clumsy Hunter, the Lazy Man, the Rogue Marabout and so on. And because the *Koteba* is eclectic, its repertory of characters and sketches has grown to reflect changing times and concerns. In the colonial period, for example, new characters emerged such as the ubiquitous Interpreter, the Native Policeman, the White Colonial Officer or Soldier, and the Missionary or Evangelist. Today one encounters characters such as the Boastful City Boy, the Been-to or Johnny-Just-Arrived. And as the characters change, so do the themes, both reflecting the times in which they are being performed.

Occasions for performance

Although the main *Koteba*, in which masks and marionettes feature, is usually associated with festive occasions, such as harvest, marriage ceremonies, circumcision, and other important moments in the life of the community, the satiric sketches can also be performed at other less grand occasions. Important disputes, acts of misdemeanour or behaviour considered anti-social could prompt a quick response through performance, in which case, the themes explored would reflect the issue which had prompted the performance. The performance in Markala was at my request, although the group still had to choose a day most convenient for all the participating members. The themes explored were of a general nature and based on existing characters and situations from the traditional repertory.

I had gone to Mali for the first time in March 2004 hoping to watch the yearly festival of masquerades and puppets called *Sogo Bo*. Unfortunately, however, incorrect information and delays in Dakar meant that I arrived two days too late, the performances had finished and only the clearing up by *ton* members was going on. But the visit enabled me to make contact with Mamadou Keita who works at the Ministry of Culture in Segou. Mamadou became my guide and introduced me to Moussa Diakhite, the leader of the *ton* in Markala. The *ton* is an umbrella association to which all young people between the ages of fifteen and forty-five belong, for women it is between fifteen and twenty-five years. The *ton*, initially an all-male organization because of its paramilitary history, is now open to both sexes. It is a central element of Bamana social structure and organization, and it is usually responsible for a multitude of activities very important to Bamana society, such as collective farming projects, maintenance of communal roads, cooking at community fetes (the last done by the women) and so on. In addition to these, the *ton* is responsible for organizing cultural and artistic events, such as the *Koteba* performances. Those responsible for organizing cultural/artistic activities are called the *kote-ton* or *koteba-ton*, the play or theatre team, while the work or agricultural team is known as the *ngonson-ton*. The *ton* provides the organizational backbone for *Koteba*.

Moussa Diakhite agreed to organize a special performance for me, but he needed about three weeks in which to ask members who had returned to their places of work after the *Sogo Bo* to come back to Markala for the show. Commissioning a special performance was necessary, as it was the only way I could watch a performance, unless I was prepared to spend months in the town waiting and hoping for one. It also turned out to be a very good thing because it enabled me to work closely with the performers, as well as have unlimited access to them for interviews and general discussions. As I had to return to the United Kingdom, we agreed for the performance to be in July and for the venue to be the *ton* compound, which was in the centre of the town and easily accessible to the public. In return for agreeing to perform for me, the group asked me to make a contribution to their *caisse* – any amount that I could afford or felt their effort was worth. That was a smart move on their part – the groups in Dakar and Zaria had asked for fees – since the pressure was on me to determine what was a fair and respectable amount. In the end, advised by Mamadou Keita, I offered one hundred and twenty thousand francs (approximately £120.00) which the group gladly accepted. I gave Moussa an extra five thousand francs plus the ten thousand francs, which I had given him during my first visit in March.

The performance

Having spent almost the entire day clearing, constructing and decorating the *ton* compound in Markala, we all returned to the venue at around 7.30 p.m. as agreed (**Fig. 5.1**). By then, the place was teeming with an enthusiastic crowd eager to get into the compound and find seats for themselves. This was the first performance of the comic sketches in well over a year, and so the excitement and anticipation was understandable. Ushers kept most of the people out to give the performers time to get ready, until

Figure 5.1 Ton members prepare the *Koteba* stage in Markala.

with a sign from the 'stage manager', the spectators were finally let in. There was a scramble for the limited seats, some belonging to the association, but quite a number borrowed from neighbouring compounds. Some spectators brought their own seats. Everything about this audience was relaxed and good natured – greetings, handshakes, hugs and backslapping went on all the time as people made their way to the seating section of the compound.

The musicians – four in number, playing only percussion instruments, three double-sided cylindrical and one large dome shaped drums – emerged first from the enclosure at stage right, which was being used as the dressing room for the evening. They played a steady rhythm accompanied by songs through which the performers announced themselves. The music was made up of two beats – a one-two : one (1-2 : 1) played on the dome drum and a quicker one-two-three : one (1-2-3 : 1) provided by the other three. The music consisted of variations on these two and a third beat, one-two : one-two-three (1-2 : 1-2-3).

The performers, eight in number and all men, followed. They were dressed in an assortment of traditional Bamana costumes. The first dancer, in particular, was striking in his big white *boubou* on top of which was an open black, lightweight overcoat. On his head he wore a white cap covered over with a pink scarf, round his waist a violet sash was tied and he held a second pink scarf in his right hand. Across his left shoulder hung a length of rope which went down to his right side and on it were strung a folded mat, a goatskin bag, a calabash plate, a drink bottle, two cups, and a spoon. In fact, he seemed to carry all his worldly possession with him on his body. Others, although in different colours and with less items of clothing and props, were similarly dressed. Their faces were painted white – I later learnt that this was to symbolically disguise the identities of the actors. They danced in a single file into the centre of the stage where the musicians had already taken up a position for the introductory song and dance. Their entrance dance, called the *bamuko*, was a slow two-step, outward and forward and one-step, forward and inward. This movement was then reversed to two, inward and one, outward. At the third – whether in or out – both hands were lifted into the air and brought down as the first step of the next move began. This meant that the dancer's whole body was involved in the dance, lifting, turning and moving forward. They encircled the musicians, danced round the stage twice and then, opening up like a big snail emerging from its shell, they slowly danced back into their changing room – which was a big enclosure stage left or directly opposite spectators sitting on the right side of the stage. The *bamuko* dance, in its opening and coming-together sequence and the harmony of movement among the dancers, reflected the solidarity of the *ton*; the theatrical activities of the *koteba-ton* complemented and reinforced those of the *ngonson-ton*. The musicians, still playing, moved backwards to a park bench, on which a group of youngsters were sitting. The latter, realizing their error, scampered away as the musicians approached. This brought laughter from the audience because the youngsters who believed they had vantage seats for the show suddenly found themselves right at the back. There was also clapping to acknowledge the end of the opening routine. This opening scene clearly animated the audience, who now began chatting excitedly to each other, as they waited for the dramatic sketches to come.

Because this performance was arranged for me, the group had reserved five front row seats for us. However, only the driver chose to sit, the rest of us preferring to move around so that we could capture the audience as well in our videos and photographs. There was a mini scramble for these choice seats once it became known that we were not going to use them. The audience was made up of mainly women, young girls, boys, and children. A few young men were also present, but there were no male elders – this, I learned later, was because the elders were often the butts of the satiric comedies. The conservatism of the elders and their control of most social processes and materials were sources of tension between them and the younger generation. This provided subjects for the satires, and so the elders usually kept away from the performances. Women and foreigners were also favourite subjects for the comedies.

The drums sounded again to signal that the actors were ready, and they soon emerged – in the same costumes as before. But instead of the eight actors of the introductory dance, there were only five for the second scene. While they did not acknowledge the audience in their first appearance, this time around, instead of dancing round the stage, they stood directly in front of the now seated musicians and raised their arms; when they brought them down, the music stopped. They then turned to greet the audience. One of the dancers withdrew, one went and stood down stage left (he was later to become the *dugutigi*, the village chief), one went and stood in the centre, and the other two went across to greet the audience again. The latter responded as loudly as they could. Apparently unimpressed and disappointed by the unenthusiastic response, the two actors moved to the side to have a private chat about the audience and their lukewarm attitude, after which they went back to greet the audience yet again. And this time, the spectators, appropriately chastised, produced a much louder response. For the performers, this was a signal that they had the full attention they wanted. The two moved to the side again for further gossip and then back to work the audience again. Finally, they engaged the audience in a kind of banter, a more or less question and answer session. They asked the audience if they had a *dugutigi* to preside over the evening's proceedings, as is the custom at all public events in Bamana society. Spectators exchanged words among themselves, and the two actors taking this as a sign of confusion or the absence of a chief, informed the audience that they, the actors, had appointed one for them. As they were informing the audience about this, an attendant brought a mat in and placed it beside the actor down stage left. The latter produced a hat, which he put on and a staff, and sat down on the mat to become the *dugutigi*. The two chatty characters turned from the audience and ran up to him to welcome him and ask him to supervise the evening's show. With the *dugutigi*, now installed, the two made a hasty dash back to the dressing room, much to the amusement of the spectators.

With everything in place, the music started again, to indicate the actors' entrance and the start of the first play. Four actors entered to a hilarious welcome, prolonged outbursts of laughter, and rhythmic clapping from the audience, which kept time with the entry song and music. The cause of the laughter soon became apparent, for three of the four characters were men dressed as women. Because all the actors were men, the spectators, who were predominantly women, found this extremely funny. These usually macho brothers, husbands, lovers, and uncles had turned themselves into women and girls. The incongruity of bulging muscles struggling to be contained inside the female frocks, rugged looking men trying to move in dainty feminine ways, and hoarse masculine voices trying to be mellow but resulting in all shades of shrilly girly and womanly tones, had the audience in

Figure 5.2 Koke and family entering the stage.

stitches of laughter for a long time after these actors had entered (**Fig. 5.2**). The laughter was also because the spectators immediately recognized which story was to be enacted – a polygamous family with its usual problems is a favourite skit for Bamana audiences.

The characters were Koke (husband), Mariamoufin (first wife), Nyebaje (second wife, played by Moussa), and Jeneba (daughter). The family sang and danced in a single file as they came onto the stage, with Koke leading the way, followed by Nyebaje, Mariamoufin and bringing up the rear was Jeneba, who was carrying a calabash bowl on her head. Nyebaje sang the solo, and the others the chorus. They danced round the stage once, and ended near to where the *dugutigi* sat. Koke walked up to address him:

Koke: Good day, Dugutigi
Dugutigi: Good day, stranger
Koke: Dugutigi, we have come to your village to look for a field to cultivate. But I have got two wives and I don't want anybody to come near them. This one that you see here is my little wife, Nyebaje. That one that you see there is my first wife, Mariamoufin. (*The spectators laugh at this introduction*).

Nyebaje:	Dugutigi, have you had a good day?
Dugutigi:	There has been no mishap this day
Mariamoufin:	It's I who am the first wife, but that shameless person that was recently added to me . . .
Koke:	Mariamoufin! Mind your words!
Mariamoufin:	This does not concern you!
Dugutigi:	Go to the east of the village, there is a clearing there where you can install yourselves.

The four moved to centre stage to put their belongings down and set up their home, and straight away, the squabbles of the wives resumed. Nyebaje wanted to occupy the best room, the one with the cement floor, with Mariamoufin insisting that would only happen over her dead body. Koke, as expected, decided in Nyebaje's favour, and so Mariamoufin and Jeneba resigned themselves to the room with earth floor. For them though, that was only the beginning. The two moved to the side and spread a piece of cloth to signify their hut, while Koke spread a nicely decorated mat to stand for the better hut that he and Nyebaje were going to occupy. As soon as this had been done, Nyebaje was at him again, reminding him that they had had nothing to eat since the day broke. Koke immediately jumped up to order Mariamoufin to go prepare the meal, but she refused and told Koke to go ask the favoured wife to do the cooking. Instead of doing that Koke threatened her with a thorough beating if she did not get up and do the cooking. Reluctantly, Mariamoufin and Jeneba went across and began preparing the meal. After a while, Jeneba walked off to get some more stuff for the cooking, while Mariamoufin started pounding the millet, with a song to match. The pounding was done to the beat of the song, a one: two: three (1-2 : 1-2 : 1) beat, with the pestle lifting on the one-two : one-two and falling on the one which is when the audience's clap came in. Her song was a complaint about her co-wife:

> Where did this one come from to supplant me?
> The bad co-spouse came to supplant me
> Where did she come from to supplant me?
> Where did this shameless person come from to supplant me?

> Nyebaje (*Getting up from the mat and taking the pestle from Mariamoufin, started pounding to the beat of her own song*):

>> I came from there where the others came from!
>> Me, I came out from there to supplant you!

Nyebaje sang and pounded to a faster two beat – apparently meant to suggest her youth, quickness of hands and tongue. The audience also joined her in her song and pounding. But her action also brought roars of laughter from the spectators. After her demonstration, Nyebaje handed the pestle back to Mariamoufin and returned to the mat to sit down again, where she continued preening herself. After a while, she reminded Koke that she was still hungry, that Mariamoufin was taking too long to get the meal ready, and that the smoke from the cooking was getting in her eyes and hair. Koke responded by ordering Mariamoufin to move the cooking place further away. Nyebaje kept coming up with complaints against Mariamoufin, and Koke promptly ordering the latter around in response. Nyebaje cleverly used Koke as a weapon with which to fight and whip her rival. Having finished cooking and serving the meal, Koke subjected Mariamoufin to further insult and humiliation by asking her to present her cooking to her junior rival for appraisal. Mariamoufin was livid with anger and refused to do so. But Koke passed the food to Nyebaje to inspect. The latter disdainfully lifted the plate, touched and smelt it, and promptly pronounced it dirty and badly cooked. This was the final straw for Mariamoufin and she and Jeneba packed their belongings and left for her parents' village, to triumphant jeers from Nyebaje and Koke. The audience sided with the aggrieved first wife, although it did not stop them from laughing at the comical nature of the situation.

Once her rival had gone, Nyebaje began to revel in her new role as sole wife who had her doting idiot of a husband at her beck and call. Meanwhile, Koke was starving because Nyebaje would neither cook nor clean the house. She just sat admiring her fingernails, and expecting Koke to do the chores. For a Bamana man, that was totally unacceptable. But Nyebaje's new freedom and power did not last long, as news came to Koke via his friend, Jeliba, of how well Mariamoufin was doing at her parents', and especially worrying for Koke was the news that there were talks of many suitors waiting on her and plying her with gifts to win her love. As the two men talked about Mariamoufin, Nyebaje began to get worried and kept calling on Koke wanting to find out what they were talking about. Jeliba wanted to find out from Koke if he and Mariamoufin were divorced so that, either the suitors got the green light to court her, or he, Koke, could try and win her back for himself. Being the jealous man that he was, Koke resolved to bring Mariamoufin back, and went off with Jeliba.

He began pacing the stage in 'his search' for Mariamoufin, only to be called back by the now suspicious Nyebaje. Into this scene walked a well-dressed and physiognomically different Mariamoufin, and her changed appearance and presence completely had Koke in thrall. He could not take his eyes off her; his lustful gaze firmly fixed on her bouncing buttocks. Finally, his lust getting the better of him, he began following her sheepishly around the stage, while she, for her part, pretended not to know who he was or to have noticed his interest in her behind. This brought much laughter from the spectators who instantly began reminding and teasing Koke about his maltreatment of Mariamoufin earlier. But Koke was determined to win her back by any means. Mariamoufin's condition before she would speak to him again was that he slapped Nyebaje. Obviously pleased and relieved to be getting away lightly, Koke went across the stage straightaway to where Nyebaje sat and began to order her around. But she would have none of this and bluntly refused to do anything she was asked to do. Koke, arms raised, threatened to really beat her up if she continued to disobey him. He did this many times, but each time stopped short of actually hitting her. He then went back to Mariamoufin, claiming that he had slapped Nyebaje as he was asked to do, but Mariamoufin gently pushed him away, telling him she had seen everything. Koke again crossed over to Nyebaje to order her to do the cooking, but the latter calmly informed him that she was not the cooking type of wife. He still could not beat her, but Mariamoufin would not budge either and the hapless husband kept being shoved between the two women. At one point he just brushed Nyebaje's cheek pretending it was a slap, but Mariamoufin told him it was just a caress, and that he was not getting her back until her rival was rolling on the ground in agony. Now quite desperate, Koke went back and confronted Nyebaje:

Koke:	Nyebaje!
Nyebaje:	I told you that I am not a wife who prepares the meal.
Koke:	If you don't prepare the meal, I'll strike you!
Nyebaje:	You'll die of hunger
	(Koke strikes her and pushes her down to the floor)
Mariamoufin:	You slapped her only two times. You have to slap her three times
Koke:	Nyebaje!
Nyebaje:	If you don't let me have my peace, you and the woman will have it hot!

And this time Koke really went to work on Nyebaje, the latter verbally fighting back and berating him in tirades, and occasionally she took swipes at Mariamoufin, the flavour of the moment. Mariamoufin, satisfied that her opponent had been put in her place allowed herself to be embraced by Koke, and both sat down on a new mat away from a furious Nyebaje, who was still verbally attacking the two reconciled couple. Koke did not seem to care as he was now blissfully ensconced in Mariamoufin's laps. The latter at this point broke into a triumphant song and dance, joined by her daughter; the two women teased and tormented Nyebaje, to the immense delight of the audience, who apparently saw her behaviour as unacceptable. Mariamoufin's song was an attack on her rival, and the dance mimicked the way a thin, flat-bosomed woman would walk or dance:

> Woman with flat buttocks, you are not liked
> There is no place behind you to place the hand
> Woman with the rounded buttocks, you are liked
> There is some place behind you to place the hand.

The sharp-tongued Nyebaje responded with her own song about the fickle ness of men who she accused of being 'like a branch of a false acacia tree', whose branch would let down anyone who leant on it for support. For her, men were untrustworthy and she was better off without Koke who was truly fickle, flitting between two women like a spineless reed blown about in the wind. Thus the play was as much a criticism of Koke as it was of Nyebaje. In fact, only Mariamoufin won the approbation of the audience. The play ended with the two women engaging in a war of words, which gradually degenerated into fisticuffs. Koke's attempts to separate them, like everything he did, was comically ineffectual and he only found himself being mauled by the two women. Finally, he was bundled into an undignified heap on the ground as Mariamoufin and Nyebaje carried on their fight as they made their exit, with only the flustered Koke and his daughter left on the stage.

A change of music marked the transition from this scene to the opening scene of the second sketch. Only Koke, Jeneba and Dugutigi were on stage. Koke went across to address him. He informed Dugutigi that his two wives had left him, and only his daughter was left. Dugutigi made an inaudible reply before Koke went back to Jeneba. He asked her to look after his chicken while he went to look for food for them. As soon as Koke left, a scruffy looking young man entered. He wore what probably were meant to be western clothes – flannels, jacket, a scarf, a shoulder bag and a funny-looking cap. His style of walking – a cross between moonwalking and a macho shuffle – nearly brought the whole place down. He apparently was a well-known type – the 'been-to' (a derog-atory term used for someone who has been abroad), who had completely remade himself and totally rejecting his or her old identity for a new and often not too clear one. He immediately confirmed this stereotype, to hilarious shouts and catcalls from the spectators, when he reacted angrily to being called his former name of Madou by Jeneba. He dismissively informed her that his new name was Wankyu, repeating it several times for emphasis. Jeneba obviously impressed and excited embraced him, and invited him to sit down, while she hurried around to fix him something to eat.

Wankyu's every move and gesture, up to the manner of his sitting down on the mat, arranging his clothes, turning his cap round his head, or the way he elaborately wrung his hands, had spectators in titters. And as is always the case in *Koteba*, the actor played this to the full, prolonging and exaggerating these actions in response to the audience's reactions. While Wankyu was regaling and entertaining the spectators with his antics, Jeneba hurriedly finished the cooking and returned with the food. Wankyu meticulously loosened his scarf, stretched both arms, flexed and un-flexed his fingers, all in readiness to begin eating. At last, he began eating and with a bit of food in his mouth he proudly announced to Jeneba that he had just returned from Peking, China. Greatly impressed, Jeneba begged him to take her with him. In fact, she pleaded with him that they should flee before her father returned. Wankyu said he would be glad to do so, but that he needed first to teach her a few things, such as how to speak and pronounce certain words correctly in Chinese. After the hilarious language session, he left to go and find flight tickets for both of them. Jeneba escorted him out and then returned and lay down on the mat and went to sleep.

Koke's voice was heard off stage, and soon he rushed in. He was quite surprised and indignant to find Jeneba fast asleep in the middle of the afternoon. Ignoring her protestations of tiredness, Koke began cooing to attract his chicken to where he was standing. After a while, he started to feed, talk to and count the imaginary chicken and then horror on his face as he realized that something was amiss:

Koke: Jeneba, not all the chicken are here. Are some still locked in? And why are you still lying there?
Jeneba: There were some animal predators here while you were gone.
Koke: Eh?
Jeneba: Some animal predators came here and their footprints resembled those of humans.
Koke: Some of the footprints should be mine. You claim there were some animals of prey? Okay. There are still five chickens left. Look after them!

Koke again left, and as he exited, Wankyu entered, this time wearing a different costume – traditional Bamana trousers, a western European coat and scarf, and no shirt. He informed Jeneba that the tickets were ready and she should get her baggage for them to leave. She hurried out and returned with more food for him and then hurried out again. And as he was about to begin eating – after his usual ritual – she rushed in again in great panic to inform him that her father had returned.

To hide him, she hurriedly threw a piece of cloth over him on the spot where he sat. As she was doing this, Koke came into the room, and looked the other way. Jeneba kept fussing over the crouching Wankyu in the middle of the room and, finally, she managed to put the cloth over him, although some parts of his body still showed. Satisfied that her lover was now hidden, she walked up to her father:

Jeneba:	Oh, father, you have come back from the fields?
Koke:	Yes. I will go into the bedroom to change my clothes.
Jeneba:	(*alarmed and preventing him*) Father, give me your clothes. I will put them in the room for you.
Koke:	What is in the room that I can not enter?
Jeneba:	A wedding procession entrusted me with a drum, which I have put in the bedroom and covered with cloth. The owner told me that nobody is allowed to touch this drum.
Koke:	This has come at the right moment. It's been a long time since I danced. I will go look for my friends to come and have a dance party with me.
Jeneba (*to audience*):	My father will play the drum, which has been entrusted to me. Is this possible? Is this fair?

While she was speaking to the audience, four of Koke's friends entered. They began to sing and dance around the covered object. When they finished their dance and song, the object echoed the last line of their song. The men were understandably taken aback. They gingerly moved closer to the drum, poked at it and said things to and about it, and each time, the drum mumbled something or made grunting noises in reply, to the great delight of the audience. The men retreated to one side to confer about what to do (**Fig. 5.3**).

Some spectators made suggestions to the men about what to do with the drum. The drum also responded to the spectators' suggestions. All the time, Jeneba pleaded and remonstrated with her father and his friends, telling them to leave the drum alone, since they'd be breaking the stranger's injunction to her if they touched or uncovered the object. But the men ignored her entreaties, began to hatch a plan to get Jeneba to leave the room so they could remove the cloth. But when she would not leave, they removed the cloth to reveal the crouching Wankyu. Koke, enraged, threatened him with a stick:

Figure 5.3 Koke and friends discuss the mystery drum.

Koke: It was you that ate all my chicken!
Wankyu: The chicken was for you? They are all in my belly now!
Koke: Wait! I will open your belly today!

The exposed Wankyu slowly rose, carefully folded and put away the mat and the cloth used to cover him, before finally acknowledging and accepting Koke's challenge. He calmly went through a ritualistic demonstration of his mastery of Chinese martial arts, to amused laughter from the spectators. And when Koke attacked, he deftly stepped aside, and delivered a rapid succession of kicks and slaps all over Koke, the latter stuttering across the stage unable to cope with the speed and accuracy of Wankyu's feet and hands. They eventually came to grips with each other and wrestled themselves off stage, to music and claps from the musicians and spectators.

A brief interlude followed before Sketch Three, between Sarakole (a donkey seller), Leper, Police Sergeant and Superintendent of Police. During the interval, the spectators returned to their customary chatting among themselves, while some of the musicians stretched their legs or smoked cigarettes or had something to drink. The interval lasted approximately fifteen minutes. Then in walked a man and his donkey. He was the over-dressed first dancer of the introductory scene. The actor playing the donkey – the same actor who had played Wankyu in the previous scene – wore only a traditional Bamana cotton trouser and a brown sash across his bare body. A pair of rubber slippers placed on each side of his face and tied with a piece of cloth across his forehead served as the donkey's large ears. Because he had to walk on all fours throughout the scene, cloth pads were tied to his hands and knees to protect them against the rough ground. The man was singing and his movements and that of the donkey kept time with the song and the supporting rhythm from the musicians. The man stopped and pulled his donkey forward to stand before Dugutigi, who had sat in that same spot all through the previous two sketches and only occasionally becoming part of the action when other characters came to him or involved him, as Sarakole did:

Sarakole: Good evening, good evening.
Dugutigi: Good evening to you, stranger.
Sarakole: I am Sarakole. The Bamana language is very difficult.
Dugutigi: What is up? What is happening?
Sarakole: Me, I am Sarakole. I left Nioro and I am travelling through the Sahel. I trade in donkeys. I buy them and I sell them. This is my trade. Are there some donkeys in your village?
Dugutigi: Plenty of donkeys. You can set yourself up in the eastern part of the village. Your luck may find you some there.

Sarakole returned to his song again, and began to make his way to the eastern part of the village as suggested by Dugutigi.

After a while, the musicians changed the beat, and another character sang as he danced onto the stage. The lyrics of his song clearly pointed to his ungrateful nature and the scenario in which he would be involved. As Sarakole and his donkey had done before him, he circled the stage and this took him to Dugutigi as well. From the way he walked, the manner of his cropped hand and fingers, his tattered clothes, as well as the thickness of his white facial make-up, the audience immediately recognized him as the leper. He exchanged greetings with Dugutigi, and then informed him that he wanted to go to Bamako (the capital city of Mali), but that he was ill and tired and was therefore looking for a kind person who could help him continue on his journey by letting him ride on their cart or the back of their donkey. Dugutigi advised him to sit by the roadside and that if he was lucky somebody would come along prepared to help him. While this brief exchange was going on between Leper and Dugutigi, Sarakole began another song as he started walking round the stage again with his donkey in tow. Soon he crossed by where Leper had installed himself. The latter noticed him and called to him:

Leper:	Hey, good day! Hey, you there, good day!
Sarakole:	I don't understand Bamana.
	(Laughter from the audience)
Leper (getting up and approaching him):	Sarakole, good day! Can you let me ride your donkey?
Sarakole:	Didn't I tell you that I don't understand Bamana?

Sarakole continued on his journey, gently touching and leading his donkey along. Leper walked up to him and tapped him on the shoulder to get his attention. He offered to pay Sarakole any amount to let him ride on the donkey. But the latter, unimpressed by the offer, told him that his donkey was for sale and so nobody was going to ride on its back. Leper changed tactics and pleaded with Sarakole:

Leper (pleading):	So, for the sake of Allah, let me ride on your donkey.
Sarakole (relenting):	All right, for the sake of Allah, I'll let you ride on my donkey. But, you must not beat it because I am going to sell it afterwards. Besides, you have got a big belly. Pay attention and be careful because often he gives kicks with his hooves if he is not happy.
Leper:	I understand, I understand (*Struggles to mount the donkey with so much difficulty. Succeeding at last, he waves gingerly and triumphantly to the audience, and then to Dugutigi*). We are off! (**Fig. 5.4**).

The pair began their journey towards Bamako, Sarakole walking in front, and Leper following behind on the donkey. But without wasting any time at all, Leper smacked the ears of the donkey; the latter buckled under

Figure 5.4 Leper: 'For the sake of Allah, let me ride your donkey'.

the enormous weight of and the beating from Leper. This brought an immediate angry reaction from Sarakole. He warned Leper that if he beat the donkey again he would ask him to dismount and find his way to Bamako on foot. At which Leper promised not to hit the donkey again. Off they started again, but as soon as Sarakole's back was turned, Leper whacked the donkey across the ear, and the donkey again wobbled but managed to remain on its feet. Even though the spectators tried to alert him to what was happening behind him, Sarakole carried on walking and singing. However, a third whack across the ear and flanks brought the donkey to its knees with a wail. This enraged Sarakole and he turned to confront Leper. They started fighting and when Sarakole accused Leper of hitting his donkey, the latter said the donkey he hit was his. The audience greeted this twist with much laughter, while Sarakole was reduced to utter disbelief and dismay. Leper meanwhile walked across to possessively pat the donkey on the flanks, telling Dugutigi that he'd just found the donkey which he had lost. Sarakole, properly incensed, hurriedly put his things down in readiness for a real fight. Leper would not even allow him near the donkey. The two squared up to each other, as they physically contested for possession of the donkey. They finally engaged in a fight, and were only stopped by the arrival of Police Sergeant, who quickly put himself between them as he questioned them about what was happening.

Leper:	Ask him, he started it.
Police Sergeant:	You, why were you fighting him?
Sarakole:	Police Officer, you know that since the beginning of time, the work of the Sarakole has been the trade in donkeys. Leper asked of me, because of Allah, to let him ride my donkey. Out of pity, I took him. But I asked him not to beat my donkey and he beat it three times.

At this, Leper attacked him again and another fight ensued, but they were promptly stopped and reprimanded by the officer. Sarakole was still very incensed by Leper's ingratitude and effrontery that he pounced on him to continue the fight. Again, the policeman pulled them apart, with a stern warning of severe consequences if either of them started the fight again.

Leper took the sergeant aside, owned up that the donkey belonged to Sarakole, but offered a bribe for the sergeant to 'arrange' for him to become the owner of the disputed donkey. Sergeant pocketed the bribe, and walked back to Sarakole and accused him of trying to steal Leper's donkey. The latter was so enraged by this sudden and unexplained turn of events that he attacked Leper again, but was forcefully restrained by Sergeant and Superintendent, the latter having walked into the scene. When Superintendent asked to know what the matter was, Sergeant took him aside to explain the situation to him, and in the process gave him some of the bribe money. Having accepted the bribe, Superintendent came up with an ingenious 'donkey test' as a means of ascertaining who the real owner of the donkey was:

Superintendent (nodding):	Yes, okay. No problem about that! Since Leper has given some money, a testimony will be established in his name. Normally, the donkey follows his master. We are going to let the two persons walk away from here.
	When Sarakole begins to walk away, you will hold the donkey back so that he does not follow him. And when Leper takes his place, you will push the donkey towards him. You understand?
Police Sergeant:	Yes, yes.

The test was carried out, with the officer sitting resolutely astride the donkey as it strained to follow Sarakole when he walked away from them. And when it was Leper's turn, Sergeant did all he could to get the reluctant donkey to follow, but without success. Instead, the donkey kicked out, first at Sergeant, then Leper, and finally, Superintendent who was completely floored by a very vicious kick. At this point, Sarakole came back to attack Leper again, but was once again restrained by the combined efforts of the two officers, at which point he turned to plead his case with the audience:

Sarakole:	You see! The policeman hindered my donkey from following me. They deprive me of my good in front of all the people.
Superintendent:	If you don't hold your tongue, I will shut you up forever!
Sarakole:	To take away my donkey in front of these people!
Superintendent:	Neither you nor any of your parents ever possessed a donkey!

Sarakole became angrier at this, but the police officers bombarded him with words to the effect that he had lost his donkey, and that Leper was now the recognized owner of the said animal. It soon became obvious to Sarakole that nothing was to be gained by continuing to talk to or plead with the two officers. He calmly invited the sergeant to the side, pretending to want to have a quiet word with him in private, and the latter followed, hoping apparently for a bribe as Leper had done previously. What he got instead was a hard punch to the abdomen which completely knocked him over, and then a series of kicks and punches all over his body as he struggled to get back on his feet. He was finally kicked and punched out of the stage, to applause from the spectators. Superintendent, realizing what was happening, rushed to rescue his colleague, but was too late to save him from the deserved punishment and loss of dignity, which he was suffering at the hands of Sarakole. Superintendent finally decided it was time to deal with Sarakole himself, but the latter in full fighting flow was much too nimble, mentally and physically, for the charging officer. As Superintendent charged at him, Sarakole raised both hands, in a gesture of surrender and this succeeded in stopping the superintendent's charge. Sarakole walked up to the bewildered police officer and began an earnest conversation with him in which he kept flattering and heaping praises on him:

Sarakole (walking towards him):	Boss, your eyes resemble those of a panther!
Superintendent (quite puzzled):	What?

Sarakole (coming closer):	My Superintendent! There was an abnormal phenomenon today!
Superintendent (more puzzled):	What?
Sarakole (pointing to the sky):	Look! Two moons in the sky today! Look at the sky very well.
Superintendent (looking up):	Oh. Where? (**Fig. 5.5**).

Superintendent looked up and in doing so bent backwards slightly and thus positioned his enormous belly properly for Sarakole's vicious punch. This almost lifted Superintendent off his feet and flat onto his back, while Sarakole, ever nimble with his hands and feet followed this up with more blows and kicks all over the prone Superintendent's body. The latter, however, managed to get to his feet, and with murder in his eyes, charged after Sarakole. Again, Sarakole put his two hands up in the air in a gesture of a truce, and again, Superintendent fell for it and stopped his chase, allowing Sarakole the chance to move in with more belly blows and Superintendent once again found himself flat on his back. This gave Sarakole the opportunity to find a long stick, which he now used to beat and chase Superintendent off the stage, to musical accompaniment and applause again from the audience, the latter feeling rightly that justice had been done.

Figure 5.5 Sarakole pleads with Superintendent.

Dugutigi finally got up – having sat there all through the three sketches – to announce that the show was over, and he thanked the audience for coming. The latter clapped and whooped as they made their way to the exit; there were also animated discussions about the performance they had just seen.

Organization and training

Koteba performances are usually organized and performed by the *ton*. The *koteba-ton* in Markala is not a professional theatre company, as members are in fairly steady jobs from which they derive their livelihood. Moussa, for instance, as well as being an actor, singer, dancer and theatre director, mainly works in the local health ministry as the community dispenser. His brother, who played Wankyu and later the donkey, is a self-employed radio technician. Others work at various professions in and out of Markala. For them, organizing *Koteba* is more of a civic responsibility, and like the other activities of the *ton*, performances are expected to be of benefit to the community. The satire is designed to teach moral lessons, and ultimately to correct deviant or unacceptable behaviours, but in doing so the performers also provide much needed entertainment for their community. Not being a professional activity brings difficulties, such as incentives and levels of commitment. But the group keeps the performances going for two major reasons; it is fun to do, and they desperately want to ensure that the *Koteba* tradition does not disappear in their time for lack of interest from the younger generation – the average age of all the actors who performed in Markala was approximately forty-four years.

For this group commitment was not a problem, however, and, under Moussa's enthusiastic leadership, members seemed willing to contribute physically and materially towards the successful presentation of performances. Democratic principles govern decision-making, such as where to hold the performance, the number of characters and sketches, and who was going to play what character. All group members were invited to an open meeting where my contribution was discussed, but how the payment was shared out or utilized was done after we had left. They usually shared the money equally between those who took part but very often, in keeping with the spirit behind all *ton* activities, they used some of such contributions for communal projects or to assist indigent members of the community. During the discussion, members' views were canvassed and welcomed, but two or three members assisted Moussa in the specific task of leading the association.

Once the approach was made in March, it was Moussa's responsibility as leader to inform the group, and to persuade his members, especially the renowned actors and musicians, to return to Markala for the performance. The oral and highly improvisatory nature of *Koteba* and the fact that the story outlines are well known meant that there was hardly any rehearsal immediately before the performance. Also, because the actors had been performing these sketches for a long time, they did not need too much preparation time. Most of them were ready at short notice to get into the bodies and minds of their characters. Once they had been assigned a role or roles for the evening, group members became responsible for providing their own costumes and props. Each instrumentalist is responsible for the storing and maintenance of any instruments that they play, although the association maintains a few items of clothing and some musical instruments.

According to Moussa, the group had a production meeting on the morning of the day of the performance to discuss and agree the performance structure and time of starting. After which they all went away to sort out their costumes and props. They scheduled to meet up again at the *ton* compound in the afternoon to set the stage, sweep and clean the space, erect a changing room, sort out the simple electrical connection needed since it was going to be a night performance, and arrange for a few chairs for the spectators. By 3 p.m. most had returned to the *ton* house, where we joined them as they began work. While the stage was being set, final checks were also made on costumes, make-up, props and musical instruments which members had brought from their homes. Even though this was the responsibility of each individual, the group discussed each item of costume, prop or instrument. But Moussa and his assistants had overall supervision and approval. This process of scrutiny and approval of every aspect of the performance ensured consistency in costume, make-up and props. The group also met after the show to discuss and assess individual performances, and how the whole show had gone. Most of the post-performance meetings took place at the guesthouse where we were staying and we were invited to join in the after performance analysis and discussion. The group worked until 6.30 p.m. when we dispersed, to reconvene at 8 p.m. We went away for dinner, and for some enthusiasts to catch bits of the Czech-Greece European Championship football match being played that evening. It was the match that had prompted the performance being shifted to later at night than was previously agreed; it was a reminder to me that in most African contexts events govern time and not the other way round, as in many non-African societies.

Publicizing the performance was through traditional word-of-mouth, by *ton* members, relatives and friends. The show was also mentioned on the local FM Radio station as a means of reaching a wider audience. But many heard about the performance closer to the start time when, at about

8 p.m., the musicians began playing as an invitation to the spectators and as a guide to the venue. The musicians used it also as a warm-up session and a chance to practice some of the tunes and the core music for later.

The last roles to be assigned were the ushers who controlled how the spectators entered the performance enclosure and took their seats. They arranged for the children to sit in front, ensuring no one sat on or obstructed access to the stage. Because no gate fee was charged for this performance – as is the practice in other indigenous African societies, Bamana people usually do not expect to be asked to buy tickets before watching a show – it was essential that order was created and maintained throughout the evening. Some of the ushers became stagehands once the performance was under way. And when the show was over, they helped guide the spectators out of the compound; they also assisted in dismantling the lights and dressing room and clearing up.

While the spectators were filing in, the actors began arriving to go into their changing room, immediately behind a park bench, on which the musicians were later to sit. Inside the changing room, there were a few other non-performing members to act as assistants, make-up persons and stagehands before and during the performance. One group member acted as the 'stage manager' – he coordinated, brought and removed items on and from the stage. Despite not being 'professionals', it was impressive to see how efficiently responsibilities were carried out, without any disruption to the evening's performance programme.

Training

As with most other indigenous African performances and theatres, no formal training is required. Two main ingredients combine to propel people into either taking part or becoming regular members of a *koteba-ton*. The first is an innate talent for acting or organizing theatre; this is known as *nyankoro* or the ability to recognize and reproduce comic situations through mimicry. The second is a love of performance itself since hardly any income or social capital accrues from being an excellent performer. In fact, among the Bamana, the artist, especially the actor, is regarded as a gifted vagabond or outcast. Possession of *nyankoro* gave the performer an ambiguous status: privilege and marginality, loathing and admiration. He is a person despised for being lazy, a playboy and drunkard and yet admired for his ability to entertain and tell truth to the society (see Chapter 4, p. 135 for attitudes to the *jali* in Mandinka society). This ambiguity also extends to the fact that the satiric skits on the one hand put pressure on people to conform to the norms of society, but on the other reflects the rebelliousness of the youth against the dominance of the elders. Performance, therefore, is something people do because they love to, and not because they have been trained or are paid to. All the actors at the Markala performance had main occupations from which they made their living.

Unlike the Mandinka *Jaliya* tradition where a recognized period of informal training takes place, or the Hausa *Bori* and masquerade in which an initiation signals a process or moment of becoming accepted into the *Bori* cult or the masquerade fraternity, the *Koteba* has none of these formal or informal markers of entry. Belonging to the *ton* is automatic once a person attains the age when his or her age-mates (contemporaries) are expected to be accepted as the youngest members. Within the association, individuals become involved in a lot of *ton* activities, theatre being one of these. But unlike the Igbo masquerade theatre tradition in which once a boy becomes initiated, he can then have periods of intensive training and rehearsals in preparation for specific performances, the *Koteba* seems to operate mainly on observed learning – younger members of the *ton* would have grown up watching older members perform, and they will also be very familiar with the sketches and characters. The individual brings together all these years of observation and their talent and improvisatory skills in a performance. Informal discussion sessions prior to a performance are when more experienced actors pass on advice or suggestions to beginners. The troupe members during the pre-performance meeting in early evening freely swapped suggestions between themselves. Also, comments and reactions from the audience are often taken on board and worked into subsequent performances.

The most important element of a *Kote-tlon* performance is the improvisation – how a performer brings their mastery of the character into a relationship with other characters in performance situations. The audience already knows about the situations and skits. But what they do not know and are most interested in seeing is how individual characters achieve their objectives within the performance situations. For instance, the situation of polygamy and the conflict between 'warring' co-spouses is well known, but in Sketch One, how Koke, Mariamoufin, Nyebaje and Jeneba recreated this scenario was entirely up to them, including what they chose to wear, what they said or did, and how long the scene lasted. This is what the audience watches because it is always new and often different each time, often incorporating current anecdotal material. The same could be said of the Wankyu, Jeneba and Koke scene. In the scene I watched he had just come back from Beijing, China, but I was told that he usually was from Paris, London, New York, Brussels or Amsterdam. But the fact that China is fast becoming a major economic power attracting migrants from all over the world has found its way into the plays, and this is one of the strongest evidence of the contemporaneity of *Koteba*, and why like the *Mmonwu* theatre, *Jaliya* or *Bori*, it can never become dated.

Staging technique

Space and atmosphere

The *ton* meeting compound was enclosed by four walls with only one entrance and measured about one hundred by sixty feet. There were no fixed structures or buildings within it. The stage itself was just a slightly elevated square space on the left side of the compound as one walked in. It measured approximately twenty-four feet by sixteen feet, and was covered at the back by a high wall which kept the noise from the adjacent compound out. A large piece of white cloth was tied across the left side of the stage to screen the changing room – two assistants lifted this for the actors each time they came out or went in. However, the flexibility of the *Koteba* form, as well as the adaptability of the performers, makes it possible for it to be performed anywhere – on street corners, in the village square, school halls, hotel courtyards, or private compounds. This is also enhanced by the technical economy of *Koteba*, which does not require too much scenery and props. The actors informed me that they simply adapt their performance to suit the space in which it is being staged (**Fig. 5.6**).

The main performance space was left uncluttered to enable the high physicality which the action and roles demanded. As was evident in the three sketches, the tendency was for dialogue and action to in the end transform into wrestling and fisticuffs and the empty stage enabled this to happen relatively safely. Most transitions between scenes were marked by actors leaving the stage kicking and punching each other: Mariamoufin and Nyebaje in Sketch One, Koke and Wankyu in Two, Leper and Sarakole and Sarakole and Superintendent in the final sketch. The deliberately uncluttered stage also left narrative gaps which the spectators creatively filled as they imagined for themselves the worlds being suggested through the descriptive dialogue and stylized actions. Even though *Koteba* is drama – in the sense that Finnegan advocated (see p. 6) – it is still drama which is deliberately left sketchy so that actors and spectators can together complete the details; and in this way, audience participation is ensured.

While the costume and action approximate as closely as possible to the real human situations and characters being represented, the set and make-up were rather symbolic and suggestive. No attempt was made to recreate actual places. For instance, Koke's home in Sketch One and Leper's roadside squat in Sketch Two were the same spot on the stage space, but

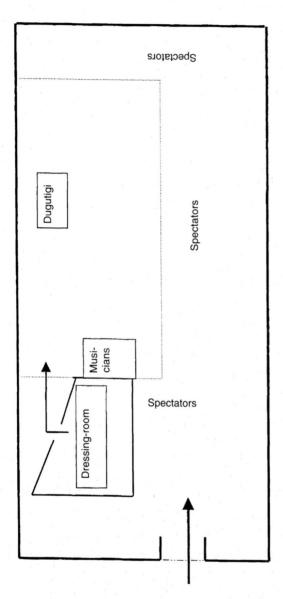

Figure 5.6 Diagram of *Ton* compound and stage.

the two locations were suggested simply by two different kinds of mat. The special staff and a mat on which he sat represented Dugutigi's place and the performers constantly orientated themselves to it as they performed. Distance was usually suggested by the characters circling the stage, the longer the distance the more times the stage was circled. Also the pace of the circling was used to suggest the distance being covered – when Sarakole and his donkey walked towards Bamako, and also when they were joined by Leper – their pace of circling was slow, whereas when Koke in Sketch Two went out to look for food for his chicken, his pace was brisk. The huts in Koke's compound were also suggested by different sizes and colours of mat – the bigger and more colourful one for Koke and his favourite wife, Nyebaje, and a dreary tiny one for out-of-favour Mariamoufin and her daughter, Jeneba. The decor and comfort of each hut was further conveyed through the dialogue.

Every bit of the stage was used, and there was constant transformation of the space into different locales, depending on what was happening at the time and point. One or two spots on stage were fixed, the rest changed as needed. The slightly elevated stage ensured that a demarcation was created and maintained between audience and performer. This small distance was constantly annulled by the reality of the performer–spectator engagement and interaction, but, despite this, the elevation created a tension which at all times was a reminder that it was a performance – with neither party physically crossing over to the other's space. This was quite unlike the physical relationship in Igbo masking performances where such periodic crossing over was implicitly factored into the performance dynamic. Even though it did not readily give the spectators direct access to the perform-ance area and vice versa, the actors/characters were still very close to the audience. The characters would walk up to the audience when they wanted or needed to communicate directly to them, or wanted the latter to join in the singing or clapping. This closeness and openness was achieved by the semi-arena staging style of the performance and, crucially by the fact that the 'stage' was not that removed from the audience space. The two areas were on the same level and, even though there was a slight suggestion of where one ended and the other began, the line demarcation had an air of impermanence and permeability which allowed the first row of seats to begin right where the stage stopped.

Make-up and costume

Make-up was used mainly to symbolically transform the actor into the character. At Markala, it consisted of white chalk from the beds and banks of the River Niger nearby, ground and mixed with water into a slightly thick paste. The actors covered their faces with this but, unlike *Kathakali* performers in India, the make-up was not intended to hide the identity of the performer, since underneath they were easily recognizable. Instead, the white face conventionally signaled the change from performer to character, that is, from reality to fiction. The make-up was not changed throughout, even though the actors performed different characters in the course of the night's performance. Costumes marked changes in character, while the faces remained the same throughout. Moussa Diakhite played many roles such as Lead Singer, Nyebaje, one of Koke's friends and Leper and he wore the same make-up, but underwent three significant costume changes. Make-up was not used to suggest character, age, gender or ethnicity either. However, throughout the evening the actors, some more than others, put on more make-up to replace what was washed away by sweat. Make-up acted merely as a symbolic mask or disguise for the actors, behind which they could perform many of the ridiculous roles and antics that the comic characters got up to in the sketches. But at the same, all of them said that they did not want the disguise to be so complete that their individual identities were erased. They still wanted the audience to be able to recognize and appreciate their individual performance skills.

While in principle the characters' costumes were meant to reflect those prevalent in Bamana society, there was also an element of exaggeration, in keeping with the temper of the *Koteba* itself. While clearly illustrating both social standing, ethnic origin, gender and occupation, the costumes also endeavoured to achieve a degree of distance from the everyday, so that both spectators and performers were able to stand away from the characters, and laugh at them because they had been made the 'other'.

Because the characters were stock-characters, costume helped to make them easily recognizable to the audience. The props they had and what they wore gave them away as soon as they entered. Sarakole's headgear, long walking stick, assortment of pots, pans, spoons and sleeping material immediately suggested he was a nomad. The donkey by his side reinforced this as it also indicated his ethic origin. Wankyu's costume, for instance, was a mass of contradiction – a European coat on an African trousers with a scarf to go with these. He was a mishmash of different cultures, neither sitting comfortably with the other, a fact that was also reflected in his actions. And when he played the donkey, he was marked by the absence of most of what he had worn previously and by a pair of rubber slippers for the donkey's ears. Costumes served as a signifier of character change for the actor who played Koke and Police Sergeant, and for the very versatile actor who played a dancer and one of the two gossips in the *bamuko* dance scene, Mariamoufin in Sketch One, one of Koke's friends in Sketch Two, and Sarakole in Sketch Three. Playing Mariamoufin, he went through two costume changes – first as the despised first wife and later as the very beautiful, large-bosomed and self-confident Mariamoufin. It would have been difficult to effect all these transformations without the help of costumes.

In general, there was a tendency to use exaggeration in both acting and costume as a means of characterization. This was most pronounced in the female characters whose breasts, hips and buttocks were in most cases extravagantly stuffed to achieve the 'feminine' look (**Fig. 5.7**). Two other characters with exaggerated physiognomies were the two police officers – the Sergeant had a protruding belly, while the Superintendent

Figure 5.7 Mariamoufin and Nyebaje (Moussa Diakhite).

wore a heavily stuffed shirt and largely bloated trouser legs and foot-wear. The overall effect was caricature, which is an underlying tone of this theatre. The audience was invited to take serious note of these char-acters and their behaviours even while laughing at them. While it was in fact difficult to identify with any of the characters, each was accurate enough to strike a chord of recognition in the audience which enabled the latter to critically engage with the images and actions being represented on the stage.

What struck me most about the performance was the economical nature of the theatre itself. Most of the materials used, including the costumes, were everyday home items, sometimes modified and temporarily pressed into theatrical service. The performers, who played the female parts, simply borrowed from their wives, sisters or girlfriends. Moussa – the group leader who played Nyebaje, Leper, singer, dancer, and one of Koke's friends – in real life has two wives and he freely helped himself from their wardrobes for his female parts. Part of the fun, and for which the female characters drew most laughter from the audience, was the recognition of whose clothes a particular character was wearing. The troupe has no costumes exclusively intended for performances. The male characters appear in a variety of traditional Bamana male attire – most usually made to look worn. The only other costume of note was the donkey's – a role performed brilliantly by Moussa's younger brother. The donkey, practically speaking, was bare bodied, with a strip of cloth tied round his waist. For ears, two brown rubber slippers were tied around the actor's ears and across his forehead. He had padding for his knees as he had to walk on all fours all the time. The slippers around the ears were the most suggestive and effective costume. He had the audience in stitches of laughter all the time he was on stage, especially in his attempts to deliver two-legged donkey kicks to Leper and the two corrupt police officers.

Props

A variety of props were used in the performance and a property person silently and almost surreptitiously moved in and out to remove items during the performance, sometimes bringing in something characters needed or taking out some that had been forgotten by the performers in their occa-sionally chaotic exits from the stage. Although some real props were brought on to the stage, most were mimed or suggested by the actors. Props used included cooking pots and pans, a sweeping broom, a basket for Jeneba, three walking sticks, a water bottle for Sarakole, a small shoulder bag for Wankyu, mats, an imaginary mortar, rope, cane for the donkey, whistle, police officers' staff, another longer staff for Dugutigi, handkerchiefs for the dancers, scarves, a Fulani raffia/grass hat, calabash bowl, animal skin bags for the elders, fly whisks and so on. For the first two sketches, not many were used, even though they were all on show as part of the characters' costumes, for example Sarakole's water bottle, cup, walking stick and grass hat. The use of the props was flexible; one item sometimes serving a variety of purposes: a 'pestle' used by Mariamoufin in Sketch One later became a walking stick when the same actor played Sarakole in Sketch Three, and Wankyu's slippers in Sketch Two became the donkey's ears in Sketch Three.

Flexibility and mobility of the props were also reflected by the group of dancers at the beginning and Koke's companions in Sketch Two. Koke and his friends had goatskin bags and walking sticks; some of them had a few odds and ends, including chewing twigs and small sticks which they carried on their persons all the time, except when they had to put all these mobile props down to do the final vigorous dance around the 'mysterious speaking drum'. They picked them up again immediately the dance was finished and carried on with the scene.

Themes and characters

Kote-tlon performances usually are situational comedies in which a range of social themes are explored. In general, because the characters are stereo-typical, situations and themes are treated in a stereotypical manner. The stereotypical nature of the characters is also responsible for the way the audiences respond during performances. The responses at the Markala performance were as expected – passionate engagement and a willing-ness to contribute when asked to – and remained consistent throughout. Characters who have communal approval, such as Mariamoufin in Sketch One or Sarakole in Sketch Three, enjoyed the approval of the whole audience, irrespective of what they did. Those, like the ungrateful Leper in Sketch Three or the fickle and foolish Koke in One and Two, were derided and booed most of the time. There did not seem to be a ques-tion of some spectators supporting a character, while others disapproved of them. Even when gender or generational issues were being explored, such as the marital situation, or the father-daughter-lover scene, the audience was never split on any of these issues because of the seeming apoliticized treatment.

On the whole, however, there was a condescending acceptance of the characters as flawed but likeable. The spectators felt superior to them because they felt that the weaknesses and mistakes of the latter were quite beneath them; most audience members questioned saw the characters as extremely foolish, naive, selfish or incompetent. But they were still liked because the spectators were able to recognize elements of themselves in the caricatures. This acceptance and denial of oneness with the characters was made possible by the technique of comic distancing achieved by the clownish white faces, outlandish clothes and stylized acting. Also because of the one-dimensional nature of the characters and thorough knowledge of the stories, the audience seemed to know what to expect from each of them and so their responses were determined in advance. They seemed to know the characters more than the characters knew themselves because, no matter what the situations were, the outcomes were always predictable. Since characters hardly deviated from type, the audience remained comfortable in their knowledge of them.

The three sketches in Markala explored a variety of themes, with each handling a multiple number of themes. Sketch One was about a family of four who arrived in a new town to settle. It explored the classic theme of rivalry and favouritism in a polygamous relationship. Usually the arrival of a new wife almost always signals the sidelining of the first or older wife. In the play the new wife refused to do anything and instead played her husband like a musical instrument and a weapon against the older wife. The husband, totally blinded by his amorousness and desire to please his new wife, fell into the trap, but got his just desserts once the first wife left him and the new wife refused to do any of the house chores. In the end, he was brought to his senses, but not before the two women had made a complete ass of him in public.

Sketch Two explored a number of themes, ranging from filial deception and disobedience, the gullibility of an inexperienced village girl, to the brazen and comic artificiality of the been-to who had completely given up his African name to assume a Chinese one, as Wankyu had done. As in the preceding sketch, these themes were treated in a comic way so that the audience laughed at the foibles of the characters. The purpose was to make others refrain from such absurd behaviour. Sketch Three explored the themes of ethnocentrism, selfishness, ingratitude and corruption. The story of the naively kind stranger or outsider imposed upon by an ungrateful Leper, with the support and collaboration of two very corrupt police officers is popular with Bamana audiences. Sarakole, out of kindness, allowed Leper to ride on his donkey, and the latter, apart from beating the donkey mercilessly contrary to the wishes of the owner, turned round to make a brazen claim of ownership of the donkey for himself. The corrupt police officers arranged an ownership test, which they then proceeded to openly manipulate by preventing the donkey from following his rightful master. But the last laugh belonged to Sarakole, as he cunningly managed to get the better of the two policemen. He got his donkey back, the donkey having almost kicked the life out of Leper instead of following or carrying him as intended by the policemen. There was harmony in the end and justice, in the eyes of the spectators, was done.

The plays, in general, started out with harmony and a state of equilibrium, but in the course of the action, this state was severely threatened by the actions of some of the characters – disharmony and dis-equilibrium reigned momentarily – but in the end a state of harmony and equilibrium was restored. The plays seemed to suggest through this structure that these momentary disruptions of harmony were necessary to enable society learn and then return to calm, all the wiser for the experience and knowledge which these brought.

There are a host of stereotyped characters in the *Kote-tlon*, but the inherent flexibility of the form enables each *koteba-ton* to devise and incorporate these characters into scenarios of their choice. Each performing group creates and maintains a repertory of its own sketches on existing characters, but is always on the look out for new story lines and characters. The stereotype, to a large extent, determines the structure or plot of the plays. However, although the characters are very well known to the spectators the structuring of how these characters are portrayed or the kind of situational interaction between different characters is the responsibility of the group and the individual actors performing the roles. In effect, although circumscribed by the characters, each group retains the freedom to pair characters up and develop dramatic situations for them to play. Thus, a character such as Leper appears in many plays and in many situations. In Pelengana, a small village on the outskirts of Segou, one of his popular sketches is the one between him and the Blind Man, in which the Leper has an adulterous relationship with Blind Man's wife, right there in front of him. The essence of Leper is his ingratitude to those that have done him good or helped him. All his sketches revolve around this key objective, irrespective of who he is performing with or against, or whatever situations he is placed in. And his scenes end with his customary comic fight in which he just barely manages to hold his ground, despite his obvious severe handicap of not having full use of his fingers and arms. His fast mouth is his greatest weapon in dealing with his opponents. Blind Man is basically a kind person, who is usually put upon by people who wish to take advantage of his lack of sight – but he still manages to sense things and deal with these adversaries of his. He is similar to Sarakole whose kindness was grossly abused by the ingrate, Leper.

Music and dance

Even though *Koteba* performances are prinicipally dialogue driven, music and dance feature in equal measure as part of the structure of this theatre.

A typical *Kote-tlon* performance is in two parts: the first section of a night's programme is made up of a sequence of music and dance. This first section is called *kotedon* or *kotebadon*, while the main dramatic part is referred to as *niogolon*. It is during the danced part that the *koteba* or concentric circles formation from which the theatre derives its name is displayed. The Markala performance, however, had just one circle of dancers/actors enclosing the musicians because of the number of performers involved. It was clear from this introductory entrance that music and dance were going to be key structural elements of the night's performance. The songs and dance routines were definitely codes that informed the spectators about the specific sketches that the group had chosen to present for the night. The first song and dance to start the night programme off began once the musicians and actors emerged from their dressing room:

> They are here!
> The actors of the *Koteba* are here
> You pass your time beside another person
> Beloved child
> Welcome us
> Welcome us with the drum and the *balafon*
> Only a noble child keeps his promises.

During the singing, dancing and the formation, the characters were vaguely suggested for the audience to begin to piece together the possible sketches to follow. Following on from this dance, two of the dancers detached themselves to engage the audience in a banter which lasted approximately three minutes. They then asked the audience if they had a leader and as the latter conferred among themselves, the two announced that they had appointed one for them. At which point they gleefully skipped across to a lone figure sitting on a mat at the opposite end of the stage to acknowledge him as Dugutigi, did a comic dance round him and then ran off to allow the first sketch to be under way. The musicians played them out with this comic dance and song:

> Only one husband!
> Me, I can't marry only one husband
> During the night
> The night began
> The husband cries like a donkey
> The donkey is useless to me!

The song is ostensibly about marital infidelity, but at the same time it is about the fact of one husband for more than one wife, which it is believed leaves the husband too tired and useless in meeting the sexual needs of his wives. The song was also a hint to the Leper, Sarakole and donkey scene of Sketch Three. Into this song and the comic antics of the duo, walked Koke, Mariamoufin, Nyebaje, and Jeneba. It is significant that Nyebaje sings the solo (perhaps suggesting her domineering nature and role in the sketch), while the other three, and later the audience, provide the chorus. All through the sketch, comic songs and dances punctuated the dramatic action – sometimes elaborating on what was going on, and sometimes signaling the end, such as when Mariamoufin and Nyebaje fought to signal the end of the first play, or Wankyu and Koke to end the second. In all three sketches the fights, dances and music were used to mark transitions within and between scenes and between plays. The big fight between Sarakole and Superintendent was used to bring the play and the entire performance to a climactic conclusion.

Music and dance did not just act as transition or end points, they sometimes constituted the dramatic action, such as when Mariamoufin and Nyebaje were pounding millet. The conflict between the two women came out quite clearly in the lyrics of the songs they sang, in the manner they pounded the millet, and in the staccato rhythmic accompaniment to the music provided by the musicians. The frenetic tempo of this scene was also conveyed by the energetic clapping from the spectators, who knew the songs very well and were always ready to join in when called upon by the actors. Single actions, such as kicks, punches, slaps, and even slight gestures and body movements, were punctuated or echoed by the drums or by supporting claps and whoops from the spectators. It is in fact hard to imagine the *Koteba* without music and dance, which work in perfect balance with the dialogue to provide a scintillating theatre of images and sounds, a theatre in which each medium can sometimes become the main transmitter of the dramatic action.

Performer–spectator encounter and interaction

As with the other African theatre forms being studied in this book, the *Koteba* is a totally participatory theatre and the audience at Markala were enthusiastic and vociferous in their engagement with the performance. Their knowledge of the characters and the story lines, of course, gave them a firm critical standpoint from which to engage with and analyze the show – they must have seen good and the not so good renditions before. Thus each new performance is measured in terms of these past presentations of the same or similar material. But having said that, a similar critical attitude is adopted by the performers in terms of what level of contribution they expect from the spectators. Because African performances, in general, operate on the understanding that a performance is a collaboration between performer and spectator – that is to say that a performance does not exist until it encounters its audience – the success or failure of any performance encounter becomes as much the responsibility of the performer as it is that of the spectator. Although this is not a uniquely African phenomenon, what is unique is the immediacy and vociferousness of the audience members in response to what is going on in front of them. This vociferousness is both collective and individual; the audience, although a group bound together by a common purpose, is a number of individual persons making their own judgements. They see themselves as an integral part of the performance. The performers therefore expect them to fully play their part – through their interjections, clapping, singing, sometimes dancing, exclamations and laughter.

In fact, watching the Markala audience arrive and take their places was like watching a performance. It was animated, slow and deliberate, boisterous and noisy (especially the younger members of the audience some of whom ran round the space, even on to the stage, to try out a few comic antics of their own before the main draw). As they filed in, people chatted to those nearest to them, or called out loudly to friends further away, handshaking and backslapping. Mothers carried sleeping babies on their backs, and not being able to find seat, because of the limited number of chairs available, negotiated with or tried to persuade younger members to give up theirs. There were also people milling around in the background – young men and women chatting each other up, while they waited for the first sign that the show was about to begin. It was definitely an occasion, and people came to see as much as to be seen – as was pointed out in the introductory chapter, the constant shift in position and role between spectators and performers is a major characteristic of indigenous African performance (see pp. 3–4). The atmosphere was good-natured and expectant, but once the drums sounded, it all went quiet very quickly. And as soon as the dancers came out and began singing and dancing, the spectators joined in straightaway with clapping, and snatches of the theme songs.

Having done the opening song and dance routine, the actors returned to the dressing room, and the spectators to their chatting and so on. The audience's rhythmic clapping and a new music and song welcomed the actors' second entrance. The song over, two of the dancers detached themselves to have a direct engagement with the spectators in a question and answer session. It was obvious from these early exchanges that the audience expected to be fully involved, and thus were pleased to be acknowledged and included by the performers. And in spite of the unending chatter which always returned whenever nothing was happening on stage, neither masked nor blunted the alertness and attentiveness of the audience once action

Figure 5.8 Koteba audience watches attentively.

returned. In between their chatter, eyes constantly darted to the dressing room entrance, and ears primed to pick up the first music cue. Even the children were as good at this as the adults. The entrance of Koke and his family for the first sketch drew great laughter and animated comments from the audience, some actually calling and teasing the cross-dressers. But once the scene opened these stopped immediately and there was rapt attention as everyone became intensely tuned to the action, keeping quiet when it was expected and really letting go when the scene demanded such a response. As if by an unspoken contract, the actors always allowed the spectators their interval or space for interjection – waiting for them to stop before proceeding with the action. Between the spectators and performers there was great intimacy and a shared understanding of roles, responsibilities and expectations (**Fig. 5.8**).

Social functions

Although ostensibly a theatre that brings immense entertainment and joy to its audience, the satiric sketches of the *Koteba*, like most traditional theatre and performances all over Africa, perform other social functions. *Koteba* is '*le grand escargot bambara*', the big Bambara snail which symbolically carries on its shell the entire Bamana world and experience. This graphically captures the thoughts and feelings of the people who produce and view this theatre. Its scope is wide and its canvass is broad – a theatre in which all aspects of society and life are periodically subjected to scrutiny. Its satiric and comic mode, coupled with its sometimes larger than life style of acting make it an easily accessible but effective weapon in highlighting and correcting anti-social behaviours or challenging the domineering authority of the elders.

At a more socio-political level, *Kote-tlon* sketches provide a context for conflict management between two generations. The elders control all socio-economic and political processes – fathers still have executive and moral powers over the affairs of their children and wives. They decide and direct every aspect of their lives, including whom, when and how their children marry. They also control the material resources, with the result that sons work for their fathers, who then provide them with sustenance, shelter and other needs. Bamana sons are not expected to and neither do they disobey or challenge their fathers. The sketches provide the youth with the only avenue for dissent and an instrument with which to challenge or speak back. The plays may appear hilariously funny, but they are not as innocent as they seem. That is why the elders keep away, because the last thing a self-respecting Bamana elder wants is to 'lose face' in public, by being the object of laughter or mirth for the community.

On the surface, therefore, it would seem that the entertainment was the most important element or goal of the *Koteba* sketches. One saw from watching the plays in Markala, from the acting and extremely farcical nature of the situations that the performers took the spectators' amusement and enjoyment very seriously. Listening to and speaking with audience members afterwards, and hearing them recollect and make cross-references between the characters and certain individuals, behaviours and situations from their community, there could be little doubt that the messages of the performance got through and audience members were thinking about the issues raised. This is the *Koteba* tradition – a theatre designed to enable Bamana society to critically reflect upon itself from time to time. It does not preach to its audience, nor do the characters assume a position of knowledge or superiority in relation to the audience. They accord the spectator creative intelligence and moral competence to sift through the satiric bumble, waffle and baseness to the ethical issues embedded in the dramatic action, songs, music and dances.

Being a member of a *Koteba* audience was an uplifting experience, because for almost two hours, one was in the company of exuberant but accomplished performers – part clowns, part vagabonds, yet human enough to make one feel happy and grateful to be human and alive. Even the Leper in his odiousness elicited feelings of warmth and a few smiles from the audience – he was more like a likeable rogue, a part played excellently by the accomplished Moussa Diakhite. This theatre was, like its owners, the Bamana, very friendly, welcoming, and giving, supporting the point made earlier in this book about the mutual affectivity between cultures and their performances (see p. 21). The memory of watching and being part of it, of meeting its weird but delightful characters, is as fresh and endearing now as it was at that first encounter on a not brightly-lit stage in Markala in June 2004.

6   Conclusion

This study has touched on key theoretical issues and debates about drama, performance and theatre in Sub-Saharan Africa. Having looked at four examples of indigenous African performances, interesting facts have emerged. One was the misconception among scholars about drama, theatre and performance in Africa. Foreign scholars encountering indigenous African performances analysed them using Western European dramatic criteria. The misreading was repeated and reinforced by African scholars who continue to use the same critical framework to analyse performances that are clearly not drama. This study, however, looked into conceptions of performance and theatre found in African cultures: did drama exist in Africa before contact with Europe, and what are drama, theatre and performance perceived to be by African peoples. In answering these conceptual questions, the study showed that the indiscriminate interchanging of the word 'drama' with 'theatre' and 'performance' had been responsible for the confusion surrounding most discussions of performance in Africa.

One major fact revealed by this investigation is that indigenous performances and theatres in Africa are still very much alive today as they have always been throughout the continent's history. These performances still have their core audiences flocking to come and watch them, while attracting newer ones in the process. The indigenous performances continue robustly alongside the European influenced literary theatre, strongly challenging African theatre scholarship that oftentimes differentiates between these two forms, by using the terms 'traditional' and 'modern' respectively. These two terms are misleading since both traditions are contemporaneous with each other, and both in their respective ways address issues of tradition and modernity. Besides, the indigenous forms, while not clinging on to any sense of aesthetic purity, have kept their development paths firmly rooted in their native cultures, unlike the hybrid literary theatre which has borrowed from various sources in search of its own identity. And while the literary theatre has increasingly borrowed from the indigenous theatre, the latter does not show any awareness of the former, let alone borrow from it. Even the *Kote-tlon* comedies, which are the closest to the literary dramatic tradition, do not show any evidence of being aware of the latter. Nothing in indigenous performances – costume, props, make-up, dialogue and acting style – show any influence from the staging techniques of the western influenced literary theatre.

Performance and theatre are forms and contexts of cultural expression whereby societies and cultures articulate and interrogate their identities and values. The cultures studied have developed forms that satisfy their artistic and social needs and do not need to become like any others, as the evolutionist scholars advocate: their difference from other performances and their uniqueness and rootedness in the respective African cultures give them their identities. Their functions, the aesthetic perceptions and expectations of their makers and viewers, provide the inspiration for these performances. Each theatre or performance operates within its own aesthetic framework and principles, and generates its own performative, descriptive and analytic vocabularies. To understand a culture and its performance, according to Turner (1990), requires patient engagement with its grammar and vocabulary, which is the approach adopted in this book.

History and change in indigenous performances

Change has been so subtle in indigenous African performances that, on the surface, they seem to have remained the same while, in fact, aesthetic revisions have been taking place all the time. The four performances studied show that each has, in its own way, coped with the pressures of modernity and post-modernity, as well as with advances in technology. Their eclectic nature has enabled each performance to accommodate the movement of history, as each has had to contend with external forces, such as colonization, Christianity and Islam. And internally they have had to deal with factors such as the impact of western style education and the gradual erosion of autochthonous communities. In *Bori, Mmonwu,* and *Koteba* performances this was achieved through a systematic and selective incorporation and assimilation of the foreign intrusions as performances expanded their range of characters and themes. *Bori,* for instance, added Muslim, Arab and colonial European characters, while *Mmonwu* and *Koteba* created colonial police officers, as well as European administrators and tourists and native 'been-tos'. Negotiation also took the form of an increase in the number of occasions and events in which performances are presented, such as Christmas, Easter, national feast days, state arts festivals and political rallies. And because contexts affect themes in indigenous theatres, most have expanded their thematic scopes, moral universes and characters to accommodate the changing contexts in which they are now performed.

By adapting their themes to accommodate new experiences, the performances have managed to remain relevant to their respective communities, retaining their functional roles as critical and aesthetic mirrors for society, as well as providing sites for the societies to confront and negotiate social and cultural revisions and change.

The performances dealt with the problem posed by the urban drift in the first instance by continually expanding and renewing their performer base. In *Mmonwu* areas new male members who move into the communities are encouraged to become initiated into the masquerade fraternity. *Bori* groups eagerly recruit and initiate anyone interested in joining a *Bori* compound, irrespective of where they come from. The mobility of *Bori* and individual cult groups make access easy for new members wishing to join, especially in the urban centres. And in *Jaliya* people who are not born into *jali* families are easily accepted if they decide to become *jalolu*. Secondly, and of equal significance, because most of these societies have, in spite of urbanization and modern education, retained their underlying communal ethos, it has been easy for individuals to keep their communal loyalties, irrespective of where they live and their level of education. Among the Igbo, for instance, parents still take their young sons back to their home towns or villages to be initiated into the masquerade fraternity – this applies to both Christians and adherents of the indigenous religions. The crucial thing is that once initiated membership is for life, even when individuals are so old that they can no longer physically take part in the performances. The same is true of *Bori* adepts and *jalolu*; individuals belong to their groups for life. Every Bamana person becomes a member of their local *ton* once they get to the age of fifteen irrespective of their level of education and place of residence. Women remain members until they get married and men until they reach the age of forty-five. Even after that they continue to act as advisers and supervisors during rehearsals and performances.

But while quick to respond to current pressures and trends, indigenous African performances have held on to their original structures and aesthetic principles, adapting new or foreign materials and responding to the constantly changing social conditions of their respective cultures, on their own terms. The motivations, functions and the processes by which these performances are made and viewed have remained the same. *Mmonwu* and *Koteba* have refused to allow women to become actors, in spite of the inexcusable anachronism such exclusion represents, when in most other things societies have moved on to bring about equality between men and women. Asked why women never performed the masquerades, the elders' responses ranged from an evasive 'that is the way it has always been' to 'women do not really want to cover themselves with such filthy rags'. Only one elder admitted that perhaps one of the reasons masquerades came about in Igboland was that the men wanted an institution and instrument with which to control the women and so logically the latter could not be let into its secrets. At *Koteba* performances, women provide the main bulk of the audience as well as a good number of the characters, yet they are excluded from representing themselves. These two performances inadvertently reflect the male dominance of their societies; and if there is any area in which these indigenous performances need change, it is this and not the clamour by the evolutionists for *Mmonwu* to develop plots, storylines and individual narratives (see p. 12).

The relationship between a theatrical performance, or, indeed, any form of artistic expression, and its cultural context is a series of mediations and counter-mediations between them. The four performances studied show that they constantly engage with, modify, and are in turn modified by their social and cultural contexts. *Mmonwu* performances are aesthetic mirrors by which the Igbo examine themselves and make adjustments when necessary. But in changing society *Mmonwu* has changed over the years as it has had to cope with new experiences. *Koteba* has done the same thing for Bamana society, as has *Bori* for Hausa culture. The *jali*'s art and function has equally changed as Mandinka society has changed – some old roles have ceased to be relevant or applicable and new ones have emerged to replace them. Each performance is a product of its environment, but, equally, each contributes in the shaping and re-shaping of that environment. It is this dialectical relationship which helps the performances to remain socially and aesthetically relevant within their respective cultures and societies.

Common grounds

The four performances studied have a host of characteristics in common. These include a shared notion of performance and theatre. In African cultures, what usually marks an activity or event as performance or theatre is the presence and interaction of three key elements: performer, space and spectator. Such events or activities usually take place outside normal time and in designated or accidentally found spaces. They occur when performers meet and engage with spectators and together they define the space of their encounter. Their roles also interchange from time to time because of the fluidity of the space. Performance events usually involve what Eugenio Barba (1991) refers to as 'extra-daily behaviour' (pp. 9–10) and Schechner (1985) calls 'restored behaviour'. This means that actions and body techniques from daily life are employed, not for their communicative ability but because of their capacity to carry coded information. Equally significant is the fact that performances are understood to be events that are done for show and therefore ultimately for the non-performers. However, this other is seen as being an integral part of the performance-making process, and comes to the show to be seen as much as to see. This explains why African performances are major social occasions, which can sometimes involve entire communities.

A second similarity is that indigenous African performances are mainly improvisatory. The four performances studied rely on both the improvisation skills of the performers and the willingness of the spectators to contribute. Nothing is pre-packaged since the actors are greatly dependent on the spectators' contributions in order to generate a performance text. Particularly for *Mmonwu, Bori* and *Koteba*, this means that performances are character-led and it is the combined efforts of the character/actor and the audience that eventually gives rise to a story or plot. Even *Jaliya*, which usually has foundation texts to work from, is as un-predetermined as the other three because the *jali* also has to rely on the patrons' response to determine in which direction and how far to take his or her performance. What is surprising and quite remarkable is that such theatre traditions in which the processes of training the actors are mainly informal should rely so much on the acting abilities of the performers. The practice of leaving performance encounters open-ended and free of any pre-contact content is responsible for keeping African indigenous theatres and performance always fresh; they draw audiences because, while the characters may be familiar, the spectators are always in the dark about the stories. Audiences also come because they are excited by and pleased with their contribution in the making of the stories.

African cultures it was found use similar terms to refer to or explain theatre and performance as social and cultural activities. In these cultures, the idea of play is evident in the descriptive terms used for performances which suggests that despite some, such as *Bori, Koteba* and *Mmonwu*, having religious/ritual undertones, the performances are underpinned by a sense of play. The Igbo, for instance, see themselves as 'playing' with their ancestors and spirits through the masquerades; the Hausa are able to establish a playful relationship with their deities during *Bori* possession and trance performances; while the Bamana use the ludic ambience of the *Koteba* satiric sketches to negotiate the social tensions and problems of their society. The *jali*, even though he or she is dealing with 'historical' or mythological facts, equally adopts a playful attitude in his or her relationship with the material and the audience. The pretended anger, exaggerated gestures, flamboyant costumes and loud make-up well known of *jalolu*, are totally recognized by the spectators or patrons as pretence, but they willingly play along and try to placate the *jali* by offering her or him gifts.

Another area in which African indigenous theatres and performances are alike is in the way they are used. Like all art forms in Africa, performances satisfy a variety of social needs, ranging from being used to socialize the young as in *Mmonwu* and *Koteba*, cure the sick as in *Bori*, to acting as collective memory of history as *Jaliya* does for the Mandinka. The four performances showed the centrality of theatre or performance in the lives of various African peoples. While performances provide entertainment for audiences, their other uses include providing spaces and means for the exploration and resolution of individual and communal crises as in *Bori*, *Mmonwu*, and *Koteba*. *Bori* is, however, unique in being an instrument and space for the marginalized in Hausa society to express a shared but oppressed identity. It also allows them to challenge and sometimes subvert the structures of their oppression. Almost all of the performances act as mirrors and a gauge of the pulse of their respective societies. Societies use them to critically examine and assess themselves, and take remedial action should that be found necessary. Some *Bori* and *Mmonwu* performances are redressive acts themselves: not only finding the causes of problems, but actually a means of providing solutions to them. The current use and popularity of theatre-for-development in Africa has developed out of this redressive function of performance and theatre.

The four performances also resembled one another in their styles of staging, their open-air spaces and arena staging style. These two elements combined to provide the flexibility and fluidity which indigenous African theatres demand, both in realization of the actions and in interaction between the spectators and the performers. Fluidity was maintained in all four performances because, in general, spectators at African performances are never expected to be passive, and so for them to fully take part, performances are structured in such a way that barriers, such as the fourth wall and rigidly fixed seating positions, are eliminated or non-existent. Although the *Jaliya Balundo* took place in a hall and there was a raised stage, the other three took place in communal open-air spaces. In the other three theatre traditions there are no designated buildings and the spaces used are usually multi-purpose, only becoming performance spaces at agreed times. Arena staging was used to ensure the flexibility and spatial fluidity already mentioned. But even during the *Balundo*, despite the attempts to separate audience, performer and orchestral spaces, movement between the three areas occurred throughout the performance. In its original context, *Jaliya* is a performance for open spaces and mobile audiences.

The stage space at the *Balundo* was left bare, its elements not too defined or fixed. Props, for instance, were always mobile in their use and signification so that, while at times scene specific, they remained flexible enough to be defined by whatever context in which they were used. In *Bori* and *Mmonwu* this flexibility was slightly reduced because of the highly symbolic nature of the performances. The major advantage of a bare stage was that it helped the suggestive styles of communication characteristic of these African performances by giving the spectators responsibility for deciphering and filling in the gaps left by the performers. The well-informed audience came ready to assist in the creation of meaning, encouraged in this task by the absence or deliberate sketchiness in the performances of storylines or plots.

The impermanence of their settings always gave a distinct feeling that performers and spectators have found each other by accident; there is an element of pretended surprise but with each party genuinely happy and eager to meet and engage with the other. African audiences recognize their important role as the third and final element in the process of performance and take it very seriously. They are therefore vocal when they need to be, supportive or critical as need be, and always letting the performers know how they feel. The performers, in turn, are constantly aware of the presence of the spectators, and therefore orientate their performance with this in mind. In this non-voyeuristic theatre engagement both sides openly play to each other; it is a theatre that is unashamedly theatrical.

A reciprocal respectfulness governed the spectator–performer encounter and relationship. The performers in each of the performance I watched never approached the spectators as if they had prior knowledge or inform-ation of events or situations which they were hoping to communicate, as would have been the case if they had fixed linear plots. And the spectators, for their part, approached the performances mindful and appreciative of the performers' artistic endeavour and integrity. Each went into this rela-tionship accepting that both were going to explore and discover together in a spirit of equal partnership. Both were respectful of each other's role, knowing that neither could exist without the other.

These African indigenous theatre and performance traditions resembled one another in the informality of their training processes. While, on the surface, this sometimes gave the impression of an absence of training, the informality was in reality a reflection of a similar informality in the processes used for the socialization of the young into roles and respons-ibilities in African societies. The seemingly non-structured training may also be a result of the fact that performances, in general, are regarded as non-professional activities that require no specialization. Everybody is believed to be capable of performing at certain moments in their lives (and they do), even though it is accepted that some people do it better than others. Surprisingly though, this recognition has not prompted these African cultures to formalize their methods of training since the perception is that the ability to be a good performer is an innate talent which can be improved through practice, not through any structured process of learning. Performers therefore are expected to learn their art as they learn everything else in life, while doing it.

Some performances, such as *Mmonwu* and *Bori*, require a formal initiation as an entry point into the practice, and from then the members learn their art as they performed. Initiations in themselves do not teach the art of *Bori* or *Mmonwu*, but are keys that admit the young boy or *Bori* patient or novice into the practice of masking or the worship and performance of *Bori* spirits. *Koteba*, although not requiring a specific initiation, still requires performers to become members of their local *ton* and within it to belong to the *kote-ton* (performance) sub-group. Once a member, the young Bamana male begins to informally learn how to perform, by observing, copying and performing. *Jaliya* performers and *Bori* musicians are different as they undergo prolonged training, which, although appearing informal and unstructured, has very obvious and easily identifiable stages. To become a *jali* or a *Bori* musician usually requires a semi-apprenticeship period when the pupil is attached to a master or mistress, even if these are the pupil's parents or other relatives.

The occasions for performances in the four cultures are mainly during communal events, such as festivals, feast days, group celebrations, times of communal crises, and periods of significance to individuals (births, initiations, weddings and funerals being particularly favoured). But festivals are the most frequent contexts, especially for *Mmonwu* and *Koteba*, together with privately sponsored showings, visit of dignitaries to the town, or instances when groups decide to showcase new plays or introduce new characters to the communal repertory. Overall, performances in African cultures are major occasions for those involved, whether as performers, designers or spectators.

Appreciation and assessment of performance is done by both performers and spectators. And as the study has shown, responses and comments were usually instantaneous, with the audience showing their feelings and views while the performance was going on and then continuing their discussions afterwards. *Jaliya*, in particular, demands immediate response from the spectators usually in the form of a gift to the *jali*. *Mmonwu* and *Bori* performers also receive immediate response from the spectators, sometimes in the form of monetary gifts and sometimes by the spectators joining the performers on stage to dance and sing. The *Koteba* audience was the only one which did not offer money instantly to the performers – those who wished to reward the actors did so afterwards – but they too were quick with their comments and show of pleasure when they felt an actor had performed well or an act had been done particularly well. After each performance, the performers had a post-performance cooling down and reflection period. I was able to take part in the post-performance analyses of the Ochammili group and *koteba-ton*. The *Bori* performers had theirs too from what I was told, but another post-performance reflection took place when I returned with the videos and photographs some months later.

Both the on-the-spot comments and the after-performance reviews were intended to improve subsequent performances. While the negative comments from the spectators were demands for instant improvement, the positive comments were endorsements of what was being done and an encouragement to the performers to do more. Spectator assessment, it emerged, was based on whether or not the actor was performing and satisfying the expectations of a role – were the movements right, how suggestive of the character or situation were the dance and mannerisms. This was more so in the symbolic performances, such as *Mmonwu* and *Bori*, in which the traits of the characters or details of scenarios are deliberately sketchy. Assessment was also based on how comfortable the performer was in the space – was he/she inhibited through self-consciousness, did they use the stage well, and what was the level of interaction with the spectators? Among the Igbo, for instance, an inability to hold up in all or any of these aspects of performance was seen as the performer suffering from the dreaded '*iyi ogbo*' or stage fright. Stage savviness is an essential quality which a performer must have in abundance. One thing I noticed when reflecting on the nature of assessment and appreciation was that, in the four performances, spectators seemed especially pleased by the enthusiasm and effort which performers put into their performances. This was usually taken into account in the overall assessment. That is not to say that a highly skilled performer who seems aloof and economical in acting or dancing is not appreciated in equal measure. But it indicates that when the two – skill and flair – meet in one performer the atmosphere becomes completely electrifying and thus pleasing to the audience.

These areas of commonality suggest that it is possible to talk about an African theatre and performance sensibility, one that sees performance and theatre as artistic and social activities which enable individual African societies to study, understand, manage and come to terms with themselves and their environments. It is also a means through which they are able to celebrate their respective cultural identities.

Major differences

Although they have these common grounds, the performances also revealed major differences in the sense that no two are alike. Each reflected their respective cultural, social and political context. This goes to show that ultimately performances are products of their contexts: a text always bears the imprint of its context. Because no two contexts are ever the same, each performance text is unique and to some extent will remain specific to its context, irrespective of whatever close similarities it may share with other texts. Some performance forms were found across the continent, while some were culture specific. The masquerade theatre and ritual performances exist in most African cultures, while *Koteba* is specific to the Bamana. Of the four, *Koteba* is the only one that is 'drama' – in the western sense of dialogue, linear plot and easily identifiable story lines, makeup as symbolic disguise and skits which dealt directly with immediate social reality. However, it was not straight dialogic drama as it was also part dance drama and part music theatre. Although *Jaliya*, like *Koteba*, uses a lot of words, its dialogue was totally different from the information exchanges of the latter. The *jalolu* used words in two ways – to praise the patrons who reciprocated by giving material gifts or to other *jalolu* who merely repeated or embellished what they had heard. There were hardly any dialogic exchanges of words or information between two *jalolu* since, in all case, one merely echoed or translated the other to the spectators.

The types of characters found in the performances and the themes explored were also main areas of difference. In *Bori* and *Mmonwu*, they were generally spirits, ancestors or otherworldly beings, but occasionally representations of humans or animals. These characters were never real or specific human beings, with a history or past against which they could be placed and assessed. Neither were they ever explored psychologically in any depth to enable their individualities to become the central focus of the performances as Ukaegbu recommends (see p. 11). In *Bori*, the spirits were individualized – in fact, their *kiraris* contained a lot of biographical information about them – but in performing them, these traits were neither contextualized nor were extended story lines developed for them. In effect, they remained as one-dimensional as the *Mmonwu* characters. In *Koteba*, the characters were made to appear as individuals who had stories and contexts, and yet they remained types because they too had no personal histories, and also because they were treated with the same superficiality as the *Mmonwu* and *Bori* characters with the result that they too were one-dimensional. Because they had these other qualities lacking in the previous two, however, and because their everyday human characteristics were close to those of the audience, the latter were able to understand and relate to them more easily than audiences could with the characters in *Bori* and *Mmonwu*, who were seen as the ultimate others.

A final differentiating characteristic between the performances was the fact that while *Jaliya* presented characters purported to be real historical and mythological human beings, *Bori*, *Koteba* and *Mmonwu* presented fictional ones. And while the latter fore-grounded the fiction that they were dealing with, in *Jaliya*, the aim was to erase the boundaries between fiction and reality, and between the past and the present. The *jali*'s aim in performance always is to make the two into one. The distance in time and the fact that the characters were heroes created some distance which made identification with them rather difficult. Even when the subject of a performance was well-known, as Mandogo was, being framed and talked about in the same breadth as his illustrious dead ancestors removed him from the present into a rarefied realm in which his behaviour could be dispassionately presented and dissected by all present. The *jalolu* perform as themselves and the characters they talk about are meant to be real historical or mythological personages. Moreover, while the other three were representational, with the performer disappearing into the character he or she is presenting; *jaliya* is presentational, the performer remains and almost stands outside the character, keeping his or her distance from it all the time. The *jali* constantly analyses and comments on the characters he or she is presenting while in the other three, this function is left for the spectator to perform.

The future of indigenous African performance and theatre

The fast pace of technological advancement, tourism and urbanization in Africa at the present time have given rise to genuine concerns that indigenous African oral performances are under threat of either contamination or extinction. Taking all factors into account, what directions can the performance and theatre forms take in order to survive, be competitive, and remain relevant?

Cultural tourism presents a real danger if for any reason cultures are forced or economically seduced to give performances out of season and context to tourists or to scholars. Of the four performances that I watched, *Enemma* and *Balundo* were not special performances for me as were *Bori* and *Koteba*. There is the feeling that an over-exposure to the pressures from cultural tourism and the changing demography of the local communities are bound to affect the artistic purity and integrity of the indigenous theatres and performances. Questions are being asked about commissioned performances for outsiders, whether they are genuine as the ones the communities put on for themselves. But the two performances I commissioned suggest that these fears are unfounded. *Bori*, which because of its religious nature was the one most at risk of being adulterated by being performed out of context, but the group was still able to make the two-day performance fit into an on-going programme of healing. The group maintained that that was always the case since you could not summon the spirits unless you had a need for them. Besides, *Bori*'s use as curative ritual performance means that it is also flexible and often responds to demand.

As for the *Koteba* performance, the satires have already moved away from their religious and spiritual base and have developed to a point that they can be performed at any time and in any place in the community. Besides, the native audiences attended the commissioned shows and there was no way that they were going to stand for adulterated versions of what they were used to. Personally, I see commissioned performances as having some positive influence since they can increase the occasions, and provide new characters and themes for the communal repertoires. But, while one cannot with any certainty pinpoint what detrimental impact the change in context and motivation had on the commissioned performances, it would be naïve to believe that there was no effect.

The second concern is that in a lot of communities in which these performances used to be the main sources of entertainment, the emergence and availability of technological alternatives such as radio, television, film and video, has meant that the performances are increasingly facing major challenges to their dominance and their continued existence. The younger generation, whose continued interest in indigenous performances can help keep them going, are the ones who are more drawn to these techno-substitutes. But that said, it is difficult to see how these alternatives could become adequate replacements for the live indigenous performances. The communal nature of the performances, plus their immediacy and impermanence are the very qualities which make them appealing. Some of the performers were strongly opposed to being photographed or recorded on video or film, believing that these mediums are unnatural by attempting to capture and permanently imprison art forms that are not meant to be fixed or exactly repeated. This resistance, I believe, is born of a feeling that the electronic mediums of film and video essentially reduce a multidimensional art form into a mere two-dimensional lifeless object which in the process of its conversion loses its dynamic relationship with the audience, as well as its ability to recover and change itself in the process of performance.

The *Mmonwu* performers did not particularly want to watch themselves when I offered to bring the video back to show them. They strongly objected to the video being used for any commercial purposes, such as showing it to a fee-paying audience or copies made for sale. They were okay that the video was for academic study and private viewing only. The *Bori* performers' reactions, on watching themselves on tape, were rather ambivalent. On the one hand, they were distrustful that the performance had been turned into a product owned by other people and could be reproduced unchanged at will, with all the mistakes that were made on the day. But on the other, some members acknowledged the potential benefits of recorded performances which they could use as a learning tool, the video showing them how they had performed, so they could repeat it or make corrections accordingly. A few also saw the business potential of having the video since they could use it to advertise themselves to future clients and enthusiasts like myself who approach them in future to request a performance. The video would provide a sample of their work to new sponsors. But everyone agreed that live and recorded performances were two different things and that they were never going to be substitutes for one another.

But having to perform for the camera always affects a performance because performers suddenly become self-conscious. Even during *Enemma*, most of the Ochammili performers, because they were aware that I was recording them, kept looking to see where I was. It is always a problem if a performer has to shift focus between the spectator and the non-responsive camera. The problem was slightly less at the *Balundo* since the organizers had hired a professional cameraman to record the evening's performance and so they were able to divide their focus between audience and camera. My presence therefore did not unduly affect or influence how they performed, most of the time they ignored me and it was I who had to constantly manoeuvre myself into position to get good photographs or video-recording. During the *Bori*, *Mmonwu* and *Koteba* performances, on the other hand, my camera was an accidental intrusion which the performers had to deal with, and some ignored it while some could not.

Of the four performances looked at in this study, *Jaliya* seems the least threatened by innovations in technology. In fact, it has successfully absorbed technology into its practice. The *Jaliya Balundo* showed how modern technology has been adapted by an indigenous oral performance. The orchestra was a mixture of indigenous instruments and foreign ones, *kora*, *balafon*, *djembe* and *tabou* combining very well with the electric guitar and microphone. *Jaliya* seems made for the technological age and already is maximizing its benefits in many other ways. Many *jalolu* now frequently embark on prolonged overseas tours, and some are so internationally known today that they perform at major charity concerts, such as the recent Band-Aid concert held simultaneously in many countries. Very often these tours and international exposure lead to or follow recording contracts. It is now possible for fans to buy video, CD and DVD recordings of their favourite artists. *Jaliya* can do this because it is essentially a musical performance and it is easy for audiences to be content with listening to the recorded music, whereas *Bori*, *Koteba* and *Mmonwu*, even when they are recorded on video, lack the same appeal since they depend on their liveness to make their impact on audiences. However, *Bori* too has shown its adaptive ability by modifying its indigenous instruments so that the *garaya* and *goge* are now electronically amplified, and the lead singer and *maroka* use microphones during performance. But *Mmonwu* and *Koteba*, on the other hand, seem to shun technology. *Koteba* has changed from oil lanterns to kerosene lamps and, now, electricity for night performances, but there has been no attempt to incorporate technology into their perform-ance dynamics. Costumed *Mmonwu* performers have to retire before dusk, and so the need for light has never arisen and is not likely to. And neither *Koteba* nor *Mmonwu* has modified its musical instruments as the other two have done.

Rapid urbanization has affected the practice of all indigenous perform-ances in two ways. In the first instance, a lot of the young people, who in the past would have remained in the villages and ensured the continuity of theatre traditions, are now increasingly moving to the urban centres in search of work and a better life, and as a result the pools of performers from which the performances draw are dwindling steadily. This urban drift does not affect all the performances in the same way. The depletion of the pool of performers affects *Mmonwu* and *Koteba* most, whereas the drift to the cities does not seem to be a problem for *Bori* and *Jaliya*. The explanation for this difference is somehow linked to the second reason which is the fundamental one of the erosion of the communal ethos being caused by the movement away from the villages and the countryside. Performances such as *Mmonwu*, *Bori* and *Koteba* derive their inspiration and sustenance from this sense of community, of shared fundamental values and beliefs which are celebrated in and reinforced by the performances. But in the *Mmonwu* and *Koteba* cultures, some of these, such as religious/ritual observances, communal festivals and some public ceremonies, are context-specific and so have proved difficult to transplant from their original environments. *Bori* is different, however, since unlike in the other two, belief does not just give rise to performance. In *Bori* it is impossible to separate belief from performance; where one goes the other follows. But *Mmonwu* is different since the performance has sometimes travelled to urban centres where the belief does not exist and has been poorer for it.

But, in a curious way, this is not a bad thing for *Koteba* and *Mmonwu* since it affirms and develops their survival capacities. The fact that certain *Mmonwu* or *Koteba* performances have to be given at certain times of the year in specific locations means that the two manage to retain their pull for their audiences. Young and old Igbo and Bamana indigenes living in the cities travel home during festival times and other occasions to take part in these 'site/time-specific' theatre events. The performances still mean a lot to the people and one found that the city dwellers plan their annual social engagements with their respective local performance/festival calendars in mind. Occasionally though, *Mmonwu* has travelled with the migrants to find temporary homes in the cities. But their performances remain alien forms in the cities, always struggling with the changed context of a constantly unsettled urban setting. *Mmonwu* theatre is derived from and depends on a long established tradition, communal beliefs, shared values and a homogenous system of thoughts and practices which is absent in the city with its cosmopolitan, heterogeneous and an evolving collective ethos. Every masking tradition or cult maintains allegiance to its home base, and they find it difficult to feel or see the city as home.

The surprise is that *Kote-tlon*, which is the most secular and socially oriented of the four and which should therefore find it easier to adjust to the city, seems to be the one least adapted to life outside its locality. A *ton*'s repertoire is hardly ever performed outside of the town or village since although performers sometimes find themselves in cities, they do not organize performances there. The main reason given for this was that people are very attached to their town or village *ton* and no *ton* ever leaves its local base. Moreover, the *ton* is the only umbrella organization under which *Koteba* performances are given in Bamana society, so when people want to perform they have to return to their communities to do so. A *koteba-ton* and its collection of skits will always belong to its mother *ton*. The members do not re-form in the cities and neither do they join the *ton* of other towns or communities, even if they have lived there for a long time. The Markala performance illustrated this strong attachment, as most of the actors and others members had to come back from their respective places of work for the two days needed for organizing and giving the special performance.

Jaliya and *Bori*, of the four performances, have travelled best and are comfortably established in new urban settings. The reason may be that the occasions when both are performed – such as births, weddings, circumcision rites, funerals, initiations, curative rites and other public events – also exist or can be recreated in the urban centres. Both are not as event/site-specific in the way that *Koteba* and *Mmonwu* are. People tend to travel with their cultures and wherever possible they try to recreate their communities and its practices in their new locations once they have the number to do so. Therefore, demand for performance will always exist once these contexts are provided. It also seems that *Bori* and *Jaliya* have adapted better in the cities because of their professional or semi-professional nature. Performers in both depend mainly on their theatre and other cult activities to make a living, and so they have had to find ways to recreate contexts which would enable them to practice their art. *Bori* groups have formed in and around cities in Northern Nigeria and they find ways to advertise their presence so clients can find them easily. In and around Zaria alone there are close to forty *Bori* compounds and I had no difficulty getting connected to the groups I eventually worked with. As in *Jaliya*, the basic needs of life and the events to mark them, such as people giving birth, getting married, falling ill, requiring a change of fortune or wanting to find out about the future also exist in the cities and require *Bori* possession performances to help sort the problems out.

Besides, *Bori* and *Jaliya*, while being communal and group oriented, are underpinned by a high degree of individualism, both in the way they are performed and sometimes in the materials contained in them. *Bori* may arise from a shared belief, but in practice what each group does or which spirits they choose to invite is up to them. The kind of general rules and codes of behaviour, which are found in *Mmonwu* practice, do not exist in either in *Bori* or in *Jaliya*. *Bori's* individualistic ethos is also reflected in the fact that spirits, although they belong to families, hardly ever come together during performances. Even when they accidentally find themselves performing at the same time, most tend to concentrate on themselves and their relationship with the audience. Only on rare occasions do they show any awareness of other spirits in the arena in a connected or sustained performative way. *Jaliya* is the quintessential art of the individual; each *jali* owns and controls her or his performance. The performance is about the *jali* more than it is about what he or she is performing. The importance of the paraphernalia of performance, such as costume, make-up, props and set are not as important in *Jaliya* as in other performances. And although *jalolu* wear flamboyant costumes and *jalimusolu* loud make-up, these are only to draw attention to the person of the *jali* and not to enhance their performance.

Mmonwu has been performed for new occasions in the cities, but the performances have seldom been specific or mandatory as they usually are in their original locations. *Koteba* has not even tried to move out of its locality. It is surprising that *Mmonwu's* religious dimension is one key reason why it has not transplanted successfully from the rural setting to an urban one, while the same religious element has not prevented *Bori* from moving around. *Mmonwu*, as practised in the rural areas with its spiritual element, automatically loses this enabling framework once it leaves the local environment because the gods, spirits and ancestors celebrated by the masquerades are local and usually do not have any power or relevance elsewhere.

The most pressing question for these two performances to address is how long will the pull they have for their peoples remain strong enough to get them to return home to participate? One answer is that as long as the sense of ancestral roots and home remains strong in Bamana and Igbo peoples, for that long will this desire to keep alive practices that help to ensure the survival of their cultures remain. It is encouraging that in *Mmonwu* theatre culture areas people living in the cities still insist on the having their young sons initiated into the masquerade cult at the appropriate times as their age mates living in the villages. People also still join age grades and other village and clan associations irrespective of where they live and these two bodies are usually responsible for theatre activities. A Bamana, irrespective of where she or he is born or lives, still belongs to her or his ancestral town or village *ton* and will actively take part in its activities.

Dead end or ocean of possibilities?

A lot of speculation has been going on regarding possible routes of development for indigenous African oral performances. Some scholars, notably the Igbo ones mentioned in the introduction, believe the way forward for *Mmonwu* theatre is to 'modernise' so as to bring itself into the twentieth and twenty-first centuries if it wants to survive. Some like Echeruo, Amamkulor and Uka advocate that this theatre should become fully dramatic along the Greek and European lines. This will mean developing individual themes as opposed to communal ones, by exploring personal stories and psychology which is what Ukaegbu suggests; it will also mean developing dialogue and a finite product that can easily be replicated which Ugonna believes it already does. But as this study has argued, cultures develop performances suited to their own needs and based on their own sensibilities: African cultures have done just that.

Others, Echeruo in particular, have also argued that indigenous performances, such as *Mmonwu* and *Bori,* should free themselves of their religious shackles and become secular forms of entertainments. But these suggestions fail to take into account that *Bori*, for instance, will cease to be *Bori* if it lost its ritual and therapeutic qualities. It is difficult to envisage a *Bori* performance in which the aim of the visit of the spirits is not for the purpose of curing the sick or answering spectators' questions about life. One doubts if *Mmonwu* will attract the same mass following and reverence if it was divested of its ancestral and mystical aura. Ironically, one quality of the indigenous theatre which has been successfully transferred to new theatre forms, such as theatre-for-development, is the willingness of the audience to respect and take seriously what the characters say or do. This comes from the perception of these characters as ancestors, spirits or deities who can see and understand the world far better than ordinary mortals. The satiric function of *Koteba* and *Mmonwu* is still very much valued and so their corrective power remains undiminished in Bamana and Igbo cultures on this account. The *Bori* spirits also tell people what to do or where they are going wrong so that they can mend their ways, and that is why the oppressed or marginalized use it to challenge the forces of oppression or marginalization or momentarily to turn the tables on them.

So, instead of wishing African performances to become like those of other cultures, we should ask how these performances have adapted to changing times and how best to utilize their inherent qualities and dynamics to expand their capabilities. *Mmonwu*, for instance, has been kept alive by the introduction of more contexts for performances within its original setting, as well as in the cities. There are now festivals and competitions at village, town, local government, and state levels throughout the year instituted by the Culture Ministry of Anambra State in Nigeria. Series of mini festivals and competitions culminate in the yearly *Pageant of the Spirits*, a state-wide masquerade festival/competition in which the best performing masquerades and best organized groups win prizes in different categories, with substantial financial rewards and state honours. This would be a good way forward for taking *Koteba* into the urban centres in Mali where at the moment it seems not to have penetrated. The fact that the characters which feature in *Koteba* are the same all over Bamana would enable such a competition to encourage imaginative use of the communal pool of characters among the various *koteba-tons*. Having the same characters would also make assessing individual actors and judging the competitions easier.

Even if performances, such as *Mmonwu* and *Bori* which are extremely improvisational and deliberately sketchy, were to develop extended plays and skits with complicated story-lines, it would be difficult to see the point of this since both would lose two of their essential characteristics: their suggestive symbolism and cryptic narratives. Their audiences would also lose their key role of creatively interpreting the performances as there would no longer be any narrative gaps for them to fill. Exploring individual psychology and themes, as Ukaegbu (1996) suggests, would certainly be contrary to the underpinning spirit of some of the performances which is the celebration of the community and not the individual.

Taking all these factors into account, it is clear from this study that African indigenous performances have not reached the 'dead end' which Echeruo (1981) confidently concluded from his study twenty-four years ago. It is also clear that they are neither likely to develop along Greek dramaturgy lines nor turn themselves into strange or hybridized performance forms borrowed from other cultures. Their forms and structures have not changed dramatically as a result of their respective journeys through history or their encounters with modernity and post-modernity. Individually and collectively, they have competed, negotiated with and adapted internal and external forces of history, and thereby remained relevant to their respective communities. They all still perform the aesthetic and social functions which they had always provided for their cultures; they have expanded their themes and increased their contexts, absorbed influences to cope with newer and changing realities and, in all this, they have held on to their aesthetic principles.

Bibliography

Amankulor, James (1981), 'Ekpe Festival as Religious Ritual and Dance Drama' in Yemi Ogunbiyi (ed.) *Drama and Theatre in Nigeria: A Critical Source Book*. Lagos: Nigeria Magazine.

Atkins, Guy (1972), *Manding: Focus on an African Civilisation*. London: SOAS.

Awoonor, Kofi (1975), *The Breast of the Earth: A Survey of the History, Culture and Literature of Africa South of the Sahara*. New York: NOK Publishers International.

Banham, Martin, *et al.* (1994), *The Cambridge Guide to African and Caribbean Theatre*. Cambridge: Cambridge University Press.

Barba, Eugenio (1991), *A Dictionary of Theatre Anthropology: The Secret Art of the Performer*. London and New York: Routlegde.

Beattie, John and Middleton, John (eds) (1969), *Spirit Mediumship and Society in Africa*. London: Routledge & Kegan Paul.

Beier, Ulli (1967), 'Yoruba Theatre' in Ulli Beier (ed.) *Introduction to African Literature*. London: Longmans.

Besmer, Fremont E. (1983), *Horses, Musicians and Gods: The Hausa Cult of Possession-Trance*. Massachussetts: Bergin & Garvey Publishers, Inc.

Brink, James (1977), 'Bamana Kote-tlon Theatre' in *African Arts*, 10/4.

Brook, Peter (1968), *The Empty Space*. London: MacGibbons & Lee.

Chinweizu (1988), *Voices from the Twentieth Century: Griots and TownCriers*. London: Faber.

Diabate, Mansa Makan (1984), 'Etre griot aujourd'hui' in *Notre Librarie Litterature Maliene*. Nos 75–76.

de Graft, J. C. (1976), 'Roots in African Drama and Theatre' in *African Literature Today No 8: Drama in Africa*. London, Ibadan and New York: Heinemann & African Publishing Company.

Echeruo, M. J. C. (1981), 'The Dramatic Limits of Igbo Ritual' in Yemi Ogunbiyi (ed.) *Drama Theatre in Nigeria: A Critical Source Book*. Lagos: Nigeria Magazine.

Enekwe, Ossie (1981), 'Myth, Ritual and Drama in Igboland' in *Drama and Theatre in Nigeria*.

Enekwe, Onuora (1987), *Igbo Masks: The Oneness of Ritual and Theatre*. Lagos: Nigeria Magazine.

Finnegan, Ruth (1970), *Oral Literature in Africa*. Oxford: Clarendon Press.

Finnegan, Ruth (1992), *Oral Tradition and the Verbal Arts: A Guide to Research Practices*. London: Routledge.

Hale, Robert (1998), *Griots and Griottes: Masters of Words and Music*. Bloomington: Indiana University Press.

Hoffman, Barbara (1995), 'Power, Structure and Mande *Jeliw*' in Conrad, David and Frank, Barbara E. (eds) *Status and Identity in West Africa: Nyamakalaw of Mande*. Bloomington, Indiana: Indiana University Press.

Hoffman, Barbara (2000), *Griots at War: Conflict, Conciliation and Caste in Mande*. Bloomington: Indiana University Press.

Horn, Andrew (1981), 'Ritual, Drama and the Theatrical: The Case of *Bori* Spirit Mediumship' in *Drama and Theatre in Nigeria*.

Jansen, Jan (2000), *The Griot's Craft: An Essay on Oral Tradition and Diplomacy*. Munster: Lit.

Janson, Marloes (2002), *The Best Hand is the Hand that Always Gives: Griottes and their Profession in Easter Gambia*. Leiden: research School CNWS.

Kanoute, Nding Nding (2004), Personal Interview in Dakar, 15 March.

Kerr, David (1986), 'An Approach to Pre-Colonial African Theatre' in *African Theatre Review*, Vol. 1, No 2.

Kerr, David (1995), *African Popular Theatre: From Pre-colonial Times to the Present Day*. London: James Curry and Heinemann.

McAlpine, Alison (1985), 'The Cult of Bori Among the Hausa: A Kinetic Event'. Unpublished thesis, University of Leeds.

Mahood, Molly (1966), 'Drama in Newborn States' in *Presence Africaine*, Vol. 31, No 60.

Maiga, Moussa (1984), 'Le Koteba: le grand escargot bambara' in *Notre Libraire: Litterature Maliene* No 75–76 (Juliet–Octobre) 135–136.

Nzewi, Meki (1979), 'Traditional Theatre Practice' in *Nigeria Magazine* Nos 128–129.

Obiechina, Emmanuel (1978), 'Literature Traditional and Modern _ in the Nsukka Environment' in G. E. K. Ofomata (ed.) *The Nsukka Environment*. Enugu: Fourth Dimension Publishers.

Odita, Emeka O. (1970), 'Igbo Masking Tradition: Its Types, Functions and Interpretations'. Unpublished dissertation, Indiana University.

Ogunba, Oyin and Irele, Abiola (1978), *Theatre in Africa*. Ibadan: Ibadan University Press.

Ogunbiyi, Yemi (1981), *Drama and Theatre in Nigeria: A Critical Source Book*. Lagos: Nigerian Magazine.

Okafor, Mary-Blossom C. (1998), 'Theatre of Life: Rituals, Transition and Progression Among the Igbo'. Unpublished dissertation, University of Plymouth.

Okagbue, Osita (1987), 'Theatre on the Streets: Two Nigerian Samples' in *Maske und Kothurn* 33.

Okagbue, Osita (1993), 'Invisible Presences: Masks and Spirits in Igbo Society' in *ASSAPH*. C No 9.

Okagbue, Osita (1997), 'When the Dead Return: Play and Seriousness in African Masked Performances' in *SATJ* 11, Nos 1 and 2.

Okpewho, Isidore (ed.) (1990), *The Oral Performance in Africa*. Ibadan: Spectrum Books Ltd.

Onyeneke, Augustine O. (1987), *The Dead Among the Living: Masquerades in Igbo Society*. Nimo: Holy Ghost Congregation and the Asele Institute.

Ottenberg, Simon (1975), *Masked Rituals of Afikpo: The Context of an African Art*. Seattle: University of Washington.

Rubin, Don (1997), *The World Encyclopaedia of Contemporary Theatre. Volume 3 Africa*. London: Routledge.

Schechner, Richard (1977), *Performance Theory*. New York and London: Routledge

Schechner, Richard (1985), *Between Theater and Anthropology*. Philadelphia: University of Pennsylvania Press.

Schechner, Richard and Appel, Willa (1990), *By Means of Performance: Intercultural Studies of Theatre and Ritual*. Cambridge: Cambridge University Press.

Smith, Mary E. (1981), *Baba of Karo: A Woman of the Muslim Hausa*. New Haven and London: Yale University Press.

Turner, Victor (1968), *The Drums of Affliction: A Study of Religious Process Among the Ndembu of Zambia*. Oxford: Clarendon Press.

Ugonna, Nnabuenyi (1984), *Mmonwu: A Dramatic Tradition of the Igbo*. Lagos: Lagos University Press.

Uka, Kalu (1973), 'Drama in Nigerian Society' in *The Hoe*, Vol. 1, No. 1.

Ukaegbu, Victor I. (1996), 'The Composite Scene: The Aesthetics of Igbo Mask Theatre'. Unpublished dissertation, University of Plymouth.

Wall, L. Lewis (1988), *Hausa Medicine: Illness and Well-Being in a West African Culture*. Durham, N.C. and London: Duke University.

Index